QUESTIONS ENGLISH TEACHERS ASK

R. BAIRD SHUMAN

*University of Illinois,
Urbana-Champaign*

HAYDEN BOOK COMPANY, INC.
Rochelle Park, New Jersey

For the Wolfes,
Celia and Denny,
and their two cubs,
Cary and Ashley

Library of Congres Cataloging in Publication Data

Main entry under title:

Questions English teachers ask.

   (Hayden English education series)
   Bibliography: p.
   1. English philology—Study and teaching.
I. Shuman, Robert Baird.
PE65.Q4   420.7'11   77-10545 ✓
ISBN   0-8104-6005-X
ISBN   0-8104-6004-1 pbk.

1	2	3	4	5	6	7	8	9	PRINTING
77	78	79	80	81	82	83	84	85	YEAR

PREFACE

Questions English Teachers Ask is an outgrowth of my decade and a half of working with English teachers at both the secondary and college levels. Seldom do I make a speech or run a workshop that teachers do not flock around me afterwards to ask for help in finding solutions to the professional problems which most concern them. Like others in my position, I try to provide practical and workable suggestions. However, I usually feel that such instantaneous advice given under the pressure of the moment might be ill-conceived if not downright misleading.

Therefore, I have compiled these questions and answers in an attempt to provide English teachers with thoughtful, documented responses to their most pressing concerns.

The Method

When I first decided to edit *Questions English Teachers Ask,* I sent letters to 1,500 English teachers requesting that they submit to me the question or questions which most perplexed them professionally. Letters were in some cases distributed through principals, department heads, English supervisors, or associate superintendents in charge of curriculum.

The 1,500 letters originally distributed brought responses from 374 teachers who asked a total of 946 questions. Some teachers asked as many as twelve questions; others asked only one. There was considerable overlap in the questions, as was to be expected. For example, forty-one teachers asked how they could keep up with the paperwork involved in teaching English to upwards of 130 students a day. Three representative queries about this topic were selected for inclusion in the book.

Questions on how to individualize instruction were numerous, and these are included in several sections of the book. Twenty-nine teachers wondered what sort of grammar instruction would help students to improve their writing. Since nearly all research in the field indicates clearly that a knowledge of grammar has little relationship to one's ability to write (or speak) in a manner which is considered standard, only one of these questions made it into the book.

An attempt was made to balance the book in a proportion roughly reflecting the categories in which teachers asked questions. For example, I would have hoped to have major sections on subjects such as drama, speaking, listening, and articulation among secondary schools, colleges, and universities. However, because only eleven questions had to do with speaking and listening, only seventeen with drama, and only eight with articulation, I had to conclude that these topics were not foremost in teachers' minds.

Organization

The largest number of questions had to do with areas not specifically within the framework of English curriculum; but, since they were asked, I felt that I should include them under the broad category which I have designated as "Professional Concerns." Most of the questions in this section are ancillary to curricular matters, but the questions are, nonetheless, significant ones. Of the 946 questions received, 347 could legitimately have fallen into this broad category. Some of the questions were carping—"How can I deal with a principal who was formerly a coach, is presently a fool, and has no idea of what English is all about?" Others were stated in such a way that productive answers could be provided for them—"What can a typical English teacher do to convince his superiors in the administration that high school English programs must be brought more into line with the 20th-century world as it actually exists?"

I was surprised to find that questions concerning writing were almost double the number (187) concerning reading (101). Despite the recent prominence that creative dramatics has gained in this country, only four questions had anything to do with creative dramatics.

Questions regarding grammar numbered 202, of which sixty-eight were concerned with dialect study. While dialectology is a branch of grammar, I thought it best to devote a section of the book to dialects rather than lumping this important topic with grammar generally.

The Respondents

Initially I had intended to answer personally all of the questions dealt with in the book. However, it soon occurred to me that I could get more informed results by sending questions to people in the field who might have more ready answers to them than I. The result is that each question has been answered by a person who has at his or her fingertips the specific research data necessary for a considered and informed response. The respondents are leaders in education and have supplied answers that should be of considerable use to English teachers at all levels. I am deeply grateful to all those who took the time and trouble to respond —and to those who asked the questions.

R. BAIRD SHUMAN

ACKNOWLEDGMENTS

The Editor's appreciation cannot be extended individually to all of the people who contributed to making *Questions English Teachers Ask* a reality. All of the teachers who submitted questions and all of the people who worked on answering them deserve boundless thanks. School administrators such as Charles Jarvis of Gastonia, North Carolina, Joyce F. Wasdell of the Durham County Schools, and Carolyn G. Ennis of the Smithfield-Selma School District were of enormous assistance in identifying teachers who might be asked to provide questions. Alan T. Hill, Director of the Division of Management Information Systems of the North Carolina Department of Public Instruction, provided the addresses of every secondary school in the state of North Carolina.

Numerous scholars who were invited to be respondents were unable to accept the invitation because of other pressing commitments; however, these people, virtually without exception, were warm and encouraging to the Editor even though they could not contribute to the book.

Several friends and colleagues have been valuable sounding boards as work on the book has progressed: Denny T. Wolfe, Jr., Director of the Division of Languages, North Carolina Department of Public Instruction; Celia O. Wolfe, English Department, Needham-Broughton High School, Raleigh; Professor and Mrs. Frank Mendoza, Lees-McRae College, Banner Elk, North Carolina; Professors William H. Cartwright, Allan S. Hurlburt, Ronald R. Butters and Mrs. Edith Horn, all of Duke University; Dr. Jan A. Guffin, Department of English, North Central High School, Indianapolis; Dr. Robert W. Reising of Pembroke State University; Professor Ward Cates of Kansas State University; Professor Robert Shafer of Arizona State University; and Professor Mary Jane Cook of the University of Arizona.

William J. Marcus and Robert W. Boynton of the Hayden Book Company have been unfailingly encouraging and understanding. My undergraduate research assistants as the book progressed were Richard Chase and R. Scott Edens, both of whom were helpful in checking sources and in giving their reactions to much of the material. My graduate assistants, Omer Abdelrasoul, a lecturer in English on leave from Khartoum University, and Thomas C. Richardson, assumed numerous burdens attendant upon the compiling of this book. The manuscript would not have reached the publisher in legible form had it not been for the devoted services of my secretary, Yvette Tillett Greene. Janet Robinson also pitched in whenever I was hard pressed for someone to help with typing copy.

Finally, the Duke University Research Council provided funds to cover postage, duplicating, and other editorial expenses; for this generosity, I am most grateful.

R.B.S.

CONTENTS

Section II: Writing   45

SECTION I

PROFESSIONAL
CONCERNS

Question I, 1

Of all of the topics which are huddled under the English umbrella, which do you think should be given top priority in our secondary schools today?

Martha Sofley, Holbrook Junior High School, Gastonia, North Carolina

Answer by:

JAMES R. SQUIRE, Senior Vice President and Publisher, Ginn and Company. Mr. Squire, former Executive Secretary of the National Council of Teachers of English, is the author and editor of numerous books and articles on the teaching of English, including the 76th yearbook of the National Society for the Study of Education.

More important than assigning priorities in relation to the topics and subjects covered by the content of English is considering the language needs of students in any particular classroom. Unless the student can become genuinely engaged in his reading, writing, and speaking, coverage of content seems unlikely to result in effective learning.

This means not rejection of subject learnings which have occupied our attention for so long, but rather a realization that subject learnings must involve the full play of the total human personality. It is not enough to read and study Shakespeare. More important is what each pupil feels about Shakespeare after he completes his reading. It is not enough to assure mechanical efficiency and coverage in reading instruction. What matters more than drill and memorization and review of basic decoding and comprehension skills is the desire to read and learn and communicate. Arthur Eastman points towards the shift in attitude when he calls for ". . . a preference for power rather than knowledge, for experience rather than information, for engagement rather than criticism."[1] Is it not significant that the two books reporting the Dartmouth Seminar were entitled *The Uses of English*[2] and *Growth Through English*?[3] Use and Growth, twin priorities in the English program for which we must work. As we sharpen our concern with the imaginative education of pupils, paralleling our long-time concern with rational education, the student's own reactions take on new significance—his attitudes to life, his freedom in shaping through language his own active response to the world around. Genuine engagement in the literary experience thus becomes significant as does the selection of literature to evoke deepening and ever broadening response. So also with imaginative writing and the student's experience in creating his own literary response to his surroundings. Writing becomes a part of the process of growing awareness, not merely a product to be marked by the teacher and filed for later reference. Creative speaking, acting out, role playing, creative drama—these take on new dimension. Above all we need to think through with fresh insight the problem of replacing our present concern with book, author, genre, theme, and literary history, with a program that provides a real imaginative education.

References

[1]James R. Squire. *Response to Literature.* Champaign, Illinois: National Council of Teachers of English, 1968.

[2]Herbert Muller. *The Uses of English.* New York: Holt, Rinehart, and Winston, 1968.
[3]John Dixon. *Growth Through English.* London: National Association for the Teaching of English, 1967.

Question I, 2

How might the elements of the English curriculum best be coordinated—grades 9 through 12—so that each teacher knows what the students have covered and what he or she should teach?
Wilma Simpson, Cherryville Senior High School, Cherryville, North Carolina

Answer by:
CLARENCE W. HACH, Supervisor of English, Evanston Township High School, Evanston, Illinois. Mr. Hach has long been identified with advocating sequence and articulation in English progams. His articles in *The English Journal*, "Needed: Sequence in Composition" (Nov. 1960) and "Needed: Sequences in Composition" (Jan. 1968), are often cited as being seminal influences to the establishment of sequential programs in composition.

The question of how best to coordinate elements of the English curriculum has long beset English department chairmen and supervisors and often concerned teachers of English who believe in *programs* in English. In recent years, when accountability has entered the thinking and vocabulary of school administrators and boards of education, the question of coordination has received impetus. But despite efforts of many, little really has yet been done in most schools to achieve a carefully coordinated and articulated program in one of the most important areas of curriculum, if not the most important.

Coordination implies a program. Thus, despite the fact that every English teacher knows that instruction must begin where a student is, English teaching must be based on something more than each teacher's assessment of a student's needs or perhaps that teacher's understanding of what an English curriculum should be. For too long in too many schools the teaching of English has been (and is) what each teacher has chosen to make it or not make it. Perhaps in a small school where one teacher, and hopefully the same one, has all students all four years (9-12), there is no need for a program except in that teacher's mind. Even then, however, we must hope that that teacher understands what a modern English curriculum should include and has the background and ability to implement it for all students. However, a school having only one English teacher hardly exists any more.

There are many schools today, however, that have no real programs, particularly those with electives constituting English all four years or at least in grades 10, 11, and 12. In these, English is still pretty much what each teacher makes the electives. As a result, it is possible for a student to have very little work in any kind of composition, for example, or perhaps little practice in expository writing. Another may have no work at all in language, or at least in the broad spectrum of language that should include semantics and "doublespeak," some kind of grammar study, usage, dialectology, lexicology, perhaps some language history, and other areas. Many may not receive any instruction in any of the mass media, including film. Others may never have an opportunity to try to write "creatively." Still others may graduate with a very unbalanced background in literature—perhaps no nonfiction or ethnic studies and certainly many without any study of poetry. Electives, thus, have complicated the important job of coordination.

Regardless, though, of how English is organized, coordination presupposes a program, an understanding at least, for example, of what the nature of composition, language, and literary study should be at each grade level for various types of students. Even in an ungraded, phase elective system some such program should be created and carefully monitored, though, to be sure, the problem is more difficult. A department needs to decide what English should be for its students and then plan a program, grades 9-12, that will meet both *needs* and *interests* for the kind of student population it has. Too often in recent years *interest* has been the primary concern so that today we see backlash to the so-called basics. As always, the eclectic approach espoused by the Greeks years ago, "Nothing too much," is proving the wise course.

More than program is necessary, however, for coordination to exist. That program must be monitored, to use current lingo. Thus, a system of diagnostic and achievement tests needs to be established, perhaps each year. Certainly, the possibility exists for much of language study to be tested. For example, a language test for sophomores perhaps should be given in early April so that it can serve both achievement and diagnostic purposes, achievement to determine how well a student has mastered language study of grades 9 and 10 (tests should be cumulative), and remediation to indicate what help is needed before the end of the year. If tests are properly devised so that item analyses may be obtained, such remediation can take place through many of the individualized means a teacher has to use. Some system, of course, should also be devised to pass this information from teacher to teacher, from grade level to grade level.

A system of writing folders to contain only semester exams in composition for each grade and/or ability level can be initiated, too, so that a teacher of juniors may know the achievement level of his students, for example, at the middle and end of both the freshman and sophomore years. Such a folder might also include a diagnostic composition, its nature geared to the course of study, to be written at the beginning of each year. There are some problems in distributing folders, but these are not insurmountable if a faculty believes in the system. There is accountability involved, of course, because each teacher, in a way, puts his work on display for others; but if teachers are really professional and know that no teacher saves all souls, such a system should not be a threat. The possibility of all students receiving instruction in writing and having writing progress monitored is worth the effort.

Some schools include as part of the folder system a simple reading record card to keep track of students' personal reading. Teachers who believe that one of the primary purposes of teaching literature is to encourage students to read on their own and become lifetime readers advocate this procedure. They believe that one of their most important jobs is to become reading guidance counselors, and the only way they can succeed is to know the amount and nature of their students' reading.

A carefully delineated program in literature by grade and ability levels will assure teachers of works students have read in previous years and indicate to them what works they might teach. Such a program should be varied and extensive to enable teachers to meet student interests and enable them to teach works they particularly like and will probably therefore teach successfully. At the same time, besides titles, there should be in the program a course of study that assures students' understanding of common literary concepts, such as irony, satire, tragedy, and the like. Some schools devise departmental tests designed for this purpose.

With literature, of course, arises the question of reading achievement. There is no doubt that reading proficiency needs to be monitored, too, as students progress from year to year. Hopefully, a school has the specialized staff to handle reading problems of all kinds, including slow readers. But in addition to achievement tests in reading, a department may wish to test students specifically in their ability to read literary materials and keep records on their progress. There are, of course, standardized tests that may be purchased for this purpose.

How much coordination a department should or can do will depend on the time the chairman or supervisor has, the commitment of the faculty, and, naturally, the size of the school. Coordination is easier with fewer teachers. It might even be more informal. Nevertheless, if an English faculty is to be responsible to its clients, it does need a carefully coordinated, articulated program. The importance and cost of teaching English are too great without it.

Question I, 3

What do you consider the ideal preparation for high school English teachers given the present school situation? What sorts of follow-up work most helps the teacher in service to keep current?
Jan A. Guffin, North Central High School, Indianapolis, Indiana

Answer by:
SAMUEL D. WEHR, Professor Emeritus of English Education, Temple University.

i

The academic preparation of English teachers will always remain of prime importance, no matter how much teacher training programs may be revised. However, the content of that academic preparation needs drastic revision. The heritage of great literature that is background knowledge for all literature will remain important. This is a *sine qua non*. No teacher without a fine background can teach well. All too frequently, however, though it is called "background," it is the *only* literature that prospective teachers study, even though they will teach very little of this background literature in their careers. Teachers, and the institutions that train them, must remember that, important as this basic literature is, it is only a part of what must be learned.

Most people, including students, read contemporary literature—if they read anything at all; and it is this contemporary literature which English teachers must know and have the preparation to evaluate, understand, and appreciate. It may be disheartening to know that students drooled over *Love Story*, but their teachers should have read it while students were drooling over it. The first step in leading students to better literature is to know what they are reading and to be able and willing to talk about such reading from first-hand experience.

ii

English teachers need to be communications experts today. Just as we don't lead students to better literature by scorning what they read, so we will not make them more discriminating users of current media offerings by ignoring the fare they find fascinating on TV and in the theater.

English teachers must know and believe that there exists today a number of avenues into the mind. They must explore ways of using all these avenues in their teaching. Film, recording, and cassette libraries are as important today as bookshelves. Good English teachers must be as knowing about what makes a fine movie or TV script as they are about what makes a good book, and they must be as ready and willing to use film and TV as media of literary instruction as print.

iii

Well-prepared English teachers need to have had in-depth training in what people are actually reading that is not literature as English teachers classify it. This training must include current bulletin and periodical materials, including magazines and newspapers, broadsides and fliers. It should take in science fiction, whodunits, how-to-do-it manuals, and United States government publications about such things as child care, income tax, medicare, social security, etc. Teachers hesitate to include such materials about the problems of living in our complicated society because they have never been educated to regard a government publication on "Gardening to Fight Inflation," say, as literature. But it *is* a type of literature that students must learn how to deal with.

iv

For hundreds of years we have taught teachers how to get ideas into students' heads via books, as though the printed word were the only avenue into the mind. We are living in a world where for masses of people books are not important, and most of those people are not enough aware of how much they are subjected to a bombardment of impressions and ideas via media other than the printed word. Today's English teacher needs to teach students to be aware of how this daily barrage influences our thinking.

The corollary of this, of course, is that English teachers must be prepared to use all these avenues to the mind in their own teaching. Films, tapes, records, cassettes must be used as the media of instruction as professionally as books always have been. Students should be offered as many means for self-expression as there are means for learning itself. A school's chief duty is to teach each person how to learn by the means most suited to each one's ability to learn. English teachers must be experts in helping students learn how to learn, learn how to use that learning, learn how to prove that they have learned.

v

It the past we have taught teachers *about* language and the stress has been on grammar analysis. Teachers learned to take language apart, but most have never learned the process of putting language together. The stress has not been on the language learning process, where it belongs.

While a fair knowledge of formal grammar may be a necessary part of an English teacher's background, it is certain that the processes of learning language and mastering the operations of language are essential to good language teaching.

The people of the United States ought to be the most polylingual people in the world. Instead, by an almost criminal handling of the linguistic problems of a diverse people trying to become a single nation with one native language, we have created a monolingual people ashamed of their foreign language backgrounds, people who are in some cases boastful of the fact that they can't learn languages. Between 1825 and 1925 our schools transformed a diverse population into one nation by teaching them English. This miracle should in no way be disparaged; but in achieving it our forebearers should not have abandoned mastery of the languages they brought with them to these shores.

Future preparation of English teachers may well require them to learn a foreign language, in the course of which they would learn the process of language learning. They might well be required to master a dialect of English other than their own so that they learn not to scorn the culture that produced the dialect. However it may be accomplished, the worth of language and culture must be learned. Few English teachers admit to being language teachers. They must be encouraged to understand that whether they are teaching literature, composition, spelling, reading, and all the other things English teachers do, they are English language teachers.

vi

Finally, English teachers must be professionally and academically organized. Teacher preparation must include a thorough knowledge of the academic and professional organizations for English teachers specifically and all teachers in general. None of the academic organizations has been as strong a force in English teaching as they should have been, and they have been of little help to English teachers in areas other than methodology. Partly it's a matter of numbers and partly of the active involvement of those who do become members. In matters of concern to the whole profession, teachers must know and care about their rights and responsibilities. They need to have fringe benefits spelled out as carefully as do longshoremen and electrical workers. They must have organizational protection from censoring bigots. Above all, they must administer their own organizations so they are not taken away from them for selfish aggrandizement as has been the case in many labor unions, including teachers' unions.

Question I, 4

What can a typical English teacher do to convince his superiors in the administration that high school English programs must be brought more into line with the 20th-century world as it actually exists?

Miriam R. Jones, South Point High School, Belmont, North Carolina

Answer by:

MARY BARNES, Supervisor of Secondary English, Virginia Beach City Public Schools, Virginia Beach, Virginia.

If we English teachers were casting a "devil-play," we would most often seek the protagonist in the front office. Sometimes the villain does indeed reside there. He obstinately resists any classroom where desks are disarranged and any teacher who neglects her role as disseminator of information. Nothing short of threatened dismissal by the school board can transform him. But many administrators whose schools operate this way are not villainous, obtuse, or resistant to change; they are simply uninformed of new trends in English education and beset by the demon of accountability. Everywhere headlines broadcast the news that Johnny can't read, Johnny can't write, and Johnny's scores drop on standardized tests, particularly College Boards. Why shouldn't administrators cling to the methodology and content of the past, a past where the taxpaying public believes that everything was better.

So much for the defense of some administrators. Now to the problem. I interpret the question to mean convincing superiors of a need for change in English methodology and content because of the different demands of a changed world. Much hard work must precede the persuasion, so I would substitute "teachers" for the "teacher" of the question, not just because strength of numbers is preferable, but because the reading and thinking and planning are demanding enough to be shared by a total department. The need here is to inform administrators; to set in motion improved classroom processes that they can observe; and to prove, statistically if necessary, that this new program or programs enable students to become more discriminating receivers and producers of language.

As its opener, the group should bombard their superiors with current research in English, with descriptions of exemplary programs, and with information about all new trends in English education. Since these people are busy and since they are concerned primarily with administrative duties, the information should be in digest form. This is phase one in the strategy. It seldom works, but the gesture has been made.

Stage two is a bit more subtle. The teachers prepare demonstration classes, and the students and teachers invite the administrators to attend. This phase is extremely important because it effects the transition from a theory about, or a description of, English elsewhere, to a concrete classroom situation here and now. The administrators must be shown that innovation is not to be equated with a bag of tricks, that the teacher is not using a gimmick to conceal his inability to teach. They must observe students involved in an activity for which there is a rationale and an acceptable end product; and they must understand how the activity fits into the superstructure of English. If the teachers can comment intelligently on these purposes and aims, their superiors can see honesty of intention which may decrease resistance toward a new English program. Furthermore, teachers can support their claims by referring to those articles already supplied to the principals. Perhaps the latter may read them now.

The third stage is to secure the principal's permission to pilot the new plan in one school, either with or without state funds. Here, teachers prove their desire to be accountable, because they establish their hypotheses and test control and experimental subjects to determine the validity of these assumptions. Teachers should secure the services of a good testing consultant so that measurement will not be construed as administering standardized tests, which rarely test anything but usage, mechanics, and spelling.

Another method of convincing administrators to update English programs is to involve them in curriculum planning. This courtesy might be, in fact should be, extended to students and community members. These persons, along with representative English teachers, can constitute a curriculum committee to recommend new programs and critique curriculum materials developed by English departments. If such committees exist, English teachers at least have a visible group to whom they can direct appeals and upon whom they may exert some influence. They also have aides in the students who stand to gain or lose most in the decision about English.

Administrative animus to change, if such animus exists, may be a valuable protection against innovation for innovation's sake. It forces teachers to evaluate the present state of their English programs, to collect and study research and theory, to assess the needs of their school district, and to plan for their future state. Thus they may avoid playing the game of following the fads.

Question I, 5

What recent books are most frequently recommended by English teachers as the most useful for professional development?

William R. Wise, Encina High School, Sacramento, California

Answer by:

THEODORE W. HIPPLE, Professor of Education at the University of South Carolina at Spartanburg, where his area of specialization is secondary education. Mr. Hipple has written and edited numerous books and articles, including *Teaching English in the Secondary Schools* and *A Time to Teach, A Time to Learn*.

No evidence that I am aware of indicates what English teachers are reading, but there does appear to be some data that suggest what English teacher trainers believe English teachers *ought to read*. The reasons for this distinction between "are" and "ought" can be discovered amid the competing reading priorities English teachers encounter. They have to read student written themes and exams, a task that can take hours each week. They feel compelled to reread the novel they will soon teach and perhaps some criticism of that novel. They are aware that their students are reading the most recent adolescent literature and the current best sellers and rightly believe that they, too, must be familiar with this significant, growing, and ever-changing body of literature. Unfortunately, reading for "professional development" can sometimes get lost in the shuffle; like Scarlett O'Hara's thoughts, it is put off until a tomorrow that never comes.

Thus, when a little professional reading time does exist, the English teacher must choose wisely. What follows is an attempt to suggest what those choices might fruitfully be.

Probably every English teacher ought to have read carefully, and ought to reread periodically, one or more of the standard English methods texts, the "what-to-do-and-how-to-do-it" books of our trade. In a recent survey about the practices in the undergraduate English methods courses at more than 100 different teacher training institutions,[1] a question was asked about the textbooks students in such courses were required to buy. The most commonly mentioned were these seven books, listed here in rank order, any one of which, but ideally several of which, every English teacher ought both to own and to make his own:

1. Walter Loban, Margaret Ryan, and James R. Squire. *Teaching Language and Literature*. 2nd ed., New York: Harcourt Brace and Jovanovich, 1969.
2. Theodore W. Hipple. *Teaching English in Secondary Schools*. New York: Macmillan, 1973.
3. J. N. Hook. *The Teaching of High School English*. 4th ed., New York: Ronald Press, 1972.
4. James Moffett. *A Student-Centered Language Arts Curriculum, Grade K-13; A Handbook for Teachers*. Boston: Houghton-Mifflin, 1968.
5. Dwight L. Burton. *Literature Study in the High Schools*. New York: Holt Rinehart & Winston, 1959.
6. John Dixon. *Growth Through English*. 3rd ed., Urbana, Illinois: NCTE, 1975.
7. Theodore W. Hipple. *Readings for Teaching English in Secondary Schools*. New York: Macmillan, 1973.

These are valuable books for professional development, just as are the methods texts published after the survey was taken, like Stephen Judy's *Explorations in the Teaching of Secondary English* and Bryant Fillion's, Ken Donelson's, and Dwight Burton's *Teaching English Today*. No teacher of English should fail to study and restudy such books.

A second category of useful professional books includes those about education in general, and here the list can be an extensive one. Many teachers of my acquaintance have found the following ten books good sources of provocative insight and practical help.

1. Mary Greer and Bonnie Rubinstein. *Will the Real Teacher Please Stand Up?* Pacific Palisades, California: Goodyear, 1972.
2. John Holt. *How Children Fail,* 2nd ed., New York: Pitman, 1969 and *How Children Learn.* New York: Pitman, 1968.
3. Neil Postman and Charles Weingartner. *Teaching as a Subversive Activity.* New York: Delacorte, 1969.
4. George Leonard. *Education and Ecstasy.* New York: Delacorte, 1969.
5. Carl Rogers. *Freedom to Learn.* Columbus, Ohio: Merrill, 1969.
6. Charles Silberman. *Crisis in the Classroom.* New York: Random House, 1970.
7. Louis E. Raths, Merrill Harmin, and Sidney B. Simon. *Values and Teaching.* Columbus, Ohio: Merrill, 1966.
8. Joe Wittmer and Robert Myrick. *Facilitative Teaching: Theory and Practice.* Pacific Palisades, California: Goodyear, 1973.
9. J. Doyle Casteel and Robert Stahl. *Value Clarification in the Classroom: A Primer.* Pacific Palisades, California: Goodyear, 1975.
10. Herbert Kohl. *The Open Classroom.* New York: N.Y. Review, 1969.

Books like these, though not written specifically for English teachers, nonetheless may inform the judgments of English teachers and excite them with a renewed sense of important purposes and practices in their teaching.

Finally, one must go beyond books. Though the question to which I am to address myself calls only for the mention of books, the term "professional development" in the question gives me latitude to mention two additional and extremely important sources of such development: the *English Journal* and *Media and Methods.* Most English teachers are familiar with these, though by no means all of them.[2] The *English Journal,* the official organ of the secondary section of the National Council of Teachers of English, regularly contains a combination of theoretical and practical articles and columns that belong in the "must read" category. Ditto *Media and Methods,* which for the past decade has been on the cutting edge of new developments in English education.

These books and journals, then, comprise my suggestions. Through study and reflection on their many-splendored offerings, every English teacher can be "professionally developed" in ways that will pay positive dividends to his students. And that, at bottom, is what professional development is all about.

References

[1]Theodore W. Hipple. "What Goes On in the English Methods Course?" *English Education,* 5 (1974), pp. 225–237.

[2]Theodore W. Hipple and Thomas R. Giblin. "The Professional Reading of English Teachers in Florida." *Research in the Teaching of English,* 5 (1971), pp. 153–164.

[This piece of research is worth examining, as it relates in stark and depressing ways how woefully inadequate is the professional reading of many English teachers.]

Question I, 6

I am still much concerned with the task of providing a variety of learning activities for a wide range of learning abilities. With no clerical help, it seems an overwhelming job, and I invariably find myself violating copyrights and placing myself in potentially illegal situations. Any comforting words?

Jane S. Shoaf, Jordan High School, Durham, North Carolina

Answer by:

ROBERT E. SHAFER, Professor of English at Arizona State University, whose specialty is English Education. Professor Shafer is author or co-author of more than one hundred articles and ten books, the most recent of which is *Decisions about the Teaching of English,* Allyn and Bacon, 1976.

Obviously, teachers need a wide variety of learning materials to develop appropriate learning activities in their classrooms. Your statement that you believe yourself to be "in violation of the copyright law" is a common misconception held by many teachers who are systematically being brainwashed by publications relating to the copyright law currently under revision by the Congress. Actually, the Congress has been in the process of revising the copyright law since 1963. Bills have been introduced in the Congress for the last several years proposing a new copyright law for one reason or another, but these bills have never passed.* For more than a decade the copyright law has been under intensive study by a variety of interested parties such as the Authors' League of America, the American Book Publishers' Council, the National Textbook Publishers' Institute and the Ad Hoc Committee on Copyright Law Revision. The Ad Hoc Committee on Copyright Law Revision has been for many years under the chairmanship of Dr. Harold Wigren of the National Education Association. Its objectives are (a) to protect the public interest in the revision of the United States Copyright Law; (b) to obtain a copyright law which will enable teachers to teach as well as they know how to teach; (c) to make teaching and learning materials as accessible as possible without affecting the potential market for such copyrighted works.[1]

---

* *Editor's Note:* New copyright legislation has been enacted since Professor Shafer wrote this contribution.

The Ad Hoc Committee representing more than 40 consumers of copyrighted materials has been concerned with the concept of "fair use" which has grown up since the 1840s in case law and which has been incorporated into the new copyright law to be a legal doctrine that permits a limited amount of copying of copyrighted materials without infringement of copyright. The Ad Hoc Committee has actively attempted to persuade the Register of Copyrights in drafting the new bill to provide a limited "educational exemption" under the doctrine of "fair use" which would provide the following:

1. Reasonable access to print and nonprint materials for instructional purposes.
2. Reasonable certainty that a given use of a copyrighted work is permissible. Under-the-table uses must be eliminated.
3. Certainty that the present law's "not-for-profit" principle, granting special exemptions for nonprofit uses of copyrighted materials, will be extended.
4. Assurance that teachers who innocently infringe the law will be protected.
5. A new copyright law that will support, rather than thwart, the use of the new technology in the schools.
6. Assurance that the doctrine of "fair use" will be extended to the use of instructional television, computers, automated systems, and other developments in educational technology.[2]

While the various organizations have been studying the copyright law, an unusual court action has affected the attempts to pass a new law. A small Baltimore publishing company, the Williams and Wilkins Company, which publishes 37 scientific journals, many for nonprofit learned societies, claimed infringement by the National Institute of Health Library and demanded "reasonable and entire compensation" in the form of royalties. Suit was brought before the Court of Claims under a 1960 statute which permits persons who have had property taken from them by the government under eminent domain to sue for compensation. The Court of Claims ruled for the government and the Supreme Court deadlocked, thereby upholding the decision of the Court of Claims that essentially the free circulation of scientific knowledge in the public interest was the guiding principle in the decision. The decision, or perhaps one should refer to it as the lack of a decision, caused much reaction in both the educational and publishing worlds. The publishing community has continued to call for a law to be passed by which libraries would have to pay royalties to make copies of articles and indeed proposes that royalties be paid on certain kinds of photocopying.[3]

What is even more worrisome, with respect to the case of the individual classroom teacher, is that large publishing companies are making their own interpretations of what will be in the new copyright law (which has not yet been passed) and are sending out guidelines to teachers and school districts which attempt to interpret the doctrine of "fair use." Such materials as the following anticipate what the publishers hope the new law will contain, when in fact it has not yet been passed. This sample recently mailed to thousands of teachers by a large educational publisher is particularly misleading to teachers and librarians working in schools:

> This fair use doctrine was purposely drawn with a broad brush. To be more explicit would be to limit its effectiveness when as-yet-unconceived technologies present new possibilities for uses of copyrighted works. The drawback to this general approach is that it makes it impossible to list dos and don'ts for teachers, librarians, and others who want to know what is and is not a legal use of copyrighted work. But, rough guidelines are possible:
>
> 1. For educational use, much broader leeway would be given to copying items of general interest, such as a news story or a recipe (all other factors being equal), than copying materials specifically designed for classroom use.
> 2. Consumable materials, such as tests, answer sheets, workbooks, etc., would not fall within the bounds of fair use if duplicated for classroom use.
> 3. Making copies of films or audiocassettes without permission is almost always a violation of copyright.
> 4. Making a single copy of an article for personal use is generally considered within the bounds of fair use. The problem arises when the article is duplicated many times either in a single mass duplication or on a one-by-one basis which, in the aggregate, amounts to multiple or "systematic" duplication.
> 5. A creative teacher develops a "textbook" using a magazine article, a chapter from a textbook, a portion of an encyclopedia item, and some lengthy excerpts from a scholarly journal. This collection is duplicated and distributed to the class. This is clearly beyond the bounds of fair use.[4]

Such statements as those above are in direct conflict with the doctrine of "fair use" as it has evolved since the 1840s in case law. This doctrine provides that *each case is to be judged on its own merits* and such generalized statements as those above might or might not be judged to be "fair use" in a specific case by a specific judge in a specific school at a specific point in time. If a publisher chose to sue a teacher for an infringement of copyright, the judge would apply certain criteria to the case; that is, the judge would ask certain questions concerning the alleged infringement, such as:

1. What is the purpose and nature of the use?
2. What is the nature of the copyrighted work? Is it out of print? Is it consumable or is it easily available from a recognized publisher?
3. What is the amount and substantiality of the material used? Is it a single poem, story, or article within a collection, an excerpt from that collection, or is it considered a whole work in itself?
4. What is the purpose of the use of the work? In other words, has it been used in some of the "time honored" fair use ways which are not considered infringements such as teaching, research, news reporting, etc.?

5. What is the effect of use on the potential market or value of the work? Has the copying displaced what realistically might have been a sale no matter how minor the amount of money involved?

Only after applying such criteria to a specific case would a judge be able to make a decision as to whether there had been an infringement. Since each case of copying would differ with respect to all of the criteria above, no one is able to predict in advance whether a judge will decide a teacher might be infringing or be under "fair use" in any particular case. It seems clear, however, that historically most of what teachers do in duplicating copyrighted materials for the students in their classes would fall under what has been considered the doctrine of "fair use." This would mean that *all* of the items with the exception of Number 3 indicated by Engelhart above are directly misleading or designed to mislead the teacher into thinking that he or she would be infringing on a copyright when actually they would be, under the law as it stands and as it is proposed, entitled to copy copyrighted materials for use in their classrooms.[5]

Teachers need to become informed on issues concerned with the use of copyrighted materials and also with the effects of what our new copyright law will be if it is passed. It would seem clear that we will soon have a new law. As teachers we should be active supporters of the rights of the users of copyrighted material in the knowledge that ultimately the users of copyrighted material make the creative acts of authorship and publication possible, the products of which are to be legitimately protected under the copyright laws and agreements.

References

[1] Harold E. Wigren. "Ad Hoc Committee on Copyright Law Revision," National Education Association, Washington, D.C., p. 1.

[2] *Ibid.*, p. 2.

[3] Richard R. Lingeman. "Copyright and the Right to 'Copy'." *The New York Times Book Review,* November 17, 1974, p. 47.

[4] Susan Engelhart. *Scholastic Teacher.* Volume 22, No. 11, May 1, 1975, p. 1.

[5] Robert E. Shafer. "Fair Use of Copyright Law and Instructional Materials." *Forging Ahead in Reading,* Volume 12, Part I, Proceedings of the Twelfth Annual Convention, International Reading Association, Newark, Delaware: pp. 153–161.

Question I, 7

If an English teacher is lucky enough to choose his own textbooks, how can he know which are superior and what he has available to choose from? Are there any complete lists of English textbooks and any rating systems for them?

Lucy Ellis Parker, South Granville High School, Creedmoor, North Carolina

Answer by:

JOYCE F. WASDELL, Assistant Superintendent for Curriculum and Instruction, Durham County Schools, was a former English teacher and is currently chairperson of the North Carolina Textbook Commission.

Since the question is posed by a North Carolina teacher, some specific comments will be made regarding textbooks that are available for purchase by North Carolina teachers in grades 9–12 with the designated annual textbook allotment of $8 per student. Twenty-six states have similar procedures, and in those, teachers should become familiar with their local or state education agency policies.

An extensive listing of textbooks is found in the *North Carolina State Adopted Basic Textbooks* catalog and in similar guides issued by other state departments of public instruction. (If a catalog is not available in the principal's office, write to the Director, Division of Textbooks, State Department of Public Instruction, in your state capital.) Only textbooks listed in the Division of Textbooks' catalog may be purchased from the annual state allocation.

Readers and advisors to the Textbook Commission usually represent a cross section of English teachers and English educators throughout the state. In the case of North Carolina, criteria for the review and final recommendations of these textbooks are furnished to the Commission and readers by the Language Division of the State Department of Public Instruction.

If these listed textbooks do not meet the needs of students, the Division of Educational Media publishes a bi-annual annotated bibliography of supplementary materials which have been submitted to that department for review and evaluation. Many of these materials could appropriately be used as a supplement to, or instead of, a textbook. These can be purchased with the state allotted instructional materials funds in the "624" category. Each school in North Carolina receives this mailing bi-annually from the Division of Educational Media, and each school library or media center has a copy. These books and other instructional materials are reviewed and annotated by professionals in local school systems as well as in the State Department of Public Instruction.

Publishers are informed about the procedures for textbook adoption and review in each state and their submissions are handled accordingly. In North Carolina, most textbooks or other instructional materials appear on these lists.

A complete list of available textbooks may be found in *Textbooks in Print*, published by R. R. Bowker Company, New York, N. Y. There are no annotations, but the books are categorized by subject areas and grade levels. In addition, the National Council of Teachers of English publishes a list of textbooks and materials submitted to them with the publisher's annotation. This publication is the *1974–75 NCTE Guide to Teaching Materials for English, Grades 7–12*, and is not a complete listing, but yearly supplements are planned. Both of these sources would be helpful as a first step in locating titles and publishers.

All English teachers should become familiar with the review and selection procedures for their state or local districts. Lists of English textbook selection criteria as well as evaluation sheets can usually be secured from a district consultant or supervisor, or from your state agency.

Question I, 8

Does a humanities approach offer secondary school students any sort of unique experience that cannot be offered by the conventional English/social studies/art/music curriculum?

Celia O. Wolfe, Needham Broughton Senior High School, Raleigh, North Carolina

Answer by:

EDWARD M. KELLY, who received his Ed.D. from Boston University with a concentration in humanities education. He has published a number of articles on humanities education. Dr. Kelly is presently Education Director of the nonprofit Institute of Certified Travel Agents.

The uniqueness of the humanities is found not so much in the approach as in the effect. In a successful humanities program, the secondary school student integrates a variety of disciplines. Hence, in the humanities, the student has an opportunity to synthesize as he cannot in specialized electives. More often than not in the well-planned humanities curriculum, taught by able and enthusiastic teachers, the high schooler sees that there is a music to science, that contemporary art is insightful about contemporary poetry. Conventional divisions between subject matters disappear in the light of the humanities.

In direct response to the question, yes, the humanities do have a uniqueness not offered in the music/art/literature/social studies classroom singularly. For example, a senior chooses the following semester-length courses: American history, physics, English literature, and music. Rarely do teachers have time to touch on the connectedness of those subjects. But in the long view, all of these courses at least impinge upon one another. If the same courses were to be included in a humanities aproach, in all probability the students would be focusing on how history exerted its force on literature, the differences and similarities between a law in physics and the conventions governing parody. Another approach might be the thematic, the "19th century world view," where each of the disciplines mentioned could be examined in light of the theme. The possibilities of a humanities approach are manifold.

But a humanities program is not without distinct obstacles also. Unless a teacher exercises great care, the program can be a mere dilettante's tour through disparate bits of knowledge. A prominent danger in a humanities program is this: too much is attempted and depth of understanding may be sacrificed to "coverage."

Those proposing a humanities approach must remember that if "coverage" of content is paramount, content coverage will likely be superficial and gained at the expense of depth. More realistic is the aim to limit the content which will be covered, but to allow for a greater probing of the content. The overriding purpose of a humanities program is not to give secondary students a 2000-year itinerary of Western civilization, but to lead them to an awareness of how all subject matter converges. Later on, if inclined, the students will have ample time to explore the specialized branches of the humanities.

The humanities are best offered in a program rather than as a single elective. Offering the humanities in this manner gives a curriculum design freedom because more subject matter can be included and, usually, a greater time can be allotted to a program than to a course. Most important, a single elective humanities course runs the risk of all electives—specialization. As a result, the student fails to use the interconnectedness of all knowledge and views the humanities as he would creative writing or British writers, isolated bits of content. But, if a choice has to be made whether to offer a single humanities course or no work in the humanities, at least the elective course would be a beginning on which to build.

Question I, 9

Given the diversity of high school populations today and given the public clamor for more attention to the teaching of basic skills in English classes, what do you see as the role of the high school English department? Is it more or less accountable than ever for teaching such skills to all students?

Jan A. Guffin, North Central High School, Indianapolis, Indiana

Answer by:

A. GRAIG PHILLIPS, North Carolina Superintendent of Public Instruction. Dr. Phillips is in his third term as Chief State School Officer for North Carolina.

Regardless of what is taught in English classes, to whatever heterogeneous mix of students, basic skills instruction is fundamental and crucial. While searching the second edition of Webster's *New World Dictionary of the American Language* (New York: William Collins and World Publishing Co., Inc., 1974) to consider the standard meanings of *basic,* I discovered that the phrase *Basic English* itself is included as an entry. Its definition is: "A simplified form of the English language for international communication and for first steps into full English, devised by C. K. Ogden; it consists of a selected vocabulary of 850 essential words and is copyrighted." Incidentally, two dictionary meanings of *basic* are "essential" and "fundamental."

As far as considering the teaching of basic skills is concerned, one must ask, "*Basic* for what?" For international communication (which looms increasingly large as an issue of deep concern), perhaps C. K. Ogden's 850 words are enough. Again, enough for what? For ordering from menus? For asking for a glass of water? For asking directions? For greetings? For saying "Please" and "Thank you"? Perhaps. But only individuals can answer these questions for themselves. And the answers depend upon the extent of academic, occupational, social, and cultural involvement which individuals wish for themselves. *Basic,* considered in this light, becomes a relative term. It is not the responsibility of English departments, which are often considered as bastions of basic skills instruction, to define for students the parameters of involvement they desire. But it *is* the responsibility of English departments to help students acquire the tools of communication they need to arrive at their own definitions and decisions about the involvement they desire. Mastery of basic skills is critical to asking questions, not to mention discovering answers.

For an English department to consider how *much* basic skills instruction it should give is to presume more than is prudent about what students "need." English departments must provide basic skills instruction within the context of all substantive content taught, i.e., instruction in such skills as reading, writing, listening, speaking, observing, and critical thinking. The emphases must never be upon *minimum* but upon *maximum* learning for each individual, according to his or her individual capacity to achieve a mastery of skills.

No advocate of educational reform seriously suggests downplaying basic skills instruction. Even Ivan Illich, perhaps the most radical school reformer, says basic skills instruction is "fundamental, . . . such skills as reading, typing, keeping accounts, foreign languages . . ." (*Deschooling Society,* New York: Harrow Books, 1971, p. 130). The substantive content of disciplines does indeed change and require constant re-evaluation. Methodologies change and expand, as new and effective instructional approaches evolve. Curricular designs are continuously restructured and redirected out of future-oriented thinking. But attention to the basic communicative skills must always permeate any other changes and redirections that affect the lives of students in schools. Such a stance is necessary if we really believe in enabling students to be truly wide-open and flexible about the decision-making processes which affect their futures. Deficiency in basic skills obviously limits such decision-making.

Now for the matter of accountability. In North Carolina recently, I appointed a committee to study the issue of accountability. The title of their report is "Becoming Accountable in Education: An Interim Report" (Raleigh, N.C.: Department of Public Instruction, April, 1975). The committee defined accountability as "the mutual acceptance by individuals and groups of shared responsibility for the status and continuing improvement of the total educational process" (p. 4). The committee was composed of legislators, laymen, and educators. Accordingly, no single individual nor narrow group of individuals can be held legitimately accountable for the success or failure of any educational enterprise. English departments can be held accountable for adequate and effective instruction in the basic skills only to the extent that they have concrete support from state education departments, local boards, school principals, parents—in short, all members of the educational community. If adequate support is present and agreed upon by all, then teachers can and will perform their tasks effectively. Assessments must be conducted to determine the quality and the quantity of student learning, with the full realization that always there will be failures in the learning process. Realistic judgment and prudence by all are necessary for accountability to be a viable and useful concept.

For students to be able to make decisions about their futures and to act on those decisions, basic skills must lie at the heart of any effective instructional program. And for English departments to be held accountable for instruction, all members of the educational community must share in the responsibility.

Question I, 10

I know that high school students love to play games, and I suspect that many games can be used in the English classroom to help students polish their basic skills. Can you suggest any?
Robert C. Baird, LeRoy Martin Junior High School, Raleigh, North Carolina

Answer by:
STAN COX. Mr. Cox received his A.B. in Social Anthropology from Harvard College and his M.A.T. in English from Duke University; he is presently an English teacher at Sea Pines Abroad in Faistenau, Austria.

The popular suggestion that "learning should be fun" has led many English teachers to design assignments which trick students into learning or which challenge and build upon area(s) of natural curiosity. I am all for such innovation and have made an early reputation among my students as the crazy English teacher who "has you do weird things in class." But this question doesn't ask about disguised or innovative English assignments, but rather about actual games which can be played in the English classroom. The difference between an innovative English assignment and a game involving English is readily apprehended from the student point of view: assignments are work; games are play. No matter how cleverly I lead into a creative writing assignment or supplement a lesson on paragraph unifying techniques, Susie eventually figures out that I mean for her to hand in a paper with some writing on it that will count for a grade. Though I start by reading "Jabberwocky" and end up by giving Mitch ten fictitious words labeled noun, adv., etc., Mitch knows that if he doesn't turn in "them crazy sentences," it will go none too well for him when report card time rolls round. Such learning activities may be fun, but they are still work.

The first suggestion I make concerning a game, then, is to let it be a game: don't count it for a grade; don't set it up so that only good students are rewarded for their participation in a good students' type of class drill. Let game day be noticeably different from class days. Letting the game be a game includes such things as: (1) giving prizes to the winning team (candy, gum, etc.); (2) suspending or modifying normal classroom rules of conduct (more talk, different seats); (3) allowing the natural high school competitive spirit to surface (even occasional taunts are permissible); (4) helping as moderator to create a mood of excitement and tension (counting off the clock;

continually saying "are you ready, team?"); repeating the score in a close game; doing many other things to show that this is a contest which one team will actually win. Once students realize that game day is definitely not work day, they respond with appropriate enthusiasm. Students like to play games.

And though the students think they are completely getting out of work, they are in reality playing a game involving English. The teacher can use a game to introduce concepts really not of major import- ance to a unit but still worth covering, and the teacher can use a game to review and polish old skills in a fun context. Yet the main value of the game is probably not directly educational. The game primarily provides a diversion from the regular routine for both teacher and student. By dissociating the English game from the English class- work, several educational side benefits can be reaped. The apathetic or rowdy student is more likely to turn in regular work and behave if he feels his privilege of "having a fun game" might otherwise be taken away. The talented yet troublesome student who won't do good school- work because he "hates school" might allow some of his talent to show forth in a game clearly labeled "not schoolwork." And the competitive game allows the teacher to see vividly who are the peer leaders and what are the class interpersonality relationships. So a game can be sound strategy even if only a questionable amount of academic learning takes place.

What kinds of games can be played? There are many possibili- ties, and I would encourage every teacher to find or develop his or her particular favorites (it is always easier to get excited about a game you helped build yourself than about one borrowed *in toto*).* I give for the remainder of this article the outline for one of my own games, not confident that it will work in every situation, but hopeful that by seeing what has been successfully practiced by one teacher (myself), other teachers will be encouraged to invent and refine their own games.

The most popular game in my classroom has turned out to be a vocabulary game. I usually divide the class into two teams (two seems to provide the most competition). Since students do not know in ad- vance which days are to be game days (a privilege promised has a way of transforming itself into a right owed), they are eager and surprised when I begin to count them randomly as "ones" or "twos." When chairs have been shuffled, teams have conferred, a timer/scorekeeper has been chosen, and quiet has begun to prevail again, we start the game. One team gives a letter, the other team adds a letter to form a word; the first team adds another letter to form a new word, etc.—that is the simple format of my vocabulary game. Each team receives however

---

*There are many places to start looking for ideas. Scholastic Book Services through its Teen Age Book Club regularly offers game aids, many of which are quite good. Several books also provide game suggestions. (One such book is *Games to Improve Your Child's English,* New York: Simon and Schuster, 1969.)

many points as there are letters in the word it forms. Whenever a team feels it cannot add a letter to the existing word to form a new word, the team submits a new letter, worth one point (thus a team always scores on its turn). A typical round might proceed as follows:

Team One: "a" = 1 pt
Team Two: "at" = 2 pts
Team One: "hat" 3 pts + 1 prev. pt = 4 pts
Team Two: "heat" 4 pts + 2 prev. pts = 6 pts
Team One: "heats" 5 pts + 4 prev. pts = 9 pts
Team Two: "hearts" 6 pts + 6 prev. pts = 12 pts
Team One: "r" (new letter signifies the start of a new round)

Team Two would be seen to have the advantage at this stage since it was the last team to add to the existing word. Some original letters cannot be added to form words so we have made it a rule that a letter can be started only once. Team members are required to use the words they submit correctly in a sentence if there is any doubt in the teacher's mind about the students' knowledge of the words. A dictionary is kept handy to settle disputes about "hard words," but in truth I often use the dictionary when I already know the answer, just to set an example for future student use (if students see the teacher naturally turn to the dictionary when he is in doubt about spelling or meaning, students are more willing to turn to the dictionary when they are in doubt). Though a team may confer before giving its answer, I call on individual members one by one for the team answer. Not only does this insure some measure of participation by all, it also allows everyone to be "king cheese" for his team at least once. Peer pressure is strong enough that even a slow, apathetic student makes sure he has been told what the word means, how it's spelled, and how it's pronounced before he answers. No one wants to cause his team to lose and thereby cheat himself out of a piece of candy.

Not only is this game fast moving (a 30-second time limit for formation of new words insures this), unembarrassing to slow students (the word submitted is a team effort, even though only one person gives the answer), and a challenge to brighter students (scratch paper is always filled with unused vocabulary words that have been formed on the possibility of what the other team will do); but this game can be easily modified to become a new game each week.

One variation is to allow substitutions of one letter for another at a value of, say, four points (provided the word has at least four letters). A round under this variation might go as follows:

Team One: "best" = 4 pts + prev. pts
Team Two: "belt" = 4 pts + prev. pts
Team One: "belts" = 5 pts + prev. pts
Team Two: "beats" = 4 pts + prev. pts
Team One: "beasts" = 6 pts + prev. pts
Team Two: "feasts" = 4 pts + prev. pts

Another variation is to allow for the formation of antonyms, synonyms, homonyms, etc., for a bonus of, say, five points for each such word recognized and given. By building gradually on a simple game, students after a few weeks are able to play a much more complicated game, which involves several different types of vocabulary skills. Skills learned in one type of game can also be transferred to a different game. Thus, my students who had played the vocabulary game with the variations described above quickly caught on to a spelling game involving forming smaller words from a larger word (using the letters of the large word to form other words). The creative English teacher will enjoy seeing how far he or she can push a class into these complex and modified sort of games. Why? Because:

> Team One: "lode-load" = 4 pts + 5 bonus pts for homonym
> Team Two: "loading" = 4 pts for suffix transformation
> Team One: "loaning" = 4 pts for letter substitution
> Team Two: "leaning" = 4 pts for letter substitution
> Team One: "learning = fun" (8 pts for adding letter + 5 pts for synonym)

Question I, 11

At any given grade level, is there a significant difference between standardized test scores of students who are products of conventional, traditional learning situations and those who are products of nonconventional learning situations such as IGE, open classrooms, or alternative programs?

James A. Jenkins, North Central High School, Indianapolis, Indiana

Answer by:
WALTER H. MacGINITIE, Professor of Psychology and Education at Teachers College, Columbia University. His specialty is the psychology of language. He is the author of many journal articles and research reports and the co-author of the *Gates-MacGinite Reading Tests*. He is President of the International Reading Association.

Both "traditional learning situations" and each of the "non-conventional learning situations" mentioned in the question differ so much from one situation to another that I am quite unable to give an answer that would be useful to anyone wishing to compare their products. There are certainly reports of open classrooms, for example, where the students have improved their standardized test scores in certain subjects in relation to the scores that were previously obtained in that school under a more traditional situation. There are also open classrooms where standardized test performance in certain fields appears to have dropped since the institution of the open classroom. Neither of these kinds of reports provides any evidence for the guidance of someone who would be interested in instituting a new, nonconventional program.

Seldom, in these reports, is there a sufficient description of the conventional and nonconventional situations that are being compared, and even a considerable accumulation of such reports would not provide sound guidance. One thing seems clear from previous studies of educational achievement, and that is that time and effort spent by students and teachers on a particular subject matter area is an important influence on the achievement of the students in that area. The amount of time and energy spent on any one subject is seldom determined by the general nature of the particular organizational structure that a school or classroom uses.

This is but one of many factors that probably have much greater influence on students' achievement than the particular organizational structure. I personally believe it is far more important to capture the enthusiasms and interests of teachers and students than it is to establish a particular organizational structure. Oftentimes, however, a particular structure can be the basis for capturing these enthusiasms. In that case, a program based on that structure is likely to be successful.

Question I, 12

My question is a cliché complaint: How can I give personal attention to my students' varied problems in language with the limited amount of time available and the number of students assigned to me? Are there *any* personalized-type assignments that can reach the entire class and meet their needs? I use journals for writing and they seem to work on high- and low-level students, but what about the majority in the middle?

Larry Morwick, Emmerich Manual High School, Greenwood, Indiana

Answer by:
FRANCES N. WIMER, Coordinator of Programs for the Gifted and Talented, Richmond Public Schools in Richmond, Virginia. Mrs. Wimer is editor of the *Virginia English Bulletin* and the *Administrator's Newsletter* and has been active in the Virginia Association of Teachers of English and the National Council of Teachers of English.

Movement to an individualized-personalized strategy of instruction in combination with other teaching strategies would possibly offer a partial solution to meeting the needs of today's heterogeneous school population.

To a typical school teacher with an average class size of thirty students per class teaching five classes per day, the idea of individualization may appear absurd. With clearly defined goals, however, a strategic plan of teaching procedures and some student-created and teacher-created materials worked out in advance, a teacher can individualize some phases of language study.

Since both spoken and written communication are included in language study and because research indicates that students respond favorably to theme- or process-oriented units with skills studies interwoven within the unit, we are recommending two approaches with which we are currently experimenting in the middle schools and high schools of the Richmond Public Schools.

Plan I

Step 1.

Through open discussion in whole group sessions, arouse student interest in ideas they wish to explore. Use favorite poems and quotations, editorials, television programs, or any activators which stimulate students toward further discussion and study. To students who prefer teacher-suggested topics, you may wish to include these theme-oriented or process-oriented ideas for their consideration: "The Nobel Prize Winners: A Reflection of Humanistic Thought," "The Profundity Pit: Exploring Literature in Depth," "Making Decisions: How Wide Is My Window," or "The Undiscovered Individual," "The Youth Scene," "Choice in Consequences," "All Our Tomorrows," "Dreaming the Dream," "Making Do," "Finding Love," "Making a Living," "Doubting," "Believing," and many others.

Step 2.

Prepare, perhaps with student assistance and/or by teaming up with another teacher, folders of materials related to developing the themes in which the students have expressed an interest. The potpourri of materials should include both student- and professionally-written poems and essays, newspaper editorials and columns, and teacher-prepared materials. The materials should not be "textbookie" but should be both profound and light. Magazines and newspaper items are current, interesting, and inexpensive; selected anthology items add variety to the folder contents. *The Good Life/U.S.A.*, an inexpensive paperbound book, gives not only ideas for themes but also for materials for possible inclusion in the folder.[1] To develop certain cognitive skills, contracts and ideas for written compositions should also be a part of the folder contents.

Step 3.

Have the student select a folder of his choice. From the materials included and by adding others of his own, he will develop a theme independently or with a group. If the theme is too broad, variations can be selected (Example—*Theme:* THE CREATIVE INSTINCT, *Variations:* "Portrait of the Artist," "To See Feelingly," "Cinematics," "Visual Literacy," "The Phantom Script," and "Immortality through Art"[2]).

Step 4.

Have the student select books from a classroom library which includes readings related to the theme he has chosen. The books can be paperbound or hardback, classics as well as modern literature. No limit should be placed on the number of books, selections, or articles to be read.

Step 5.

Activities should be based on materials the students, with teacher assistance, have selected for study. The teacher must next direct his energies toward creating varied types of learning environments. A social atmosphere should exist for whole-class discussion which reflects freedom and liveliness and where spoken language can be natural. On the other hand, a more formal atmosphere should be created for organized discussion and for the use of language study in two components: the

development of ideas and the expression of these ideas appropriately and effectively. Occasionally an atmosphere of more restraint may be desirable for formal writing situations. The activities should encourage the individualization and continuous progress concepts of learning.
Step 6.
Evaluation of the student's work should be a continuous process. He should keep a cumulative progress folder, complete with a table of contents, a teacher-student conference and evaluation sheet, written compositions, and a record of any talks, films, tapes, or other work he has done related to his project or study. Much of the evaluation process can be conducted through student-teacher conferences.

Plan II

A second plan embodies the same basic concepts and similar procedures as Plan I. With more extensive pre-planning and teacher preparation, it can result in a greater degree of emphasis on individualized-personalized instruction on written language skills. This plan was developed by a core curriculum committee in Richmond Public Schools in consultation with Paul C. Kreuger, formerly of MacDougal-Littell Publishing Company.

Objectives	Beginnings	Developmental Activities	New Beginnings Unplanned	Evaluation Assessment
1. Affective	# 1	_____	_____	_ _ _ _
2. Cognitive	# 2	_____	_____	_ _ _ _
3. Skills	# 3	_____	_____	_ _ _ _

In Plan II, the teacher plans approximately three weeks of a six-week unit. The second portion is unplanned but not unstructured. It becomes structured while the unit is in progress as student needs arise and during student-teacher planning and working sessions.

The beginnings include ten to twenty written language assignments. The teacher uses only as many of these as are necessary for the student to begin fulfilling the objectives.

Many of the procedures used in Plan I can be used in Plan II. Spoken language, history of the language, dialectology, and some other phases of language may be taught in whole-class sistuations. Two excellent recent NCTE publications for the study of the English language as *language* have been written by J. N. Hook[3] and Robert C. Pooley.[4]

The basic difference in the two plans, however, is that the developmental skills activities are taught through the use of skill boxes, activity cards, and posters.

Several commercially prepared skill boxes and the James Moffett *Interaction* series activity cards can be used or even serve as models for teacher- and student-created cards. Skill boxes can be made with commercial materials by tearing up workbook and textbook items on several grade levels, mounting them and then laminating them. Grammatical structures and composition skills can be effectively learned in this manner. Activity cards can be made for word study, dialectology, usage, linguistic analysis, and composition. Every card should require a product—a paper, a tape, or a film. The product should be evaluated in a student-teacher conference. Answer sheets should be provided for "drill-type" exercises, and each student can check his own work.

"Individualization should be the rule," says Don H. Parker, "when we want to help the student learn basic skills." [5] Then, too, the philosophy encouraged as a result of the Dartmouth Conference in 1966—that when a child begins to grow, his growth progresses at an individual rate—makes individualization and continuous progress concepts almost mandatory.

These individualization strategies make available for students what they need at the moment they recognize that need.

Time-savers for the Busy English Teacher

1. Introduce a major sequence, then move to "laboratory" instruction.
2. Put students in groups to use a skill, to write group compositions, to evaluate compositions, to discuss parallel reading.
3. Have the student do his own filing for his English folder.
4. Tape comments and replies to the individual student.
5. Team teach as often as feasible.
6. Use whole-class instruction for subjects with common appeal or for common knowledge.
7. Use peer tutoring, peer evaluation, and student planning techniques.
8. Prepare answer keys and have students check objective-type materials.
9. In evaluating compositions:
   (a) Mark only certain types of errors based on student needs
   (b) Mark papers in teacher-student conferences when possible
   (c) Serve as a consultant rather than a proofreader for written composition
10. Prepare a "Teacher Survival Kit" to be used as needed. Place in a clasp envelope:
    (a) Good topics for short essays
    (b) Creative writing ideas
    (c) Crossword puzzles
    (d) Travel brochures
    (e) Job application forms
    (f) Several good poems by old and new masters
    (g) Word study games
    (h) Topics for classroom discussion
11. Read and use for action by your local association the NCTE publication, *Workload for English Teachers: Policy and Procedure* by Henry B. Maloney

Your problem is a universal one for English teachers. More time spent in pre-planning, however, and utilizing student resources and the newer concepts for the study of language should make both the teaching and learning processes more exciting.

References
[1]Arthur Daigon and Ronald T. LaConte. *The Good Life, U.S.A.* New York: Bantam, 1973
[2]*framework for freedom in the english curriculum 7-12* Fairfax County Public Schools, Fairfax, Virginia: 1972, p. 75
[3]J. N. Hook. *People Say Things Different Ways.* Glenview, Illinois: Scott, Foresman and Company, 1974
[4]Robert C. Pooley, *The Teaching of English Usage.* Urbana, Illinois: National Council of Teachers of English, 1974
[5]Virgil N. Howes. *Individualization of Instruction.* New York: The Macmillan Company, 1970, p. 177

Question I, 13

I teach a senior English class composed of 36 students, half of whom are college-bound and the rest of whom are work-oriented. Given a 55 minute class period five days a week, how can I make the class meaningful to both groups? Should both groups be held to the same standards?

Iva G. Dean, Tazewell Senior High School, Tazewell, Virginia

Answer by:

LEONIDAS BETTS, Associate Professor of English and Education and Coordinator of Student Teaching in English at North Carolina State University. Mr. Betts is former editor of *North Carolina English Teacher* and editor of *North Carolina Folklore Journal.*

To our delight or to our dismay, English instruction has entered the Post-Dartmouth Age. The participants at the 1966 Anglo-American Conference on the Teaching and Learning of English agreed on eleven points, including the "need to overcome the restrictiveness of rigid patterns of 'grouping' or 'streaming' which limit the linguistic environment in which boys and girls learn English and which tend to inhibit language development."[1] Indeed, the "problem" of the heterogeneous or "mixed" class may become the sought-after norm. Difficult as the acceptance of a changing perception of what an English class is or should be, the portents of widespread reassessment and reformation are upon us. Of the present state of affairs, Brinkman has observed, "Every semester we are given a diversified group of human beings. We can see them as the 'group' assigned to our classes to have a specified amount of material poured or forced into their minds, or we can care for them, touch them, share with them, and respect them."[2]

Today a watchword is "individualization" (in spite of the reassurances of some cloistered theorists, a process easier to conceptualize than to implement). Individualized instruction is possible, within limits, even in a class of thirty-six significantly different students. In spite of overcrowded classes, lack of planning time, the absence of meaningful communication among faculty members, haphazard curriculum articulation, and inadequate funding, the individual, dedicated teacher can realize a measure of success in meeting the needs of the unique personalities in a class. The situation described in the question would demand an abandonment of reliance on a singleshot approach, which invariably would be diluted for academic students and unrealistic for the work-oriented.

An English teacher first must gauge the needs of the students, taking into account personal judgment, standardized test results and subjective measures, community expectations, and students' insights and plans. The primacy of this initial step is emphasized by Swift: "It would be foolish to go into a period of renovation simply with the idea of *change:* The guiding principle should be *needs.*" [3]

These needs become translated into instructional objectives for individuals, groups, and the entire class. Strategy for accomplishing a set of objectives almost invariably entails the use of what is broadly termed a unit. *"The ideal unit of work makes the student feel that a hitherto confusing area is gradually being clarified, that previously miscellaneous observations are being fitted into a meaningful pattern. At the same time he feels that light is being shed at least in part as a result of his own efforts; that he is contributing rather than merely absorbing."* [4]

The unit takes countless forms. A student who is deficient in sophisticated usage skills but is planning to attend a university whose English department expects grammatical "correctness" may be assigned a programed text.[5] Students weak in the most basic language skills could work within the framework of other types of published materials.[6] Given adequate time, the teacher can develop units from sets of comprehensive handbooks.[7] Learning activities packages, incorporating various types of processes and materials, containing numerous choices, can be constructed to use with groups of all sizes. Some subjects are universal in their appeal and pertinence, such as uses and misuses of media. Within a media LAP could be incorporated activities for the entire scope of student needs, interests, and abilities.

The apparent educational success of *Foxfire* strongly suggests that such projects could work in many classrooms. Folklore is not confined to mountain hollows and bridgeless islands. A teacher embarking on folklore study, with all its educational potential, would need personal preparation to capitalize fully on the vast resources within the students and the community.[8] A folklore LAP would engage every student in a class-wide enterprise of nearly infinite potential, encompassing all language skills, as well as humanistic concerns. Of his use of *Foxfire* in his classes, Eliot Wigginton has said, "English . . . is communication— reaching out and touching people with words, sounds, and visual images. We are in the business of improving students' prowess in these areas. In their work with photography . . . , text . . . , lay-out, make-up, correspondence, art and cover design, and selection of manuscript . . . , they learn more about English than from any other curriculum I could devise." [9]

The problem of evaluation and standards for grading does not yield readily to solution, especially in a traditional school setting. The March, 1975, issue of *English Journal* focused upon this unsettled (and unsettling) area. One potentially useful approach is suggested by Kenneth Lewis.[10] In any case, the best guide for assessing a student's work will be the success the student achieves in meeting the needs and objectives set out in the units undertaken. If individualized instruction can be realized, then individualized grading must follow, not in the ABC sense, but in the summation of competencies demonstrated by the student within the range of his own peculiar work.

References

[1] See Albert H. Marckwardt. "The Dartmouth Seminar." *NASSP Bulletin*, 51 (1967), pp. 104–105.

[2] Sandi Brinkman. "The Public Education System: Future or Funeral?" *English Journal*, 63 (1974), p. 44.

[3] Jonathan Swift. "The Prevention and Cure of Post-Curriculum Innovitis." *English Journal*, 63 (1974), p. 54.

[4] Hans P. Guth. *English Today and Tomorrow.* Englewood Cliffs, New Jersey: Prentice-Hall, Inc., 1965, p. 352.

[5] See, for a time-honored example, Joseph C. Blumental. *English 3200.* New York: Harcourt Brace & World, Inc., 1962.

[6] A survey of any recent catalog of the publisher of instructional materials will reveal numerous possibilities. For example, the 1974-75 catalog of Scholastic Book Services contains items like *Patterns for Reading, Reluctant Reader Library* and *Scope/Skills.*

[7] For an inexpensive and comprehensive source, see William B. Ravenel III. *English Reference Book.* Alexandria, Viriginia: English Reference Book, 1959.

[8] Possibly the most satisfactory guide is Jan Harold Brunvand. *The Study of American Folklore.* New York: W. W. Norton & Co., Inc., 1968.

[9] *The Foxfire Book.* Garden City, New York: Doubleday & Co., Inc., 1972, p. 13.

[10] "Putting the Hidden Curriculum of Grading to Work." *English Journal*, 64 (1975), pp. 82–84.

Question I, 14

What is the most effective means of teaching each child in a secondary school English class at his own level?

Leona P. Parrish, Smithfield-Selma Senior High School, Smithfield, North Carolina

Answer by:

CARYL McNEES, associate professor of English at California State Polytechnic University, Pomona, California. Dr. McNees's specialization is in English Education. She teaches Secondary English Methods, Adolescent Literature, and a graduate seminar in Problems in High School Composition, in addition to regular English courses.

Educators agree that individualization of instruction is the most effective means of teaching each student at his or her own level. The problem, then, becomes one of implementation; that is, *how* do teachers individualize instruction in the English classroom?

G. Robert Carlsen[1] recommends a three-dimensional plan for individualizing literature which involves: (1) individualized reading; (2) in-common reading; and (3) thematic reading.

In describing the program, Carlsen suggests that (in the first dimension) students read novels of their own choosing. The teacher ascertains individual interests and reading levels and, accordingly, selects 30-40 titles from which students may choose.

The second dimension involves one novel which the class reads in common. Analysis of this novel should relate to ideas which were perceived individually in the first dimension reading. Thematic reading, the third dimension, is designed around a particular theme. Short pieces of literature in all genres (but on the same general theme) are read in common, whereas longer pieces of literature are selected by students to be read outside of class. These outside readings are chosen from a thematic bibliography provided by the teacher.

Thus, each of the dimensions of Carlsen's program provides for the individualization of each student's work in literature while, at the same time, the student is learning the basics of analysis.

In composition as in literature, the problem again seems to center around the means by which to individualize. Because students are at different levels of writing ability, it is difficult for the teacher to decide upon appropriate writing topics. The teacher generally solves this problem by allowing students to select their own topics—a procedure which usually leaves them floundering.

In order to give students something to write about at their own level, Hawley, Simon, and Britton[2] suggest activities in preparation for writing. These activities concern individual values and thereby offer students writing topics about which they have first-hand knowledge. The authors maintain that when students are writing about their individual values and needs, they are most at ease with composition.

Another means of meeting individual levels of learning in composition is the use of the journal in which students write their perceptions of their daily lives. This method is highly individualized and allows the students to become accustomed to writing in general. Periodically, the students may submit what they consider to be their best pieces of writing in order to obtain teacher and peer comments for revision of the work.

Recently, the use of the elective system throughout secondary schools has gained much popularity. The elective system in the English classroom may help meet students' individual needs. The teacher offers a list of reading and writing activities from which students may choose; this list encompasses a wide range of abilities and each activity is assigned a number of points. Evaluation is determined by the total number of points accrued. In this manner, students may more easily individualize work in English both as to the difficulty of the work and the quality and quantity of performance.

Last, independent study is probably the purest form of individualization. Here, the students work on their own with the teacher serving as a resource person. McNees's[3] study, based on research of English independent study, revealed four separate elements which appear to be necessary to the structure of independent study:

1. self-direction: students are given much freedom in selecting and directing their own English study;
2. interrelationship of fields: students may relate English study to other disciplines;
3. flexible scheduling: students have schedules which allow them time outside the English classroom to conduct independent study;
4. freedom of movement: students are permitted to move from one area to another in the school (school library, English resource center, etc.) and outside of the school (community library, resource centers, etc.) to work on particular study projects.

In conclusion, the answer to the question of teaching students at their own levels is individualization of instruction. Students' interests and levels of ability vary and the teacher must be aware that there are many options for individualization. Ideally, reading and writing should be a continuing interest beyond the classroom. This goal can best be achieved through making English in the classroom what it should be in a lifetime—an individual matter.

References

[1]G. Robert Carlsen. "Adolescents and Literature in Three Dimensions." *Wisconsin English Journal*, V (October 1962).

[2]Robert C. Hawley, Sidney B. Simon, and D. D. Britton. *Composition for Personal Growth*. New York: Hart Publishing Company, Inc., 1973.

[3]Caryl McNees. "An Empirical Investigation of English Independent Study Programs in the Commonwealth of Virginia Based on a Conceptual Model." Unpublished doctoral dissertation, University of Virginia, 1972.

Question I, 15

Mini-courses, which are so popular in many schools, present a major problem for me. They run for so short a time that I never really get to know my students as well as I would like. I want to know my students. Any suggestions?

Marjorie Greer Justin, Wilkes Central High School, Wilkesboro, North Carolina

Answer by:

LARRY ANDREWS, Professor of English and Secondary Education, University of Nebraska, Lincoln. Mr. Andrews has written numerous articles on secondary school English and reading instruction.

When English courses were scheduled from September to May, we had 36 weeks to teach, to learn, to get to know each other. Yet, even with that length of time we knew too little about too many students. With the advent of nine-week mini-courses in the English curricula throughout the country, the problem is intensified and more crucial.

Teachers must know their *students' abilities;* otherwise, they are forced into basing instruction upon a number of assumptions about their students' level of preparation for the content of the course. Herber[1] has described the needless boredom or frustration students frequently experience at the hands of the "assumptive teacher." Similarly, teachers need to know their *students' interests and attitudes;* otherwise, class activities, reading selections, writing topics, and the like may be so far removed from the students' interests and preferences that, again, ennui or frustration results.

A short pretest administered during the first meetings of a mini-course reveals much about the students' level of preparation for the materials and activities the teacher has selected for use. Not for grading purposes, this pretest assumes a variety of forms, depending upon the information the teacher believes will be most useful. For instance, if the mini-course requires extensive reading in a genre or topic, representative passages from the texts to be read can be duplicated and given to the class. Carefully written questions, which can be answered only after one has read the text and are therefore *reading-dependent,* reveal how easily students make out the plain sense of a poem, grasp the significance of images used, discern modes of characterization, or ascribe meaning to dialog or stage directions. Or, the pretest might assess the students' abilities to give appropriate meanings to significant technical terms which name key concepts to be studied in the mini-course; i.e., dolly, iris, fade; two-value orientation, inference, judgment; or card catalog, vertical file, *Reader's Guide.* (Obviously, terms selected depend upon the nature of the mini-course.)

The teacher could also prepare a cloze procedure for one or more of the selections the students will read in the course. Results from this informal assessment reveal at which level the students can read the material: independent, instructional, or frustration reading level.[2]

Students' preferences for independence or teacher-direction may be useful to the teacher. An informal list of questions, such as "I prefer to read when _____." or "I study best when _____.", can be beneficial to the teacher when assignments are made or groups within the class are formed. Good models to follow are the ones created by Wood[3] or by Viox.[4]

A related area, just as significant in shaping the success of the mini-course, is that of student interest. Given the need to establish an atmosphere which encourages and maintains dialog, Shuman[5] has created a series of questions which ask students to explain more about themselves as persons. Answers to questions such as "Why, aside from obeying the law, are you in school?", and "What one question would you most like to ask me?", or "What would you most hate to lose?" are invaluable to the teacher as writing assignments, language activities, viewing or reading selections are discussed in the mini-course. Fader and McNeil [6] have created a number of scales and checklists the teacher can use to understand better the students' verbal abilities, attitudes in general and toward reading in particular. Teachers might be more comfortable with interest inventories of their own making. These have the advantage of being tailor-made for one's own mini-course: "If you had three wishes for yourself, what would they be?" "Name two or three of your all-time favorite books, poets, television programs, movies, writers, words, etc." Answers to such questions, given on the first day of the mini-course, help the teacher to know immediately the students' backgrounds, interests, and concerns.

Perhaps the teacher wants different kinds of information yet, or wants to create a special climate on that first day of the course. Depending upon the nature of the mini-course, one might write on slips of paper the names of authors or characters who will be studied. Titles of movies or television programs could be used. Important people from the theater, sports, or show business might be appropriate. As each student enters the classroom, an "identity" is taped to each one's back. Three yes/no questions can be asked of every other person in the room; the student who is first to learn his identity receives a prize, either a real one or a gag. This activity can last as long as the teacher considers it convenient or comfortable.

From these individual wanderings around the room, students are then put in pairs. Give them 5 minutes to learn as much as they can about each other. At the end of 5 minutes, put the pairs into groups of four; here, each student tells the new couple everything he has learned about his partner. After an appropriate length of time, groups of fours join to make 3 or 4 groups of eight, and again each student tells all he has learned about his earlier partner(s). Finally, everyone returns to the all-class setting for a discussion of their similar/dissimilar tastes, experiences, wants, needs, hopes, hobbies, schools attended, and so on.

At some point in the discussions the teacher might arrange desks into a large circle, handing out 4 x 6 cards and felt-tipped pens, asking each student to print his name on the card and to decorate the card with his "totem." One student might draw a tennis racket beside his name, another might draw a car, a pair of skis. Whatever, the cards with the names and totems can be taped on the desks and used daily during the first week of the mini-course to proclaim everyone's name and personality.

Not one of these suggestions will supply all the information about students a teacher might want, but they'll do for starters. (The best activities are those each teacher adapts for his or her unique mini-course and students.) These initial activities will help, provided the teacher can maintain, throughout the mini-course, the idea that students are not only free to offer tentative statements, solutions, and beliefs, but that their success, and the success of the mini-course, requires it. This is the community in which we best learn and live as people.[7]

References

[1] Harold Herber. *Teaching Reading in Content Areas,* Englewood Cliffs, New Jersey: Prentice Hall, 1970, pp. 29–30.

[2] John Bormuth. "Comparable Cloze and Multiple-Choice Comprehension Test Scores." *Journal of Reading,* 10 (1967), pp. 291–299.

[3] Fred Wood. "Self-Direction and Achievement." *High School Journal,* 58 (1975), pp. 161–169.

[4] Ruth Viox. *Evaluating Reading and Study Skills in Secondary Schools.* Newark, Delaware: International Reading Association, 1968.

[5] R. Baird Shuman. "Establishing a Basis for Classroom Dialog." *English Journal,* 61 (1972), pp. 1338-1340.

[6] Daniel Fader & Elton B. McNeil. *Hooked on Books: Program and Proof.* New York: G. B. Putnam's Sons, 1968.

[7] Larry Andrews. "Responses to Literature: In Tennis the Serve Is Crucial." *English Journal,* 63 (1974), pp. 44–46.

Question I, 16

How can English teachers determine the relevancy of subject matter for non-college bound students?

Carolyn G. Ennis, Supervisor in English, Johnston County Schools, Smithfield, North Carolina

Answer by:

JAMES E. DAVIS, Professor of English at Ohio University, whose specialty is English Education. Mr. Davis is the author of numerous articles and a frequent speaker at conventions and workshops. He has edited the *Ohio English Bulletin* and is currently president of the English Association of Ohio.

Determining the relevancy of subject matter for non-college bound students is much more complex than an initial cursory reading might indicate. The terms are difficult to define, and frequently the definitions raise still more questions. Who are these non-college bound students anyway, and how did they get that way? How can teachers know? How can the students themselves know with any degree of certainty? The answers to these questions do not involve just the determining of the type of curriculum for certain students, but these answers further involve the teacher with questions of basic philosophy of teaching and the nature of people.

Are the non-college bound students the culturally deprived, the minorities, the business oriented, or the slow learners? Do they exist in a group apart from the college bound, or are they mixed and in direct competition with them? How did they get the label? Standardized test norms? Economic class? Appearance? Race? Attitude? Self-discovery? Who these students are and what they are like is the responsibility of the teacher to discover, and the teacher must live with the consequences of such discovery. Leonard Mollenkof's definition reveals the scope of the problem. He says that they are students who have been referred to in the past as a "faceless mass," who lie somewhere in between the retarded and the talented, and who present to educators one of the major challenges of the day.[1] Such students choose to terminate (or think they are going to terminate) their formal education after high school for a variety of reasons. Mental inferiority and low achievement are certainly not the only factors. In fact, some research indicates that at least two-thirds could do college work.[2]

Unfortunately, the term "non-college bound" implies a negative, even an inferior position and social stigma which aggravates even more their frequent already-present lack of motivation.[3] If this labelling is accompanied by grouping in separate classes, the problem may be further compounded by the self-fulfilling prophecy of teacher expectation.[4] Teachers may systematically favor the college bound as the more important students and demand and reinforce quality performance of them, while not demanding and reinforcing such quality performance of the students labelled non-college bound. In addition, the practice tends to segregate according to ethnic and socio-economic status and thus to make less likely flexibility and alternative thinking. After a few years of such treatment, the labels may indeed become meaningful. Such attitudes describe the rules and the final score of the game and all that is left is the perfunctory playing of it.

If not by grouping in separate classes, then how is the best way to determine what is relevant subject matter for non-college bound students? The answer is simple—individualize. But what does that mean, and how do you do it? Such students need the opportunity to work with others like and unlike themselves, and since certain communication and other process skills necessitate this, flexibility in grouping is the starting place. Individualization means that you recognize the uniqueness of each student and try to help him develop a curriculum or plan of study that meets his needs, desires, and goals. This translates into providing for the individual student things that are demonstrably related to him in terms of where he is and where he is going.

One of the best ways to find this out is to ask him, to talk with him about what he wants. The teacher's professionalism is displayed in the ability to get honest answers from the student and to use whatever expertise the teacher has in helping to create a curriculum for the student. A big drawback here is the student's distrust. One good way to help overcome this problem is journal writing. The student writes to himself about himself. The teacher can use these journals as clues to pupil interests. Then he can make available ways in which the students may further pursue those subjects that are important to them.

Another means that many teachers have found useful for individualizing instruction is the "table" or "center of interest" technique. While the teacher sits in with a small group, the rest of the students can choose from a reading table, a speaking table, a listening table, a writing table, etc. The purpose of these tables or areas would be to increase perception and self-awareness primarily, but by observation of where the individual student usually goes the teacher is provided with some pretty good clues as to what the student himself finds relevant.

Are there some common characteristics of the statistically-less-probably-college bound students that can be identified and thus provide additional clues to what may be relevant to them? Probably the most common characteristic is the position, or lack of it, these kids have in the system. The negative stigma often attached to them makes it crucially important that their need for a clear, positive self-image be met in the school. Their goals may be of a more practical and more immediate nature than intellectual and future centered. They may have less interest in and practice with abstract thinking. Their need seems to be greatest in concrete and successful experiences, especially in the classroom, and they often want the skills they learn to have obvious, marketable, cashable value after high school (and even during).

Although generalization is very dangerous, the above characteristics can be somewhat helpful to keep in mind when selecting materials and experiences for the non-college bound. For example, literature can be chosen and taught with more emphasis on emotional growth than on literary-technique development. Because of little understanding on the part of the student as to his role in the world, he has trouble seeing the human values in literature and how they apply to him. Here, concreteness is necessary. Instead of discussing the abstract nature of "good" and "evil," apply it to his immediate situation; for instance, good and bad choices in careers, resolutions of personal problems, definition and achievement of a good life, etc. Materials which don't resemble texts might be used. Many readers will enjoy digests, sports, fashion, and home magazines. Non-print media will probably be of greater use than either reading or writing because it so graphically expresses cultural and social values and lends itself to easy discussion and criticism. It is also so predictably and obviously a part of the students' after high school future as well as his present. A chance for creative success can also be made available in any form of production or media activity.

The foregoing suggestions involve teaching to fish instead of giving a fish, as the popular poster proclaims: "I gave the boy a fish; he ate for a day. I taught a boy to fish; now he can eat for a lifetime." It is the teacher's responsibility to give students, college and non-college bound alike, tools that can be used today and tomorrow, in the classroom and in the outside world. Learning to ask questions, examine viewpoints, expand ideas, to empathize, challenge, and respond make up the tools that enable life to be truly a "process," rather than a time span dominated by stagnation.

Non-college bound students are capable, intelligent, and every bit as important to the school and community as college bound students. Besides, it can never be absolutely known whether they are college bound or not until after they finish high school. The curriculum must be of such a nature that it will help them adapt to whatever they may face in the future. Increasingly, we cannot predict what will be of educational value, even for college. What we can do is provide experiences and an environment that provides opportunities for self-directed exploration. In this atmosphere where the student can help choose for himself, he should be able to determine what in terms of his purposes, achievements, needs, and abilities is most relevant to him.

Relevance is, after all, a do-it-yourself thing—a very personal aggregate of experiences which determine how value is assigned. A teacher must learn to identify and understand the values and perceptions of students, and next, to develop methods to facilitate transition from non-functional and non-rewarding to more functional and more rewarding systems. He must work to design a curriculum which is balanced and integrated, uniform where advantageous and individual where advantageous. If his program is broad enough to provide for the needs and purposes of all youth, including the non-college bound, such a curriculum offers tremendous financial, social, and psychological rewards for him, his students, the school, and the society as well.

References
[1]Leonard A. Mollenkof. "Neglect or Action for the Non-College Bound." *The Clearing House*, 40 (1966), p. 413–16.
[2]*Ibid.*, p. 414.
[3]Milton E. Larson. "The Philosophy Education Forgot! Concepts for the Education of the Non-College Bound." *American Vocational Journal*, 43 (1968), p. 22.
[4]Robert Rosenthal and Lenore Jacobson. *Pygmalion in the Classroom*. San Francisco: Holt, Rinehart, and Winston, Inc., 1968, p. 174.

Question I, 17
What kind of curriculum do you envision for the vocationally oriented high school student?
Jan A. Guffin, North Central High School, Indianapolis, Indiana

Answer by:
COLLETT B. DILWORTH, JR., Supervisor of English for Fayetteville, North Carolina, City Schools. He recently received his doctorate in English Education from The University of North Carolina, and has published articles on English curriculum and instruction in state and national journals.

The uniqueness of the English curriculum for vocational students concerns the particular vehicles or topics treating the basic goals, not the basic goals themselves. For example, all English students should study language usage, but the student going directly into the world of work must be primarily concerned with language as a process to be used rather than as an artifact to be examined. His English teacher would do well to abandon grammatical absolutes and to understand that in teaching usage, "Correction . . . becomes a matter of awakening sensitivities to social expectation" (Pooley, 1966, p. 152). In other words, the job of the teacher is to help the vocational student develop a bidialectical capability that will serve him in various social and economic circumstances. Social awareness would then be the factor eliciting standard dialect in a unit on "The Interview," not belief in some abstractly "correct" language. Pooley (1974) delineates significant aspects of the standard dialect for usage skill development.

The reading curriculum can be most effectively developed according to diagnostic information about the interests and skills of the student. Derby (1975) suggests an effective means of using trade related passages in devising informal reading inventories. He reports that his analysis of certain IRI data led to the devising of units of study which directly treat basic skills in the context of relevant topics. One such unit was "Reading for Main Ideas in Auto Mechanics." Johnson (1974) also cites specific strategies for the collaboration of the vocational teacher and the reading or English teacher in developing curriculum. She found two major areas of basic skills deficiency related to particular vocations: "1) locating needed details about products and techniques quickly, and 2) learning the unfamiliar scientific vocabulary" (p. 28). To remedy these problems, students were taught skimming techniques and word structure analysis techniques.

In teaching literature, our teachers are finding that the most worthy goal is for students to value reading for imaginative experience and to manifest this value by reading on their own initiative. The type of extensive reading program outlined in *Hooked on Books* (Fader and McNeil, 1968) has been singularly successful in addressing this goal. To implement such a program, paperback libraries of from 150 to 200 cogent titles are essential for each classroom; equally essential are class time for silent reading and clearly understood procedures for circulating the books and accounting for them. The concern for the great works as acculturating devices is perforce a minor one, because if "exposure" of the students to *Julius Caesar* does not prove to serve the basic objective, this great work is simply left on the shelf and is not treated as some sort of intellectually radioactive isotope. A valuable guide in developing specific skills in appreciating imaginative literature is Vernon Ruland's "Dictionary of Questions for Understanding Literature" used in each volume of the *Random House Literature Series*. This dictionary is readily adaptable to an individualized reading program because the questions are quite clear and reflect the first-person viewpoint.

In teaching writing to vocational students, a teacher might well be tempted to treat only certain survival skills, such as completing application forms and writing memos. While these are important skills that deserve attention, there is no reason for the vocational student to be exempt from instruction in composition relating more profoundly to his thoughts and feelings. As Hipple (1973) states, "The fact remains that writing and thinking are somehow related, that practice in the former demands practice in the latter" (p. 195). For all students, therefore, writing should frequently be a matter of developing thoughtfully realized and communicated experiences, hopes and fears. Narratives, letters and reportage concerning significant personal experiences and written to be read by fellow students as well as by the teacher are valuable activities. Autobiographies, memoirs, journals, and diaries are also very valid media, especially if the students have the options of making them intensely personal and of sharing them only with the teacher and trusted peers. In fact, nothing is more validly revealing of the effect of instruction in basic writing conventions than a set of student letters written to an anonymous pen pal in another class over the course of a semester.

In treating speech skills, one course of study stands out as uniquely effective: creative dramatics. The techniques of pantomime, improvisation, characterization, and role playing are directly adaptable to world of work simulations and make the exploration of that world much more immediate. Furthermore, the vocational student is often one who is reluctant to speak up before others or to undertake sustained dialogue in unfamiliar situations. Creative dramatics can have very positive effects on such problems by providing students with basic speech skills and with nurturant situations in which to use the skills. Duke (1974) provides an excellent guide to creative dramatics for the English teacher.

Finally, no discussion of English for the vocational student would be complete without some attention to career education. Values clarification should be an integral part of career education, and the strategies used therein are so adaptable to instruction in the basic language arts that they can easily serve to engender a majority of the learning experiences in reading, writing, listening, and speaking. In exploring specific careers, students can find several ways to relate the world of English directly to the world of work. Finn (1975) describes a unit that leads students to identify careers in which language skills play a significant part, to devise questionnaires, to interview people in the careers, and to discuss the results in class. There is a danger, however, in going off the deep end as pointed out by Caldwell and Caldwell (1973). These authors describe a number of abuses of career exploration in the English class, one of the more outlandish of which is the example of a teacher having his students study *Richard III* by listing all the occupations mentioned in the play. The point is that when taught by the best English teachers, the communicative arts are profoundly relevant for all students, so there is no reason to forsake the basic goals of English in the curriculum of those who do not intend to go directly to post secondary education.

Bibliography

Caldwell, Margueritte and Caldwell, Robert, "Career Education: Theory and Practice." *English Journal*, September, 1973, 908–914.

Derby, Thomas L., "Informal Testing in Vo-Ed Reading." *Journal of Reading*, Vol. 18, April, 1975, 541–543.

Duke, Charles, *Creative Dramatics and English Teaching.* Urbana, Illinois: NCTE, 1974.

Fader, Daniel N. and McNeil, Elton B., *Hooked on Books: Program and Proof.* New York: Berkley Medallion Books, 1968.

Finn, Peter, "Career Education: An English/Social Studies Resource." *Media and Methods*, April, 1975, 20–23.

Hipple, Theodore W., *Teaching English in Secondary Schools.* New York: The Macmillan Company, 1973.

Johnston, Joyce D., "The Reading Teacher in the Vocational Classroom." *Journal of Reading*, Vol. 18, No. 1 (October) 1974, 27–29.

Pooley, Robert C., *The Teaching of English Usage.* Urbana, Illinois: NCTE, 1974.

Pooley, Robert C., "Usage—Standard vs. Substandard," in Hogan, Robert F., ed., *The English Language in the School Program.* Champaign, Illinois: NCTE, 1966.

Question I, 18

How can secondary school English be made more relevant for the culturally deprived?

Ruth Stroup, Cherryville Junior High School, Cherryville, North Carolina

Answer by:

ALICE A. PARSONS, Ed. D. in English Education. Dr. Parsons has taught English and speech (grades 9-12) and directed drama and forensics activities in public schools for 15 years. Her doctoral dissertation, *Human Problems in Communication: A High School Textbook,* is concerned with the problems of communication among different cultural groups.

Who are the culturally deprived or disadvantaged? Each of us is culturally deprived in one way or another. We are culturally deprived because we often know little about cultures other than our own. Although no culture is any better than any other culture, we should recognize that society defines various standards of behavior and language. Many social and professional opportunities are denied to those who do not meet the standards set by the dominant social/cultural group. The National Council of Teachers of English Task Force on Teaching English to the Disadvantaged contends, "The strength of the English component will largely determine whether students will someday be able to surmount the social, economic, and educational barriers which have given rise to the present conditions."[1]

Culturally deprived students are disadvantaged in terms of experience, not necessarily in terms of intelligence. These students are slow, average, superior, and gifted in the same proportions as the school population at large.[2] According to Fantini and Weinstein, they are not prepared to deal with the abstract symbols which they must confront and learn to manipulate in the school curriculum.[3] Not only must these students deal with the multiple meanings of words but they must also deal with a multitude of abstract concepts. There is much difference, for example, between the meaning of the word *set,* as in "set the book on the table" and the meaning of the word *set,* as in the mathematical concept of group. Students must also learn how to use words in a socially accepted manner in writing and in speaking.

Consider two types of relevancy: (1) relevancy may refer to helping students develop the skills needed for them to function in a middle class society and (2) relevancy may refer to a means of providing them with a curriculum which is immediately interesting and meaningful. Fantini and Weinstein maintain that the test of relevance is "the correspondence of the curriculum to the 'condition and pattern of experience' of the learner."[4]   A close correlation of these elements results in relevancy. For the disadvantaged student, the direct purposeful experience should precede the verbal, abstract experience.[5]

The Task Force report points to a need to develop programs in oral language.   More writing and reading programs need to be built upon instruction in oral English.[6]   Tapes, records, and films are important aids. The teacher becomes a model speaker and learner.   The Task Force stresses the need to emphasize the development of oral skill in techniques of conversation, enunciation and pronunciation, and Standard English.[7] Drill and practice in oral English helps students develop a sense of appropriateness in matters of language usage.[8]   Creative drama may offer worthwhile experiences in this area.

While students should be encouraged to develop skill in the use of Standard English, their everyday dialects should be respected.   Guth suggests that a meaningful way to approach the dialect problem is to "extend the range of the student's language repertory . . . from a positive understanding and appreciation of the language resources he brings to school."[9] Pooley has pointed out that the teacher of English should "familiarize his pupils with the 'best' usage current in the area."[10]

Chernow and Chernow suggest that composition programs should stress progress more than achievement, ideas more than mechanics, originality more than stereotypes.[11]   The teacher should work to create an environment in which individual thinking is encouraged and valued.   As students wrestle with the abstract concepts provided by the curriculum, the teacher should provide a variety of activities which will help them focus on such thinking skills as drawing conclusions, predicting outcomes, and interpreting data.

Literature programs need not be composed of condensed or diluted classics.   Fader and McNeil, in *Hooked on Books: Program and Proof*, have shown how literature study may be exciting as well as relevant.   Studies in literature should be used to help students improve reading and thinking skills and to serve as springboards for group discussions.   Students should be encouraged to discuss with each other the ideas presented in literature rather than recite or report to the teacher.

Relevancy must be a prime concern in all curriculum planning, not just for the culturally disadvantaged.   Two factors should be foremost in the teacher's mind, however, as he plans for these students.   First, the concrete personal experience should precede the abstract experience. Involving students in teaching other students provides such direct experiences.   Such experiences do much to help students learn how to learn. Second, the oral language skills of speaking and listening should be emphasized.   These skills should be approached from the point of view of appropriateness rather than correctness.   Students need to understand that "I ain't got no money" is a clear communication, acceptable in some situations, unacceptable in other situations.   The teacher who really listens to students and values what they say will promote listening skills within the classroom.   From such an example, students will learn to value and respect the ideas of other students.

Lefevre stresses that "Today, people who have developed the essential skills of communication are finding more and more doors opening to let them in. But if they are seriously lacking these skills, they are likely to become linguistic cripples . . . in loss of their potential humanity."[12]

References

[1] National Council of Teachers of English Task Force on Teaching English to the Disadvantaged. *Language Programs for the Disadvantaged: The Report of the NCTE Task Force on Teaching English to the Disadvantaged.* Richard Corbin and Muriel Crosby, Cochairmen. Champaign, Illinois: National Council of Teachers of English, 1965, p. 17.

[2] *Ibid.,* p. 17.

[3] Mario D. Fantini and Gerald Weinstein. *The Disadvantaged: Challenge to Education.* New York: Harper & Row, Publishers, 1968, p. 345.

[4] *Ibid.,* p. 340.

[5] *Ibid.,* p. 347.

[6] Task Force, p. 28.

[7] *Ibid.,* p. 116.

[8] William H. Evans and Jerry L. Walker. *New Trends in the Teaching of English in Secondary Schools,* New Trends in Curriculum and Instruction Series, ed. John U. Michaelis. Chicago, Illinois: Rand McNally and Company, 1966, p. 347.

[9] Hans P. Guth. *English for a New Generation.* New York: McGraw-Hill Book Company, 1973, p. 118.

[10] Robert C. Pooley, "Usage—Standard vs. Substandard," in *The English Language in the School Program,* ed. Robert F. Hogan. Champaign, Illinois: NCTE, 1966, p. 162.

[11] Fred B. Chernow and Carol Chernow. *Teaching the Culturally Disadvantaged Child.* West Nyack, New York: Parker Publishing Company, Inc., 1973, p. 112.

[12] Carl A. Lefevre. *Linguistics, English, and the Language Arts.* Boston, Massachusetts: Allyn and Bacon, Inc., 1970, p. 347.

SECTION II

WRITING

Question II, 1

What methods should a teacher follow in attempting to acquaint students with the basics in composition?. Where does the teacher begin —with sentence structure, vocabulary, organization?

Denise Sharon Lackey, North Davidson High School, Welcome, North Carolina

Answer by:

RICHARD L. LARSON, Associate Dean of Education, Herbert H. Lehman College of the City University of New York, whose specialty is rhetorical theory and its applications. Mr. Larson is editor of *Children and Writing in the Elementary School: Theories and Techniques* (Oxford) and of articles on rhetorical theory and the teaching of writing.

One has to be sure what one means by acquainting students with the "basics in composition." To think of teaching the "basics" as inculcating rules to be observed in choosing words, constructing sentences, and arranging materials is to misinterpret the job of the teacher. In my judgment, the teacher's job is to assure that the *student* gets the chance to practice making "basic" rhetorical decisions. The job that the student must do in writing is to select words that express ideas and feelings with precision, compose sentences that establish their points with clarity and emphasis and that reveal the interconnections among their ideas, and assemble longer units of discourse (paragraphs, whole pieces) that live up to the expectations they generate, and affirm their main points with due emphasis through an orderly succession of component sentences. It is of these activities—and more, of course, including the interpretation of experiences and the discovery of ideas—that writing consists, and it is these which students must learn, whether they be called "basics" or something else.

There is no evidence yet to suggest that the direct teaching of rules about grammar or the naming of parts of sentences helps students learn to compose better papers. Richard Braddock and others, in *Research in Written Composition* (1963), brought to the attention of teachers several studies that demonstrated the point, and, despite the arguments of a few linguists during the late sixties, no studies have appeared since Braddock's book to demonstrate the efficacy for writers of teaching rules about grammar or techniques of diagramming sentences. Similarly, there is nothing to suggest that the direct teaching of vocabulary lists or the drilling of students on individual words increases the students' active vocabulary—the vocabulary on which they draw when they want to express an idea in their writing. And, though we do not have much evidence about how professionals or students connect sentences together into longer units of discourse, we do know that talking abstractly about unity, coherence, and emphasis does not lead students to the composing of good complete pieces or good paragraphs. It takes more than the presentation of conceptual notions about writing to develop good writers —student or professional.

But, if the term is understood as I urged in my first paragraph, the "basics" can and should be a part of a student's work in Language

Arts or English in *every* grade. One can learn to write only by writing, and no student is too young to attempt some writing, though the kinds of writing we invite from students will vary depending on their ages. James Moffett's "I, You, and It" (*CCC*, 16 [December, 1965], pp. 243–248), along with much of his other work, suggests ways of organizing the curriculum in writing for students of different ages, so that all students write (for example) diaries, dialogues, and narratives—of varying lengths—and older students who are ready for such work also write essays on more abstract or hypothetical subjects. The student learns by first composing and then sharing his compositions with fellow students, who discuss each other's work and assist their fellows in the solving of specific problems. Instead of giving explanations, drills, assignments to textbooks, or other forms of direct instruction, the teacher acts as guide and coach, ready to offer advice if asked, but willing as much as possible to let students learn through their own efforts at the process of composing.

Such work, which can be included in any classroom at any level, should of course be supplemented with abundant opportunities for students to read and to respond to what they have read. Reading will familiarize them with how writers construct sentences to achieve varied goals, and will also enable students to enlarge their vocabularies through seeing words in action in contexts created by their writers. From reading and discussion can also come a sense of what "organization" means—and an awareness of the possible patterns and plans by which discourse is often constructed. (See my "Toward a Linear Rhetoric of the Essay," *CCC*, 21 [May, 1971], pp. 140–146.)

Lately, at least two scholars have capitalized on the insights of transformational-generative grammar to design exercises in sentence-combining that have proved significantly helpful in enlarging the syntactic fluency of students. First John Mellon (*Transformational Sentence-Combining*, National Council of Teachers of English, 1969) and then—more strikingly still—Frank O'Hare (*Sentence-Combining: Improve Student Writing Without Formal Grammar Instruction*, National Council of Teachers of English, 1973) developed techniques for helping students to master addition, deletion, and embedding, which not only increased their control of sentences but also, in O'Hare's work, increased the total effectiveness of their writing. The work of these men is promising enough to encourage teachers who know something about transformational grammar to attempt sentence-combining exercises in their classrooms. We do not now have comparable studies on the techniques for teaching the combining of sentences into longer units, although the work of Alton Becker at the University of Michigan ("A Tagmemic Approach to Paragraph Analysis," *CCC*, 16 [December, 1965], pp. 237–242) suggests that patterns of structure within the paragraph can be identified and perhaps taught through appropriate exercises.

At every grade level, then, the teacher concerned about the "basics" should provide students with opportunities for wide reading and extensive writing in a variety of modes. Such practice, supported by free discussions of students' writing and by wise guidance from the teacher, will do more to assure that students master the "basics" successfully.

Question II, 2

What realistic goals can we set for a diverse high school population in composition?

Thomas R. Cox, North Central High School, Indianapolis, Indiana

Answer by:

RICHARD A. MEADE, Professor of Education, University of Virginia, whose specialty is English Education. Mr. Meade has written articles on the English curriculum as well as workbooks and textbooks in grammar and composition and has served a six-year term on the Curriculum Commission of the National Council of Teachers of English. He is co-editor of *Literature for Adolescents: Selection and Use* (1973).

Goals for composition in the secondary school become a problem if only some students can realize them. Actually, the major composition goal, improvement in one's writing, can be attacked by virtually all students, since anyone can seek to better his written expression. As Charles R. Cooper pointed out in the Research Roundup section of *English Journal,* the teacher of English should measure the student's growth in writing over a period of time, perhaps from the beginning of a semester to the end of it.[1] For this kind of measurement for exposition Paul Diederich recommends the Reader's Analytic Scale, which includes criteria that have long been held important,[2] although a teacher has sometimes emphasized one or two of them to the neglect of the others. This scale divides phases of composition attainment into two groups: (1) ideas, organization, wording, and flavor, and (2) usage, punctuation, spelling, and handwriting. It is suggested as a guide for the determination of composition growth. Has the writer improved in the organization of his thoughts? Is his wording better? Has he improved in his punctuation? Does he misspell fewer words?

Here, then, is a major aim of composition: to have a student improve (grow) in his written communication. It is unrealistic, however, to say that a student should improve a certain amount in a given length of time, that all pupils should improve to the same extent, or that one writer should improve just as much as another. Many factors characteristic of individual persons affect the degree of improvement for different writers.

A second kind of goal refers to what the student is to write. To be realistic, the school must expect him to write on a subject and in a form with which he can succeed and which may be or may become of interest to him. James Moffett suggests many kinds of writing a student can do.[3] An example is "memory writing," when a student recounts an experience he had at an earlier time. Almost any secondary school student can write a memory piece, especially if the teacher is willing to accept an effort in keeping with the writer's ability. Must the student engage in every kind of writing that is a part of the entire range of possible written experiences? Although some students can write well-devised short stories, can all students? Does the school need to have them try? Research has told us a great deal about certain composition problems, but no investigation has discovered whether a student should write in all possible forms, or even in most of them. Perhaps it would be satisfactory for a student to write only in those forms in which he is reasonably fluent. So long as he writes and so long as he shows growth in his writing, there may be no need to specify that he must produce any particular form. It may not be a realistic goal to specify the same form for everyone.

Many educators have advocated writing a scholarly form of literary criticism, a form which may be realistic for only a few high school students. This kind of writing may best be reserved for writers with an interest in literary scholarship. If a teacher's strategy allows the writer to choose the forms he is to use, then writing which approaches literary explication can be an option.

Sometimes the school curriculum has included much attention to the analysis of syntax as a means to cause students to write better. The ultimate goal was the improvement of the ability to write, but the immediate goals were the ability to identify a noun clause, the ability to explain the constructions in which a noun clause may occur, the ability to identify predicate nominatives, the ability to identify adverbial phrases, and the like. These goals are not realistic for at least three reasons: (1) there is much opinion and some research to question the ability of most students to learn syntactical analysis [4]; (2) most students, even many with superior ability, have little interest in reaching these goals, and (3) there has been much research since the early 1900s to show that such learnings have almost no relationship to writing achievement.[5]

Goals that indicate practice on mechanics isolated from the use in writing of these learnings are not likely to produce the intended results. Practice on usage items may not have any effect if it is unrelated to actual use. There has been isolated practice, too, on rhetorical matters, sometimes on principles used little by adult writers, like some methods of paragraph development.[6] Students learn to write by writing, hence any realistic composition objectives must relate to writing itself and not to peripheral learnings that barely touch the real act of expression.

References

[1]Cooper, Charles R., "Measuring Growth in Writing," *English Journal*, 64 (March, 1975), pp. 111–120.

[2]Diederich, Paul, *Measuring Growth in English*. Urbana, Illinois: National Council of Teachers of English, 1974.

[3]Moffett, James, *A Student-Centered Language Arts Curriculum, Grades K-13: A Handbook for Teachers*. New York: Houghton Mifflin, 1968.

[4]Meade, Richard A., "Who Can Learn Grammar?" *English Journal*, 50 (February, 1961), pp. 87–92. Strom, Ingrid, Research in *Grammar and Usage and Its Implications for Teaching Writing*. Bloomington, Indiana: Indiana University, 1960.

[5]Sherwin, Stephen, *Four Problems in Teaching English*. Urbana, Illinois: National Council of Teachers of English, 1969.

[6]Meade, Richard A. and Ellis, W. Geiger, "The Use in Writing of Textbook Methods of Paragraph Development," *The Journal of Educational Research*, 5 (October, 1971), pp. 74–76.

Question II, 3

What is meant by *pre-writing*? What are some pre-writing exercises that can be used effectively with high school classes?

Michael Tad Hippler, Alleghany County High School, Covington, Virginia

Answer by:

DONALD M. MURRAY, a writer of fiction, poetry and non-fiction, is also Professor of English at the University of New Hampshire. He won a Pulitzer Prize for Editorial Writing and is author of a text for English teachers, *A Writer Teaches Writing*.

The most serious problem in the teaching of writing is that students say, "I don't have anything to say"—and their teachers believe them.

Our students do not come to us without experience and without a language; they come to us without respect for that experience and that language.

You can't write nothing; content is always more important than form. It is the job of the writing teacher to draw out of the student the experience and the language which is within him. The teacher must employ techniques which stimulate the student's awareness of his world and its potential for significance.

The best device for doing this is to begin each writing unit with the search for the specific.

Good writing, your student should understand, poetry as well as non-fiction, is built from an abundance of concrete, accurate information. The student must realize, in the beginning especially, that he is writing with information, not language. Language is the symbol for that information.

This emphasis on information instead of language is especially important for the unmotivated student, the student who is seriously deprived of self-respect. Have your student list specifics as the student has on the right. Encourage him to explore some part of his world. He should be urged to write down specifics and not to worry, at this point, about spelling, usage or mechanics. He should simply mine his experience for concrete details.

He should record specifics from a place with which he is familiar or an experience which was important to him or a person he feels strongly about.

He should be urged to limit that subject and collect many specifics—the more the better. He should not focus on the city, but zoom into the neighborhood, the tenement, a room, part of a room. He should deal with the crucial minutes of the championship basketball game or the automobile accident; reveal the per-

my grandma
sic
paper root
bicicle
cold
two alarm clox
5:15
in the morning
still dark
6th grade
black hole her mouth
teeth in glass
upper plate
sometimes snored
frost on window
snow in window once
broke window tossin paper

son in action, doing something important. And he should use every sense to collect dozens of specifics—hundreds of specifics, if possible—words and phrases which will help the writer explore the subject.

This is the point at which the student may begin to learn what writing is: *the process of using language to discover the meaning in experience.* The writer doesn't know what he wants to say before he says it; he writes to discover what he has to say.

The student freezes before a blank piece of paper because he imagines writers and other students—brighter students—know with an easy absoluteness what will appear on the page.

There are glib, superficial students who can plunge in without fear, but the writer is frightened by the blank page just as the poor student is. He knows the page will reveal him, expose him. But the blank paper also stimulates him. When he puts words on that paper he will start on a voyage of discovery, he will find out what he knows and what he needs to know.

The teacher can share this expedition into the unknown with his students by starting his own list of specifics, by exploring a common subject—the cafeteria, the neighborhood hang-out, the crowd at the game—drawing the specifics out of the class and recording them on the board or on a piece of paper under an overhead projector. The more specific the specifics are, the more they will remind students of other specifics. And after such exercises the students—and the teacher—will begin to be more aware of their worlds.

This device for listing specifics is a good way to start any writing task. It is a gathering of the writer's raw material, a way of brainstorming new ideas, a way of making sure that the writing will be specific, not vague, a method to increase the chances that the writer will have something to say, that he will not write with inflated diction, with balloons of words detached from meaning.

When the student has an abundance of specifics collected in class or out, from memory or observation, from thinking or reading, then he can study those specifics to see what they mean. It is similar to looking at a slide under a microscope. At first nothing makes sense, then the writer begins to see the relationship between specifics. He begins to circle key specifics (often the most specific specifics), to draw lines between specifics, to start new lists which

grandma paralized
listenin
listenin in my bed
listenin at her door
goin to can
listenin on way back
listenin after paper
  root
dad said to tell him
if she wasnt breathing
sometimes she snored
one morning she scared
  me
she made weerd noises
she was singin hims
she didnt see me
nite light
neer door
lousy orange light
her left arm hangin
  down
I tiptow through her
  room to the can
sometimes she was moanin
I pull covers up
hope Im never that way
shed ask me for the jar
she never knew what
  time it was
got me mixed up
thought I was uncle
  Donald
even her uncle
she praid as if she
was talkin with Jessu
right in her room
they offer me her room
after but I didnt
want it. shes
still there.
My brother dont care
He didnt have a
  paper root
I stand at the door
you couldnt tell if
  she was breathin
youd heer sounds but
  they mite be somethin
  else
blak dark

evolve into drafts. And all the time he discovers new specifics, a process which should go on as he writes, rewrites and edits.

This technique of listing specifics is a good way of starting the research paper, and it can also be the way to introduce the student to modern poetry, for well-arranged, short lists of specifics can themselves become poems. It is an effective way to begin to draft a job resumé, a sports story, an advertisement to sell a used car, a speech.

If you get your students listing specifics before they write a first draft, then you may get papers such as the one below. This draft is the product of the *prewriting* process, and is full of potential which will be realized as it passes through the process of discovery called *rewriting*.

I didnt want to dye
grandma did
sheed see her husbands
all those kids what
dyed
Id sneak up close to
bed see if the covers
was movin
waitin
when I come home from
school one day she was
gone
her bed was empty
8th grade
I still wake up early
in the dark sometime
I listen
I can feel her
I was skeered sheed dye
she wasnt
whod want to lay in bed
and have to use a jar
it was spooky
shadows
her funny smell
like an old lady on
the subway
grandmas mouth
a black hole
white wispy hair
she couldnt turn
on her side
Id sing her hims
in the dark

In the sixth grade I had a paper root. I got up early like 5:15 in the morning. It was cold and dark. It was my job to listen for grandma. To see if she was breathin or something. I listen in my room, in the hall, at her door, Sometimes Id go rite in and stand at her bed, watch to see the covers move. Ill never forgot her mouth. She put her upper plate in a glass. That mouth was a black hole. I coulda fallen in it. I was always scarred she was dead but she wasnt. she wanted to dye and go see her husbands. One nite I woke up I didnt know what the noise was. she was singin hims.

Question II, 4

How often should students write in high school English classes? Are many short papers better than a few long ones?

Mary Colburn Commers, Lincoln Southeast High School, Lincoln, Nebraska

Answer by:

JOHN C. CARR, Associate Professor of Education, University of Maryland, College Park, whose specialty is English Education. Dr. Carr is also a visiting faculty member of the Speech and Drama Department, The Catholic University of America, Washington, D.C. (summer sessions). His interests range from general methods of instruction to all phases of English instruction and to the teaching of drama and film. He is the author of numerous articles and is co-author and co-editor of four books.

William Hazlitt, a writer whose prose still sets a standard in our language, advised, "The more a man writes, the more he can write." Simple and direct, that advice still applies.

Squire and Appleby report that 73.4 percent of American teachers of English and 71.9 percent of their British counterparts believe that "frequency of student writing is more important than less frequent, but longer and more comprehensive, writing assignments." [1]

Several advantages accrue from frequent, brief writing assignments: the exploration of wide-ranging interests and concerns; continuing practice of skills; opportunities for experimentation; and the creation of publishable material.

Adolescence is a time of exploration; interests of every sort vie for the attention of young people—sometimes concurrently, sometimes serially. Essential during this growing period are opportunities to reflect on, challenge, develop, and express ideas. Brief papers written on a regular, frequent basis are ideal for providing those circumstances. James Moffett's work in creating a "student-centered curriculum" attests to high interest and success when students have recurring chances to explore interests and concerns vital to them.[2]

Writing frequently, students develop the skills of selecting and organizing material; they also have a better chance of perfecting what one writer has called "the difficult business of putting words down in their best order." In addition, mechanical and grammatical skills are practiced automatically. Because assignments are brief and because topics are selected for high student interest, little time is wasted on feelings of failure and there is little sense that one is being forced to go over "the same old stuff."

When writing assignments are brief, many kinds of writing opportunities are possible; therefore, students can work in a variety of forms and styles. Ideally, they find through practice and variety that content and form are significantly linked and that style enhances one's ability to hold the reader's attention. Across several months, they explore the essay, short story, poetry, and drama. Although their writings will not be elaborate, they can develop a *working* knowledge of many kinds of expression.

To solve the problem of frequent writing, many teachers have adopted the practice of having students maintain a journal—a device which permits them to work briefly on a daily or many-times-a-week basis. The journal can serve also as a source for material which can be incorporated into a class publication. The class magazine is ideal for generating pride in writing since all students have work reproduced and are given bylines for their work. Either the teacher checks material in the journal deemed appropriate for the magazine or students submit items to a teacher-student editorial board. The magazine provides common discussion about all those aspects of writing on which individuals or the class have been working.

Establishing goals for improvement is easier when students talk about their work in a positive way and when teachers' comments are encouraging. In research by Gee, it has been shown that "student writers who received only positive comments on their papers wrote more than students who received only negative comments or no comments at all" and that students also enjoyed writing more.[3]

The problem of whether students write IN or FOR English classes is one that must be solved in each instance. Increasingly, teachers in every subject area report that students of the 70's refuse to do homework ("writing FOR English class") either at all or with any seriousness. Given the refusal or the inability of the schools to cope with this phenomenon, teachers need to reassess what experiences they want students to have—and the means by which those experiences will be achieved. A decision to have students master the craft, and strive for the art, of writing causes a realignment of priorities about emphasis, energy, and activity. It also causes important decisions about the integration of writing with the rest of the English curriculum.

Hooks' examination of the writings of Fitzgerald, Hemingway, Wolfe, and Faulkner shows that those writers "valued wide reading and experience and constant practice at writing while training oneself to observe life more closely."[4] Those values make good guidelines for the teaching of writing.

Generating excitement about writing and providing the time in which to do frequent, brief assignments are fundamental. "Keep the flow going and the rest will take care of itself."[5]

References

[1]James R. Squire and Roger K. Applebee. *Teaching English in the United Kingdom.* Champaign, Illinois: National Council of Teachers of English, 1969, p. 120.

[2]James Moffett. *A Student-Centered Language Arts Curriculum, Grades K-13: A Handbook for Teachers.* Boston: Houghton Mifflin Company, 1968.

[3]Thomas C. Gee. "Students' Response to Teacher Comments." *Research in the Teaching of English,* 6 (Fall, 1972), p. 219.

[4]Janice Hooks. *An Analysis of Writing Skills as Described by Selected Professional Writers.* Ann Arbor, Michigan: University Microfilms, 1973.

[5]J.N. Britton, quoted in Squire and Applebee, *op. cit.,* p. 118.

Question II, 5

How can a teacher convince low-achieving students that a theme is composed of more than two lines—especially when the student doesn't have faith in himself or in his ability?

Shirley C. Galloway, Belton-Honea Path Senior High School, Honea Path, South Carolina

Answer by:

JAN A. GUFFIN, Assistant Chairman, Department of English, North Central High School, Indianapolis, Indiana. Mr. Guffin's articles on the teaching of writing have appeared in several professional publications, the most recent being *Creative Approaches to the Teaching of English: Secondary.*

The dilemma of the low-achiever hinges on factors both psychological and logical. If the student lacks self-confidence, he likely demonstrates low fluency, which Roberts defines as "simply the ability to get your ideas on paper in a reasonable length of time."[1] Factors which contribute to a lack of fluency include the embarrassment (and sometimes the reprimand) attendant on a poor handwriting; confusion of subject matter; the fear of an inaccurate response; and, above all, poor spelling.[2]

Before the teacher can concentrate on helping the student to conceptualize a theme, then, he must attempt to remove the barriers to expression; he must be satisfied that the student has something to say and is not afraid to say it. In addition, he must see that the student acquires practice at writing his ideas with no fear of failure. Otherwise, the student may carry uppermost in his mind the very factors which most seriously inhibit his expression.

Steps which the teacher may take toward removing these barriers include sustained free and timed writing exercises for the student, both non-evaluative in nature. Free writing is, as its name implies, writing which calls for a response of an unplanned nature. The teacher may simply ask students to write as much as they can on an open-ended topic (what I did over the weekend; how I plan to spend my Christmas vacation; what I would do if I were President of the United States; the five things I would buy if I were given a million dollars, etc.). Subsequently, the teacher may wish to refine the writing assignments to include those which require everyone to write on a given subject but which still allow for a wide range of response (describe the possible feelings of some object in the classroom as it encounters its daily round of students; describe the feelings of an animal who has no home; tell what it must be like to be blind, deaf, or handicapped in some other way, etc.).

Regardless of the assignment in these early stages of composition training, the teacher should insure an audience for the student, namely, the class itself. He might ask the students to read what they have written to each other or to the class as a whole, in order to provide psychological reinforcement for the student who has bothered to communicate his ideas to another person. It is also best in this stage that the teacher not read the papers himself, in doing so, he poses a threat to the student who is overly self-conscious about the "correctness" of his writing.

As this kind of work progresses in the class, and as the students gain confidence in their ability to communicate in writing, the teacher may wish to refine the exercises further by adding a "time" restriction to the writing. At this point the assignments may also become more sophisticated: explain three things which we discussed yesterday in class when we talked about flying a plane; explain three or four important things a football (or basketball, swimming, etc.) enthusiast must keep in mind when preparing for competition. Such topics call for a more conscious organization on the part of the student and by giving only so much time in which to write, the teacher forces the student to increase his fluency. It is important that the teacher bear in mind, however, that such topics must be those about which the student is likely to have something to say, topics which will allow the student to begin responding immediately instead of having to think for a long time before writing, another obstacle to fluency.

Such writing activities may occupy as much as a semester with a class of low-achievers, depending on the degree of self-consciousness of the students. The teacher must himself be sensitive to the appropriate time for moving from one stage of refinement to another. If the timing is premature, the students may regress; if the timing is delayed, they may become indifferent.

When the teacher is satisfied that the students are gaining confidence in their ability to express themselves in writing, however, he may wish to move gradually into writing assignments which call for logical units of thought. The most logical step to take, of course, is to move to the concept of the paragraph. An excellent paragraph model for low-achievers was devised by McCabe.[3] This model contains five sentences which are taught over a period of four days. At the completion of the four-day lesson, the student will have written a complete logical unit of expression on a single topic. Subsequently, he may use the same model to practice writing on other topics.

When the teacher is confident that the students feel comfortable with the model, he may show them how to combine two or more paragraphs which deal with topics of a similar or contrastive nature to create an expository theme.[4] This kind of generative writing may also be used to build introductions, conclusions, and transitional paragraphs around pre-written independent paragraphs.

The low-achiever's progress in writing may depend more heavily on the teacher than does the progress of any other ability-level student. If the teacher tries to approach the low-achiever in the same manner that he does the more confident or higher-achieving student, he may expect negligible results. Since psychological factors are as important to the low-achiever's progress as is his understanding of the logical units of expression, such as the sentence, the paragraph, and the entire composition, the teacher will necessarily concern himself with such matters as the self-concept of the student, an environment which will allow him to make mistakes without fear of punishment, and the increase of his natural fluency before attempting to have the student compose on a larger, more conscious level.

References

[1]Paul Roberts. *Understanding English.* New York: Harper Brothers, 1958, p. 3.

[2]Jan A. Guffin. "Writing," in R. Baird Shuman, ed. *Creative Approaches to the Teaching of English: Secondary.* Itasca, Illinois: F. E. Peacock Publishers, 1974, p. 154.

[3]Bernard J. McCabe. "A Program for Teaching Composition to Pupils of Limited Academic Ability," in Michael F. Shugrue and George Hillocks, Jr., eds. *Classroom Practices in Teaching English,* 1965–66. Champaign, Illinois: National Council of Teachers of English, 1965, pp. 39–46.

[4]*Ibid,* p. 44.

Question II, 6

Does keeping a journal on a regular basis, either as an English assignment or as part of a classroom activity, result in solid gains in the development of writing skills? If so, which components of writing skill are most enhanced?

Shirley H. Strobel, Jordan High School, Durham, North Carolina

Answer by:

RUTH K. J. CLINE, Associate Professor of Education, University of Colorado, Boulder. Dr. Cline has been active in both Reading and English local, state and national organizations and their conferences, serving as the Program Chairperson for CEE in March 1975.

The journal has become a part of many language arts classrooms, especially after *Hooked on Books*[1] described how this technique was used at the Maxey Training School in Michigan. As used there, the boys wrote in their journals every day and the teacher simply counted pages to see if they were writing their quotas. The teacher did not read the writing unless the student asked her to. Teachers who use the journal in this way report that students become more free in expressing themselves in writing: they have more to say and develop a better feeling about themselves, a confidence in their ability to express themselves. Some teachers now call this activity "jottings" or "*u*ninterrupted *s*ustained *w*riting," but the lack of a particular structure is characteristic of its use. Motivation for this kind of writing must be clear to the students, or it will degenerate into "busywork" and lose its value. Clegg said, "compiling a journal or diary, when interest is dead, can only provide a monotonous and dull response . . . . To the children there must be something to write about and a reason for writing."[2]

A more structured situation is described by Jacobs,[3] in which he had children from 9-12 years old record *new ideas* in a journal each day of the week. An important part of this program was the teacher's reading of the entries, providing comments and corrections, along with follow-up to see if the children corrected their mistakes. Jacobs was enthusiastic about this project and reported great progress in terms of the quality of the students' thoughts and the writing of them. He attributed part of this to the students' expectations of this project after they heard about it from their peers who were involved.

Copeland[4] reinforces the creativity idea by stating that positive attention to the creative process will result in more competency in the skills of writing, and it will result in more success and joy in the art of writing than will the teaching of skills per se.

Denys Thompson in his Foreword to *The Excitement of Writing*[5] states that "The ability to use words well is an indivisible achievement which once learned will be used effectively in whatever kind of writing the child does." This is a nice statement, and one which I hope is true, but I did not find solid evidence to support this. As a matter of fact, I found no evidence supporting the journal project in terms of the writing skills which you question . . . a splendid idea for someone to research!

But I cannot leave this reply on that note—because so much more is involved in the writing process. I agree with Murray[6] that writing is a process of self-discovery and an ethical act, with *honesty* as the most important quality in writing. Giving the students an opportunity (through such experiences as journals) to *discover* what they know and "to satisfy their primitive hunger to communicate"[7] is most important. Students can be encouraged then to do self-evaluation and together you can begin to focus on areas of skills that need improvement. If skills are the first emphasis, you may never get the student past that to the *fun* of writing!

References
[1]Daniel Fader and Elton B. McNeil. *Hooked on Books: Program and Proof.* New York: Putnam, 1968.
[2]A.B. Clegg. *The Excitement of Writing.* London: Chatto and Windus, 1967. Foreword by Denys Thompson. P. 28.
[3]Gabriel H.L. Jacobs. *When Children Think: Using Journals to Encourage Creative Thinking.* New York: Columbia College Press, 1970.
[4]Evelyn Copeland. "What Can You Say About Jiint?" *NEATE Leaflet,* 9 (1971), pp. 22–27.
[5]Denys Thompson. Foreword in *The Excitement of Writing,* London: Chatto and Windus, 1967. P. viii.
[6]Donald M. Murray. "Why Teach Writing and How?" *English Journal,* 62 (1973), pp. 1234–1237.
[7]*Ibid.,* p. 1235.

Question II, 7

Is a composition class which emphasizes the basic skills as effective as a reading-writing course which teaches writing in conjunction with reading? What variables might account for effective teaching of either type?

Shirley H. Strobel, Jordan High School, Durham, North Carolina

Answer by:

ROBERT M. GORRELL is Professor of English and Dean of Arts and Science at the University of Nevada, Reno, and recently Director of the NCTE Commission on Composition. He has written on rhetoric, language, and Renaissance drama. Among his books are *Modern English Handbook, Writing and Language, Modern English Writing,* and *English as Language.*

As the second question recognizes, the first is virtually unanswerable. Its answer is yes or no, depending on the variables of the second question, and these are both numerous and complex. A course emphasizing "basic skills" can be as effective as any other, or it cannot be.

The most obvious variable, of course, is the teacher. A good teacher of composition succeeds with almost any kind of course. But even the good teacher does better with a sensible program.

Variables in the content of the course are hard to identify, and harder still to evaluate. Discontent and uncertainty about what to teach in a composition course have increased during the last thirty or forty years, stemming perhaps from disillusionment with the prescriptive rhetoric and usage that grew up in the nineteenth century—the notion that there are right ways to do things and one teaches the proper formulas. Teachers became conscious of the difficulties of teaching writing in a vacuum—writing without anything to say—and of the linguistic inaccuracy of prescriptive usage. A series of panaceas had their vogue— semantics, communication, linguistics, free writing, the haiku, to name a few. The uncertainty continues—and perhaps it is healthy; the 1976 Conference on College Composition and Communication had as its theme "Back to Basics."

The reading-writing course persists as the most popular variant from the course devoted strictly to writing or writing and grammar. Its advocates assert that the approach provides subject matter for writing, stimulates students to write, and offers models for imitation. Furthermore, students find it more interesting than marking up workbooks on usage. In practice, it is perhaps more significant that teachers find the approach more interesting and more compatible with the literary training that most of them have had, if they have been trained in English at all. More often than not, the reading-writing course becomes a reading course with a few more or less related theme assignments, or even a course in literary history or amateur sociology. At this point, advocates of the approach may also point out that students have trouble reading and listening and speaking and that the course has an obligation to consider these aspects of communication, as they can at least superficially in the reading-writing course. This multiplicity of genuine needs in the use of language has always plagued the composition course, tempting the teacher to try for so much that very little happens.

In other words, the reading-writing course has advantages—in sustaining interest of both student and teacher, in providing some substance for composition, and in giving the student examples in which he can observe writing techniques. The variable is the use the teacher makes of the reading. If the reading dominates completely, or is not related to writing, the course ceases to be a composition course.

The variable in the other alternative is obviously what we mean by "basic skills." If basic skills are regarded as only the mechanics of writing—ability to adhere to a set of prescriptive and proscriptive rules—then a course focusing on them is likely to accomplish little. Moreover, what it does accomplish may distort the students' concept of what composition is about, making him think that writing is only a matter of learning what not to do.

If, however, basic skills are regarded as techniques, strategies, and devices of writing—rhetoric, in a broad sense—then a course emphasizing them can be both interesting and valuable. With this approach the goal is understanding. The student is encouraged to discover as much as he can about the possibilities open to him and about the advantages and disadvantages of different alternatives for different purposes. He can learn about how language works; he can explore the differing effects of different sorts of sentences; he can examine different approaches to organization of materials; he can weigh the importance of voice, tone, and the audience; he can seek ways of framing a generalization, of finding materials for developing it; of preserving continuity in his writing. He can even study usage variants, approaching them as alternatives having different effects, not as items to be classified as right or wrong.

In other words, the course in basic skills can be a course with subject matter that justifies considering composition as a separate academic discipline. The approach requires that the teacher take writing seriously, that he knows something about how language works and about how composing occurs. With a good teacher and with this kind of broader interpretation, the course emphasizing basic skills can be as effective as any other and can have the advantage of concentrating directly on what it is presumably intended to do.

Question II, 8

How can I convince a non-academic student of the necessity of gaining proficiency in written communication? Are there ways in which I can teach him writing even if I fail to convince him or while I am in the process of convincing him?

Virginia B. Revelle, North Davidson Senior High School, Welcome, North Carolina

Answer by:

G. MELVIN HIPPS, Professor of Education and Associate Academic Dean at Furman University, Greenville, South Carolina. Mr. Hipps, who teaches courses in English Education, has written several articles, primarily concerning teaching literature for adolescents. He is the former executive-secretary of the South Carolina Council of Teachers of English.

Teachers have always felt a sense of urgency in trying to teach the so-called "non-academic" student the knowledge and skills considered necessary for living and making a living. This urgency has frequently resulted in exercises in writing for students of this sort that stress correctness above all else—correctness in spelling, grammar, punctuation, and usage. Forms of writing thought to be crucial in various vocations —letters, orders for merchandise, reports, directions, applications, and of course, the ubiquitous expository paragraph—are typically the ones stressed in composition courses for non-academic students. Such an approach might be appropriate for highly motivated students who have already chosen their niche in the business world. In the absence of this kind of goal, however, motivation must come from another source.

If the non-academic student is ever to be convinced of the importance of writing, he must come to see writing as an aid to his personal development and not merely to his vocational preparation. In discussing composition for the average student, James L. Fenner has said that "Writing out our feelings commemorates and celebrates them; it dignifies them with the aura of importance that they truly deserve. Writing down our thoughts clarifies and sharpens them and encourages in us the development of that sense of responsibility without which 'thought' verges on worthlessness." [1] If a student can become interested in writing something that pleases him personally or that produces a response he wishes to produce in someone else, he might eventually be led to see the value of more structured, objective, utilitarian writing.

Jan A. Guffin has presented a succint outline for a course in writing for non-academic students: "First, all of these students will profit from writing exercises which are frequent, brief in nature, nonevaluative, near to speech, and as creative as the interests of the student will allow. They should also probably involve a balance between structured and unstructured writing tasks. And finally, such assignments should culminate as often as possible in presentations to real audiences." [2]

In order to allow for the widely divergent interests and abilities of non-academic students, teachers should allow for a broad range of writing options. Stephen Judy has suggested a list of neglected forms: journals and diaries, sketches, confessions (real or fictional), dramatic monologues, stream of consciousness, plays, advertisements, riddles, jokes, aphorisms, graffiti, and so on. [3] Such experiences as these would emphasize for students the relationship between writing and speaking.

Students should experiment with various forms of writing keeping a particular audience in mind. Their writing should be judged on the basis of its effect on the intended audience. Obviously, the best judge of a play or a joke or an advertisement written by a ninth grader is another ninth grader. James Moffett recommends that writing classes be organized into workshops where the "role of the teacher . . . is to teach the students to teach each other." [4] If a student writes something that is meaningful to him, he should receive meaningful, thoughtful feedback from his peers as well as from the teacher. In this workshop approach to writing, students should feel free to continue with a writing project or to abandon it. Moffett also suggests that textbooks on writing be dispensed with and that the students' writing become the focus of the study of composition in class. [5]

If students experience some successes in producing a desired effect on an audience with their writing, they may become psychologically prepared to accept a teacher's suggestions on matters of grammar, spelling, usage, and punctuation. Naturally teachers have a responsibility to give students instruction and practice in traditional forms of writing. Most students can understand that following the conventions of standard English is necessary in formal writing if the writing is to produce the desired effect on the intended audience. To put this kind of writing in perspective for non-academic students may make it less threatening to them.

It is probably not possible to convince most non-academic students of the necessity of gaining proficiency in written communication unless the meaning of "proficiency" is expanded to include the ability to produce a variety of effects on a variety of audiences. Ken Macrorie contends, "Most good writing is clear, vigorous, honest, alive, sensuous, appropriate, unsentimental, rhythmic, without pretension, fresh, metaphorical, evocative in sound, economical, authoritative, surprising, memorable and light." [6] If teachers concentrate on these characteristics of good writing, along with the conventions of expository prose and standard English, they may experience more success with non-academic students.

References
[1] James L. Fenner. "Can 'Average' Students Be Taught To Write?" in *Teaching High School Composition*, ed. by Gary Tate and Edward P.J. Corbett. New York: Oxford University Press, 1970, pp. 336–337.
[2] Jan A. Guffin. "Writing," in *Creative Approach to the Teaching of English: Secondary*, ed. by R. Baird Shuman. Itasca, Illinois: F. E. Peacock Publishers, Inc., 1974, pp. 139–140.
[3] Stephen N. Judy. *Explorations in the Teaching of Secondary English.* New York: Dodd, Mead & Company, 1974, pp. 91–92.
[4] James Moffett. *Teaching the Universe of Discourse.* New York: Houghton Mifflin Company, 1968, p. 196.
[5] Ibid., pp. 200–210.
[6] Ken Macrorie. *Telling Writing.* Rochelle Park, New Jersey: Hayden Book Company, Inc., 1970, p. 22.

Question II, 9

How can I correct basic writing problems that are evident among my high school students without killing their creativity?
Janet T. Davis, North Johnston High School, Selma, North Carolina

Answer by:
KEN MACRORIE, Professor of English at Western Michigan University. A former editor of *College Composition and Communication*, he is well known for his books *Uptaught, Telling Writing, Writing to Be Read*, and *A Vulnerable Teacher.*

My experience—sitting in seminar writing courses for ten years with groups of twenty students or less ranging in ages from 18 to 60—tells me there is no such things as "basic writing problems," meaning a specialized set of errors or faults *existing* in writing cripples or "illiterates" as teachers often call students. Teachers may be teaching so that students are so crazed, unhinged, blocked by unnatural restrictions and prescriptions that they cannot find their voices in writing, but they have those voices or they would not have found the school building and their classroom or the way home.

The writing problems are in the teachers, not the students. If students are misspelling every third word and writing frequent sentences that are gibberish to readers, there is no medical specific that will cure those faults and make them healthy enough to go on and be "creative." Writing is creating, and writers must be allowed to write about things that count for them, in voices that belong to them, to tell truths without being penalized for candor *before* they will have motivation to improve their spelling or polish their sentences. The question looks elementary and small, but like most questions about writing it is profoundly comprehensive.

Every word teachers speak, every move they make, every stipulation about grades or assignments—all determine whether students will come to write powerfully in their classes. So there is only one way to find answers to the question: find students who are writing powerfully and examine their teacher's complete teaching program.

Question II, 10
How can I reward and encourage students who write creatively but use very poor grammar?
Hilda Parker, Cherryville Junior High School, Cherryville, North Carolina

Answer by:
LEE ODELL, Assistant Professor of English Education, State University of New York at Buffalo. Mr. Odell's articles have appeared in *English Journal, Research in the Teaching of English,* and *College Composition and Communication.* With co-author James Barchek, he is completing *Fantasy,* a text for eighth graders.

The answer to your question is both very simple and very difficult. The easy part first: If we want to encourage and reward students who write creatively, we'll have to give them plenty of opportunity to do this sort of work. Creative writing will have to be one of the central concerns of our English classes—not an occasional feature of the class, not something we work in when time permits, not a break from the serious, "real" work of the English class. What's more, we'll have to give high grades to papers with interesting metaphors but idiosyncratic spelling.

The difficult part is that we'll have to justify doing this—perhaps to our principals or colleagues, and almost certainly to the voice of our conscience that insists on asking, "Why are you doing this? Shouldn't you be concerned about more 'basic' things?" Answering these questions is complicated by the fact that many of us have the sense that really important writing is found chiefly in analytical/expository essays or in mere mundane and practical activities such as writing business letters, or filling out applications.

This sort of work is, of course, important. But it is not so important that it should lead us to overlook the very strong arguments for creative writing. David Holbrook, for example, has pointed out that creative writing—especially for "disadvantaged" or less able students— is one important means of increasing students' basic literacy. "Without a great deal of such work," Holbrook argues, "students can neither begin to bring their own souls and personalities into order, *nor* begin to become effectively articulate for normal social life, and literate." [1] On the basis of his work with extremely capable students, James Moffett [2] has shown how composing journal entries, personal letters, and short stories fits into a sequence of writing activities that helps students move from immature, egocentric writing to mature forms of communication that appeal to diverse audiences and deal with increasingly abstract subjects. Finally, Kenneth Koch [3] has described creative writing activities that can help students master basic intellectual processes. For instance, Koch gives examples of exercises that lead students to make comparisons and contrasts. In Koch's work, these two processes lead into writing poetry. But obviously making distinctions and seeing analogies are as important for expository essays as for poetry. These are not gimmicks for prettying up verse; they are powerful means for examining and clarifying one's thinking.

To supplement our own ideas for creative writing activities, there are a number of excellent sources we can turn to, sources which reflect teachers' practical experience in working with public school students. In *The Whole Word Catalogue*,[4] a number of teachers explain successful assignments they've used in their classrooms. (*Catalogue* also gives brief descriptions of many useful resource materials.) Peter Elbow's *Writing Without Teachers*[5] contains a brief but helpful discussion of the creative process and suggests—as does John Holt's *What Do I Do Monday?*[6]— practical ways to stimulate creative writing. Koch's *Wishes, Lies and Dreams* and Moffett's *Interaction*[7] present a number of ways to help students write dialogue, narrative, and poetry. Additional materials can be found all around us. One teacher reports having students buy comic books and, for one of the stories, tape paper over the dialogue and story line. Students exchange comics with their classmates, write in their own dialogue and story line, and then compare what they wrote with the original. Another teacher reports that he video tapes TV programs and replays them for his classes without the sound. Students have to fill in their own conversation and narration.

The discussion thus far has ignored the part of the original question that deals with grammar. Not because grammar is unimportant, but because attention to grammar (mechanics, usage, syntax) does not become crucial until very late in the composing process. The sources of writing activities mentioned thus far have dealt with pre-writing (formulating ideas, finding things to say), drafting (actually getting words down on paper), and revising (clarifying, re-thinking one's initial ideas). Only in the stage of editing, the final stage of the writing process, does grammar become important.

One very successful teacher reports that her eleventh grade writing classes never discuss mechanics until they have gone through the early stages of the composing process. Only when students have written something they're proud of, something they are almost ready to share with classmates does this teacher ask students to worry about grammar. At this stage, of course, grammar is very important—syntax has to reflect accurately the relationship of ideas, punctuation has to reveal rather than obscure meaning, and usage has to add to rather than detract from the overall effect of the piece. This teacher assumes that she can teach grammar effectively only when she responds to grammatical problems students are having when they are trying to articulate an idea or experience that is very important to them.

One may, of course, teach grammar through drill or competitive games. A good source for the latter is *Games to Improve Your Child's English*.[8] These games are fun, but there is no evidence that they actually improve students' writing. There are, however, strong arguments [9] that usage and mechanics improve when teachers respond to specific grammatical problems as they occur in students' writing.

The answer to your question, then, is that we can encourage students who write creatively if we (1) understand why creative writing is important; (2) make it a significant part of our teaching; (3) supplement our own ideas with some of the excellent materials available to us, and (4) make sure we relegate the study of grammar to the appropriate stage of the composing process.

References

[1]David Holbrook. *English for the Disadvantaged.* Cambridge: Cambridge University Press, 1965, p. 31.

[2]James Moffett, Kenneth R. McElheny, eds. *Points of View.* Signet.

[3]Kenneth Koch. *Wishes, Lies and Dreams: Teaching Children to Write Poetry.* New York: Random House, 1971.

[4]Rosellen Brown, et al., eds. *The Whole Word Catalogue.* Teachers' and Writers; Collaborative Newsletter, Vol. 4, No. 3 (1972).

[5]Peter Elbow. *Writing Without Teachers.* New York: Oxford University Press, 1973.

[6]John Holt. *What Do I Do Monday?* New York: Dell, 1974.

[7]Moffett, ed. *Interaction.* New York: Houghton Mifflin, 1973.

[8]Abraham B. Hurwitz and Arthur Goddard. *Games to Improve Your Child's English.* New York: Simon and Schuster, 1969.

[9]R.J. Harris. *An Experimental Inquiry into the Functions and Value of Formal Grammar in the Teaching of English.* Unpublished Ph.D. thesis, University of London, 1962.

Question II, 11

How much emphasis should be placed on mechanics of expression? Should papers that students submit in English classes be rejected if they fail to meet minimum standards? Are there any really positive ways of dealing with weak papers?

Mary Colburn Commers, Lincoln Southeast High School, Lincoln, Nebraska

Answer by:

ALAN M. McLEOD, Assistant Professor of Education at Virginia Commonwealth University, whose specialty is English Education. McLeod has written several articles on various topics in teaching English and urban education.

There is a place for some emphasis on mechanics of expression in the writing program, but such emphasis should not replace the primary focus of writing: the expression of ideas. Mechanical errors are important only if they confuse the ideas presented, for overemphasis on mechanics produces dull, sterile writing rather than vital languaging.

Mechanics of expression are conventions, proprieties, and not to be equated with the tablets inscribed on Mt. Sinai. Laird establishes an appropriate focus: "You should teach spelling, punctuation, and capitalization . . . as the minor virtues they are . . . for salvation is not in them. They should be taught and taught well, as devices with which to clarify meaning and to observe the etiquette of mentally cultured people, but they are not divine and they should not be taught as the holy of holies." [1] This idea is put another way by Muller: "Children's addiction to linguistic error is not a form of original sin." [2]

Sherwin reports that questionable dividends are reaped from intensive work on mechanics of expression.[3] Yet mechanics do have a role in writing, for they are conventions we have adopted in efforts to transcribe spoken language into written form. They should not, however, be elevated to a high level; such elevation grants them more weight than is warranted and reduces teachers to proofreaders. Correctness is not the main goal. As Laird states, "Any young person who produces a composition without error is not trying to do enough; he should be attempting structures which as yet he cannot control, seeking words he does not as yet command, not writing dull sentences to avoid fragments." [4]

If we see our role as primarily that of correcting, we discourage the writing process. Students need to be encouraged in what they write if they are to develop into more effective writers. We should, in evaluating writing, mark a few mechanical problems but reserve the weight of our judgment for raising questions to the writer. Raising questions can demonstrate an interest in what he has to say and open the way to dialog about the writing process.

Power over language and mechanics is a growth process and proceeds at different rates for different children. Young writers need to experience success now, not at some time in the future. The writer invests his personal identity in what he writes, and unless we want to crush that identity we should judge by achievements rather than mistakes. It is not until one gains a respect for his own writing, a sense of the worth of what he has to say, that he is likely to be receptive to learning about mechanics. It is at this point that he perceives the value of a needed skill, of the potential effect on his audience. As Smith writes, "The composing process is synthetic. It draws in mysterious, often only partially predictable, ways upon whatever resources of ideas, facts, experiences the composer has. If he uses rules or abstractions about the act of composing itself, he does it in eclectic and unverifiable fashion. The more vivid his memory of certain admonitions about how to compose, the more restricting and paralyzing may be the effects upon his thought." [5]

Writing is hard work, but students can accept that condition if their errors are not emphasized, if they are assisted and encouraged, and if they are given opportunities to write on topics of personal meaning and interest. To take positive steps in developing student writing, we must show respect for our students' efforts; allow them some freedom in writing; help them write with a specific audience in mind; establish specific goals and work on one skill at a time; be good listeners and confer with our students about their writing; be receptive to what is written; make distinctions between assessing composition and teaching it; provide examples of confusion created by mechanical problems, problems drawn from the writing of the students; encourage journal writing; explain clearly the development of conventions to aid readers. We might develop these possibilities by turning the classroom into a writing workshop wherein students select options from various stimuli and developed contexts; they work at their own pace; they seek help from the teacher and from their peers; they revise and rework their writing; and they see it published in any of a variety of ways: posted on the class bulletin board, published in the class or a school newspaper or literary magazine, read aloud to the class, tape recorded and put in a class or school library, and so forth. In such a workshop, the teacher can be a consultant, an editor, and not simply a proofreader.

It is at the point of publication a student is likely to be most receptive to studying mechanics, for it is at this point he sees a need for these conventions. Judy remarks: "The discussion of mechanical and syntactic correctness should be delayed until the last possible moment in the writing process, leaving the student free to do the basic writing and revision of papers without hesitation because of uncertainty over rules of correctness." [6] The attention to mechanics, then, occurs in a polishing session, and is thus assigned an appropriate place of emphasis in the writing process.

These are positive steps which can be taken in developing student writing. Other effective steps are recorded in books such as those written by Hughes Mearns and Ken Macrorie. Developing prevision, setting criteria, providing positive reinforcement, giving students opportunities to write freely as in journals, establishing a variety of interesting and personal options for writing, providing an audience and a goal of some kind of publication, and reserving mechanics for polishing, are all-positive steps. In taking such steps, we are not faced often with papers submitted which fail to meet minimum standards.

References

[1]Charlton Laird. *And Gladly Teche: Notes on Instructing the Natives in the Native Tongue.* Englewood Cliffs: Prentice-Hall, Inc., 1970, p. 6.

[2]Herbert Muller. *The Uses of English.* New York: Holt, Rinehart and Winston, Inc., 1967, p. 61.

[3]J. Stephen Sherwin. *Four Problems in Teaching English: A Critique of Research.* Scranton, Pennsylvania: International Textbook Company, 1969, p. 167.

[4]Laird, p. 4.

[5]Eugene H. Smith. *Teacher Preparation in Composition.* Champaign, Illinois: National Council of Teachers of English, 1969, p. 5.

[6]Stephen Judy. *Explorations in the Teaching of Secondary English.* New York: Dodd, Mead & Co., 1974, p. 111.

Question II, 12

How can I, as a teacher of creative writing, provide my students with more creative writing experiences without being completely overwhelmed by the resulting paperwork?

Edwina Hunnicutt, North Gaston High School, Gastonia, North Carolina

Answer by:

THOMAS N. WALTERS, Associate Professor of English and English Education at North Carolina State University. Mr. Walters' articles, poems, and short stories appear in a wide range of journals. He has published two books of poems, *Seeing In The Dark* and *Loblolly Excalibur*, co-edited an anthology, *The Southern Experience In Short Fiction*, and is currently working on a novel for teenage readers.

In my creative writing classes, I often use these time-saving practices: (1) have students think, write, confer, re-write and then tape a finished work for playback in class. Young writers learn from hearing their own stories in the context of a critically-attuned audience. Results may be compressed further by teaming the writers. (2) Teach the basics of film-making, then encourage students to write "treatments," short scripts, and "voice-overs" for a film they make to show the class. A similar approach may be taken with videotape or still photography. (3) Invite guest readers to visit and give evaluations of works they had had opportunity to read previously or which they hear students read in class. The guest does not have to be an "expert," but simply a perceptive and tactful reactor. (4) Sponsor in-school contests with prizes awarded by student judges. (5) Encourge pen-pal tradings of creative works—and *written* critiques of them—with students in other schools. (6) Have students do what my class once called "the Hemingway Holdup": practice writing his legendary eight pages and refining them into one. (7) Have classes plan, assign, and write chapters for a committee-written novel *a la* the Nancy Drew or Hardy Boys series. (8) Have groups engage in "creative-horse-around" sessions at the chalkboard so that brainstorming may occur for a group work. This my students called the "Blackboard Jangle." (9) And, finally, employ much impromptu story-telling, stressing what Faulkner called "the front porch voice"—that ability to sculpt from brain, heart and hot air a story of interest to listeners. Thoughtfully exercised, this craft becomes art: making the creative process more apparent, useful. I have seen students seriously transported by their muses during this activity, taking us away with them in story, delighting themselves—and us.

These are a few of the ways students may write creatively without the teacher's being the sole respondent. It appears, moreover, that students—given such opportunities and guidance—*enhance* their critical and composition skills as a result of helping relieve the teacher's reading task.

Question II, 13

What suggestions do you have for dealing with the crushing load of paperwork for beginning—and, for that matter, veteran—teachers of English?

William R. Wise, Encina High School, Sacramento, California

Answer by:

DENNY T. WOLFE, JR., Director, Division of Languages, North Carolina State Department of Public Instruction. Mr. Wolfe has had both public school and college teaching experience. He has contributed articles on English education to a variety of journals.

Whether it is true or not, English teachers certainly feel that their paper loads are far greater than those of teachers in other disciplines. And, as an English educator, I must concur. The key to any question about how best to handle vast quantities of student writing really lies in another, more specific, question: How can the English teachers best use their time, as well as that of other teachers, paraprofessionals, and students themselves to handle the task of reading and evaluating student writing? Obviously, if students write as much as they should, teachers cannot possibly read every word. Time constraints and the urgency of other tasks simply will not permit them to be exclusive "readers" or "graders" of every piece of work that students turn out.

The amount of time required to read students' writing largely depends upon the purposes of the writing. One important purpose for writing, which is aggressively ignored in too many English classes, is simply to provide students with an outlet for self-expression. Stephen Judy cites some "neglected forms of composition" [1] which help to meet this purpose. These include, among others, journals and diaries, profiles and portraits, photo essays, riddles and jokes, underground newspapers, graffiti, interviews, cartoons, petitions, and scripts. Such writing exercises as these need not be read by teachers, nor graded in any formal sense. Some students, or classes of students, will welcome opportunities which invite their initiative to write. Other students may require the teacher to place stringent demands on them to write. For the latter group, perhaps some kind of contract system will work well. [2] Also, asking students to submit the bulk of their writing at the end of a term, with points given for the quantity and the types of submissions, can be effective as a device for getting all students to write. Dealing with student writing in these ways requires very little reading time on the part of teachers. But the purpose of providing students with opportunities for self-expression still is well met.

If the purpose for writing is to help students master the skills and the mechanics of punctuation, usage, spelling, diction, sentence structure, and paragraphing, obviously the teacher must devote time to concentrated, detailed reading. But students can meet such a purpose for writing in far shorter compositions than many English teachers often require. Wolfe notes that in teaching mechanics "it is never necessary to assign a student more than a one-page essay at a time." [3] Students will commit the same kinds of errors in one page as they will in five or more. One-page writing exercises are much more sensible, in terms of reading time, than exercises which are several pages long. Writing which is even shorter than one page is often adequate to teach mechanics.

What does one mark or "correct" to improve mechanics in students' writing? Paul B. Diederich, echoing others, notes that "outpouring of red ink not only does no good but positive harm. Its most

Writing 69

common effect is to make the majority of students hate and fear writing." [4] Diederich emphasizes the need to be *positive* about criticizing student writing, and he suggests that teachers concentrate on one thing at a time. He declares, "Learning one new thing per paper is certainly more than most students learn at present." [5] Trying to correct every error in a single paper teaches students, at best, that the teacher may know a lot about composition. But such a practice is not very productive for facilitating students' mastery of writing skills.

Giving attention to *when* students write can also cut down on teachers' reading time. During the first few weeks of school—before football, clubs, plays, socials, and record keeping begin to eat up both teachers' and students' time—writing should dominate the English class. Late, when other demands begin to exert time pressures, much of the composition groundwork already will have been laid. Plotting monthly calendars to stagger "due dates" for classes of students to submit writing is essential, if English teachers are to keep from sinking in a quagmire of paper work.

Daniel Fader and Elton B. McNeil describe a program in which *all* teachers—not just English teachers—work with student writing. [6] Briefly summarized, the program places each English teacher with a team of teachers in other disciplines. The English teacher assists the team members in setting up a writing schedule which requires students to write at least one piece every other day in each class, *except* English. This writing is not always read, since one purpose is simply to get students to write frequently. Only one set of papers is read per week by each class instructor, and one set every two weeks is passed to the English teacher, who corrects mechanics only. The other team members evaluate content. Teachers can modify this program to suit themselves, out of consideration for ways to handle grades, joint assignments, and the like. Such a program can significantly cut down paper work for English teachers, since English instruction is diffused across the entire curriculum structure, thus freeing the English teacher from the sole responsibility of giving students experiences in writing. The program also demonstrates to students that the English department does not— indeed, should not—have a corner on the writing market.

If a school has paraprofessionals, English teachers can use them to get some relief from paper work. If paraprofessionals are not allowed to assign grades, they can at least check on the types and quantities of writing that students produce. Conventionally, paraprofessionals perform clerical duties and mark objective tests; however, with clear and skillful direction from the teacher, they can do much more to relieve teachers' work loads. They can begin classes, give and collect assignments, help to individualize instruction, and read papers for one or two particular purposes. They can also work with groups on various projects. If group work requires that *only one* product be submitted per group, submissions will be few, thus eliminating hundreds of individually submitted papers. This approach to group work can enable the teacher to devote concentrated reading time to the products which students submit. This kind of group work also creates a cooperative learning environment, with an emphasis upon *group* rather than *individual* rewards. Students learn to prize and to respect one another when each individual understands that he has a definite responsibility to help his peers attain success.

How can English teachers best use students to alleviate masses of paper work? An overwhelming amount of professional literature today supports the practice of making students feel that they are producing work for a clearly discernible and immediate purpose. For many students, it is not enough that this purpose be "a grade." The purpose must be actively relevant to their lives. And, if at all possible, it should in some way be pleasurable and fun, as well as demanding. Therefore, turning the English class into a newspaper or magazine staff has proved most satisfactory to a great many teachers. Eliot Wigginton, in Rabun Gap, Georgia, has achieved fame by transforming his entire English instructional program into an elaborate system of magazine and book production.[7] Each student has one or more specific responsibilities. Students function as photographers, developers of pictures, layout designers, interviewers, media specialists, writers, and editors. The teacher functions as a manager and a facilitator, who seldom acts arbitrarily and solely as an independent reader or grader of the work which students produce. This format requires students and teachers to be partners, working toward mutual goals. Paper work, therefore, becomes a responsibility to be shared among a team of individuals who have a clear view of the directions in which they are headed.

Round-robin reading among students is an excellent and educationally sound alternative to the coventional practice of the teacher's reading every student's work. Ken Macrorie has used this method quite successfully at Western Michigan University.[8] In the beginning, students write freely and exchange papers with their classmates. Only *positive* remarks about the writing are allowed. Once students feel free and comfortable to write what and how they please, formal criticism and instruction gradually develop in comments by both the teacher and the students. Students write almost constantly, developing confidence from their peers' remarks, and the teacher is not compelled to read everything they create.

Finally, the overhead projector can be an extremely valuable device in helping teachers to control paper work. By choosing two or three anonymous papers from the hundreds which students submit, teachers can give instruction that benefits entire classes. Writing can be transferred from the original papers to clear acetate sheets, which are projected on a screen or a wall behind the teacher. Using a grease pencil, the teacher can go to work marking errors, asking students questions about revisions, and attracting attention through the use of a visual medium.

These suggested alternatives to the teacher's function as sole reader and marker of papers are themselves time-consuming. But the time involved here is more for *planning* the work students do than for *reacting* to it. The choice which English teachers always must make is whether to spend some concentrated time in preparation for work or to spend perhaps more time coping with the work which students produce. Generally, careful planning gives one a sense of control over any situation. The teacher who plans carefully, cooperates with his colleagues, and uses paraprofessionals, students, and technical equipment effectively will learn to control—if not resolve—the frustrations of paper work.

References

[1]See Stephen N. Judy's *Explorations in the Teaching of Secondary English: A Source Book for Experimental Teaching*. New York: Dodd, Mead and Co., 1974, pp. 84–100.

[9]Howard Kirschenbaum, et. al., *Wad Ja Get? The Grading Game in American Education*. New York: Hart Publishing Co., Inc., 1971. Note especially Appendix B (pp. 292–307), which deals with alternative grading systems.

[3]Denny T. Wolfe, Jr., "The Case for Term Papers," *North Carolina English Teacher*, 27, No. 1 (October, 1969), p. 18.

[4]"In Praise of Praise," in *A Guide for Evaluating Student Composition*, ed. Sister M. Judine, Urbana, Ill.: National Council of Teachers of English, 1965, p. 38. Helpful information on assisting the teacher to cope with paper work appears in essays throughout this book.

[5]*Ibid.*, p. 39.

[6]*Hooked on Books*. New York: Berkley Publishing Corporation, 1968, pp. 27–34.

[7]See Eliot Wigginton's *Moments*. Washington, D. C.: Institutional Development and Economic Affairs Service, Inc., 1974. This short booklet is the author's credo for teaching, and it is most inspiring.

[8]See Ken Macrorie's *Uptaught*. New Jersey: Hayden Book Co., 1970. This book describes a humanistic approach to teaching the art of composing.

Question II, 14

How can one best teach students to write when his class load totals about 150 students? How can one best utilize both small group and large group techniques in such a situation?
  Ruth E. Bertsch, North Central High School, Indianapolis, Indiana

Answer by:
R. STERLING HENNIS, Professor of Education at the University of North Carolina at Chapel Hill, whose specialty is English Education; and THOMAS W. SCHEFT, Graduate Assistant at the University of North Carolina at Chapel Hill and candidate for the doctoral degree in English Education.

A first step in developing a writing plan is for the teacher to create an atmosphere where *everyone* is a teacher-student. Many teachers unthinkingly burden themselves with a serious misconception: *one* person must do *all* the teaching. The following recommendation will begin by at least attempting to take the sting out of the "me against the masses" approach. The initial step is grouping within the classroom. Separated into small groups of four or five, students have a natural audience to write for. Such a procedure, promising interaction and feedback, is an abrupt departure from the usual sterile, staid system involved when students write solely for the teacher.

Two of the most important goals of written communication are implied here: (1) spontaneity of expression; and (2) a specific audience to write *for*. Lack of either ingredient can result in a student's loss of motivation and failure to care what he produces, written or oral. No matters what writing skills the teacher imparts, if spontaneity is destroyed, the student may graduate to write only checks, memos, shopping lists, and banal phrases on birthday cards.

Most writers feel that one learns to write by writing. There are numerous attempts at teaching writing in the classroom, but in actuality, the student may do a minimal amount of writing. What constitutes the bulk of writing may be nothing more significant than exercises, book reports, autobiographies (year after year), and "What I Did Last Summer" extravaganzas. For the student to become a better writer, he needs to practice. For practice to be meaningful, good coaching is needed. The coach is the key to feedback, for he has the vantage point of observing what the learner cannot see. A problem is that most teachers do not understand that students can coach as well as teachers . . . sometimes even better. Often the teacher is stereotyped into a negative role, that of the un-hip adult, Mr. Morality, the policeman, and/or the "I'll get you in the end" grader. How much spontaneity and creativity can be dredged up by the student writing to that "audience"?

The teacher's role is vital in structuring activities, clearing up stylistic/mechanical/grammatical problems, and facilitating classroom effectiveness—whether with individuals or in small or large group situations. But with the students involved in groups, the teacher is freed from his previous Master Sergeant role to direct his aid where it is most needed. The important factor is that *one* person is not the sole reader/evaluator/corrector of one-hundred-fifty-plus papers.*

Under these circumstances it is not unreasonable that an English class have some kind of writing activity *every* day. The journal is a popular and effective means of free writing which allows a student to experiment with styles and explore thoughts. Various newspaper and journalistic articles can be eagerly shared among students. Film treatments, film storyboards, Readers' Theatre and drama adaptations are group-involved, audience-implied strategies that often develop into excellent culminating activities. The study of advertising provides a wealth of writing activities. Even the creation of bumper stickers offers a new

---

*It is important to note that previous attempts involving additional staff and "lay readers" were basically ineffective. The most glaring problems occurred over ambiguities in evaluation methods. With the group method being stressed, the teacher can set the guidelines for evaluation.

twist to written communication. Projects can be meaningful, interesting, and challenging if they focus on the long-range goals of writing instruction.

Again, the role of peer evaluation needs to be emphasized. The reason many teachers do not assign writing is the fear that inevitably it *all* must be read by them. If it is not assigned, it follows that it will not have to be read. But, can students evaluate competently? The answer is quite obvious when one considers the comments teachers make on papers. Most students can point out even in the early grades when a student's paper shows signs of awkwardness, lack of clarity or logical transition, redundancy, specific punctuation difficulties, or uninteresting content. This hardly minimizes the teacher's role. It is the teacher's job to explain the problems that the students confront but may be unable to articulate. The teacher can involve the class with different types of written communication varying in tone, style, and theme. But the objective for the teacher is to get students teaching each other.

Evaluation is largely through written and verbal comments. The student writer is often inhibited in his efforts through his receiving of "red" papers with low grades. Rather than being encouraged to learn from his mistakes, the student learns to adopt a non-writing game—avoid spelling mistakes with *simple* words; avoid sentence errors with the simplest of sentences; avoid what he wants to say for what he feels the teacher would *rather* hear; and avoid writing over the bare *minimum* for fear of making more errors. Mistakes are a natural part of any person's growth, and good writing inevitably involves learning from mistakes. How can a teacher expect to develop writers if they are all afraid to experiment with language, only to be punished for "breaking the rules"? The teacher's job is to remove the oppressive atmosphere of expected perfection, while maintaining important standards. One necessary prerequisite is to view writing as a long-term project, it certainly should not be treated as a "make-it-or-break-it" one year proposition as so many regard it now. To deal a student D's in the beginning may quickly turn into a self-fulfilling prophecy. The accent should be on learning through competent evaluation, not grades. Student papers should be filed to afford the teacher an overall evaluation, not the customary practice of infrequent, fleeting looks without any regard for improvement.

It is a fallacy to teach writing primarily through the study of grammar. The research on this is extensive and accurate. Grouping in terms of skill problems is advised, but not as a "day-in-day-out" practice. Pairing adept writers with struggling performers in a peer tutoring situation has been successful. And if skill work is needed, which is usually the case, it is advisable to concentrate on one specific problem at a time. A tennis pro does not simultaneously overwhelm the beginner with the proper grip, stance, weight distribution, forehand, backhand, the American Twist serve, rushing the net, the topspin lob, overhead smash, half-court volley, and the soft drop shot. Yet students are expected to make myriad corrections on returned papers while the teacher awaits instantaneous mastery.

By focusing on the goals, the teacher can create an environment which encourages self-motivation, positive interaction, and freedom to write. If we as teachers want students to write, we must let them assume the role of writers.

Question II, 15

How effective is revision? Should students be forced to revise and rewrite all papers?

Mary Colburn Commers, Lincoln Southeast High School, Lincoln, Nebraska

Answer by:

R. BAIRD SHUMAN, Professor of English at the University of Illinois at Urbana, whose specialty is English Education. Mr. Shuman is author of over 250 articles and seven books, the most recent of which is *Creative Approaches to the Teaching of English: Secondary.*

Writers and researchers in the area of writing are almost unanimous in their acceptance of the principle that student writing is improved significantly through competent revision. Royster recommends that teachers "double the amount of in-class writing [and] place more emphasis on revision, rewriting, and polishing, stressing quality rather than quantity." [1]

Donelson and Haley remind the teacher, "We need a reason to write, and we then need to analyze whether thoughts were communicated effectively in the writing process. Without the analysis, there is no hope for progress and improvement." [2] The analysis of which the authors speak is a major step in adequate revision, and it is a step that too few teachers take into account when they call for revision.

Revision and proofreading are closely akin and often are undertaken simultaneously by the writer. Some student writers, having done the all-important proofreading, think that their job is done. And in many instances they are right. They have discovered that their English teacher is a proofreader rather than a critical reader and that the paper without spelling and punctuation errors, dangling modifiers or sentence fragments, will command the high grade no matter what it says.

Little teacher evaluation is aimed at revision. Stephen Judy [3] asks, "Why hasn't evaluation worked? Obviously no clear answer to that question is available. . . . However, I want to suggest that a major reason may be that . . . approaches to evaluation have always been *future directed* rather than looking at writing as something for the *here and now.* Evaluation has emphasized getting students ready for the 'next time,' instead of helping them to find success now." He urges that "the discussion of mechanical and syntactic correctness should be delayed until the last possible moment in the writing process, leaving the students free to do the basic writing and revision of papers without any hesitation because of uncertainty over rules of correctness." [4]

Karrfalt [5] has built into his freshman composition courses a component which demands revision in the broadest sense of the word.

He divides his classes into groups of three. On successive weeks, one student in each group writes a paper, making two carbons. He comes to class and gives the members of his team each a carbon. They then "offer their criticisms, suggestions, corrections, or revisions to the student who wrote the first draft. During this first class-writing period, the team's attention [is] given to the larger problems of unity of the thesis, organization, development, order, clarity, emphasis, rhythm," the matters with which revision in the highest sense must be concerned. The writer then revises according to the first discussion and submits his revision to the group, which now is mostly concerned with proofreading for mechanical problems.

Shuman's research,[6] based upon 544 papers written by college freshmen, revealed that when students were asked to do two revisions of a paragraph, 44 out of 279 writing on concrete topics and 87 out of 265 writing on abstract topics were weaker in their revisions than in the original. Of those writing on concrete topics, 121 out of 279 were strongest in their first revision, 114 out of 279 in their second. Of those writing on abstract topics, 132 out of 265 were strongest in their first revision, 46 out of 265 in their second. He concludes that not all students should be forced to revise, but that revision is necessary for many.

Teaching writing according to the method suggested by Donald Murray in *A Writer Teaches Writing*,[7] Charles R. Duke [8] says, "Gone was the thought that every piece of writing was 'done' when it was passed in. Now we took the time to look at each piece of writing as a step in the process of discovering what it was we wanted to say. Students worked on drafts, submitted them for discussion, took them back, revised them, submitted the pieces again."

The answer to the question posed really has to be thus: Come up with a definition of *revision* broad enough to meet your situation. If you really want your students to learn how to write, you will probably have to demand that they revise. And if revision is to be done effectively, considerable in-class time will have to be allotted to it.

References
[1]Salibelle Royster. "A Backward Glance at High School Composition." *English Journal*, 56 (1967), p. 1188.
[2]Kenneth L. Donelson and Beverly A. Haley. "Some 'Basic, Fundamental Essentials' About Teaching Composition." *The High School Journal*, 56 (1973), p. 247.
[3]"Writing for the Here and Now: An Approach to Assessing Student Writing." *English Journal*, 62 (1973), pp. 70–1.
[4]Stephen Judy. *Explorations in the Teaching of Secondary English*. New York: Dodd, Mead and Company, 1974, p. 111.
[5]David H. Karrfalt. "Writing Teams: From Generating Composition to Generating Communication." *College Composition and Communication*, 22 (1971), pp. 377–78.
[6]R. Baird Shuman. "Theme Revision? Who Needs It?" *Peabody Journal of Education*, 40 (1962), pp. 12–15.

[7]New York: Houghton Mifflin, 1968.

[8]"How Does the Writer Write?" in Allen Berger and Blanche Hope Smith, eds. *Re-Vision: Classroom Practices in Teaching English* 1974–1975. Urbana, Ill.: National Council of Teachers of English, 1974, p. 51.

Question II, 16

Are there successful sequential composition programs to be used in secondary school mini-course programs?

Virginia O. Greene, Wilkes Central High School, Wilkesboro, North Carolina

Answer by:

R.W. REISING, Professor of Communicative Arts at Pembroke State University, where he teaches courses in English Education. Mr. Reising has written over 25 articles, as well as the section on teaching grammar in *Creative Approaches to the Teaching of English: Secondary*.

It is not difficult to identify successful sequential composition programs useful in secondary school mini-courses. Among publishing houses which have developed such programs, the Silver Burdett Company has produced materials with perhaps the greatest potential. Six of the ten modules making up that company's Contemporary English Modules Series center on composition, and collectively as well as individually they have proved to be effective. Although grade designations do not appear on any of the volumes, it is possible to use one at each level of the high-school program, 7 through 12. Conversely, the paperbound books, each consisting of about 75 pages, are adaptable enough to fit comfortably into other curriculum formats, including mini-courses.

The Art of Composition, by Barbara Pannwitt, is probably the best-done of the six volumes, all designed for students of average ability. Consisting of twenty-one lessons, plus "Composition Workshop," six composition-stimulating situations, in eighty readable and heavily illustrated pages, the book takes students through a sequence emphasizing paragraphing, point-of-view, and creativity. *Teacher's Guide: Composition*, a paperback which provides lesson plans for very volume in the series, is an additional feature that can assist in the development of sequences appropriate for mini-course programs.

Although not specifically designed for use in such programs, *Developing Writing Skills*, written by William W. West and published by Prentice-Hall, has nonetheless enjoyed excellent success in them. West is an experienced writer of high school materials, and nowhere is his expertise more evident than in this hard-cover volume, the second edition of which appeared in 1973. Eleven of its thirteen chapters treat forms of writing (for example, personal narrative, description, and opinion), and each form is presented in a prescribed sequence. In a very real sense, then, the book outlines eleven sequentially focused mini-courses in composition, each one of them culminating in a major writing assignment. Encouraging oral as well as written composition, the book takes on additional strength because of the teacher's manual that accompanies it.

Another approach to successful sequence in mini-courses in composition focuses upon sentence-combining, a technique for writing improvement that results from two research reports available from NCTE: John C. Mellon's *Transformational Sentence-Combining: A Method for Enhancing the Development of Syntactic Fluency in English Composition* (1969) and Frank O'Hare's *Sentence Combining: Improving Student Writing without Formal Grammar Instruction* (1973). William Strong's *Sentence Combining: A Composing Book,* published by Random House in 1973, and O'Hare's *Sentencecraft: An Elective Course in Writing,* published by Ginn and Company in 1975, are both designed for use on the high school level. Equally important, each moves from easy sentence-combining exercises to difficult ones, thus providing a sequence that is pedagogically as well as linguistically defensible. There is no question that students who complete either paperback are more competent writers as a result of their efforts.

The secret to sensible sequences in mini-courses in composition does not lie with materials, but rather with teachers. Because they are the best judges of their students' needs and abilities, they are bound to be the best judges of what will work with and for those students. Textbooks can help, definitely; but, as Jan A. Guffin suggests, textbooks can also be misused, hindering rather than encouraging growth in composition.[1] Teachers must constantly remind themselves of this point. Likewise, they must always stay alert to several other considerations important to effective composition sequence:

1. Sequence should be based on psychological rather than logical patterns of organization.
2. Sequence in written composition should be based on planned programs of oral language development.
3. Sequence should be based on what is known about the developmental characteristics of children.
4. Sequence should introduce students to the problems of expressing ideas in various forms.
5. Sequence in composition should provide for balanced and adequate attention to all important aspects of writing.[2]
6. Sequence in written composition must be premised on the belief that people learn to write by writing and that mastery of a grammatical system, even a linguistically based one, is not tantamount to mastery of written discourse.[3]

Finally, teachers hoping to achieve a successful sequence in mini-courses in composition should study (or re-study) three classic articles from *English Journal* which bear on their concerns: James M. McCrimmon's "A Cumulative Sequence in Composition" (LV: April, 1966, pp. 425–34); Alan D. Engelsman's "A Writing Program that Teaches Writing" (LVI: March, 1967, pp. 417–21, 442); and Ken Macrorie's "To Be Read" (LVII: May, 1968, pp. 686–92).[4]

References
[1]Jan A. Guffin. "Writing." *Creative Approaches to the Teaching of English*, edited by R. Baird Shuman. Itasca, Illinois: F.E. Peacock Publishers, Inc., 1974, pp. 133–185. Guffin provides a useful discussion of sequence in composition in a sub-section of this chapter: "Generative Writing," pp. 174–77.
[2]James R. Squire. "Five Rules for Sequence." *NEA Journal*, 53 (1964), pp. 14–16.
[3]For a full discussion of this point, see R.W. Reising's "Back to Basics in Composition . . . Huh?" *Indiana English Journal*, 9 (1975), pp. 16–18.
[4]The three articles also appear in *Teaching High School Composition*, edited by Gary Tate and Edward P.J. Corbett. New York: Oxford University Press, 1970.

Question II, 17

Do you think that students in junior and senior high school should be required to do a specified number of book reports each year in English classes? Are there any imaginative means of having students approach book reports?

John Thomas Culbreth, Jordan Senior High School, Durham, North Carolina

Answer by:
FRAN SILVERBLANK, Associate Professor of English Education, New York University.

I have heard several opinions expressed about requiring a specified number of book reports from students. One point of view holds that such a practice (1) exposes students to a greater number and variety of books, (2) gives students the opportunity to know themselves better and more clearly understand their relationship to others and the universe, (3) forces students to organize their time and ideas, and (4) prepares students for the rigors of college.

Another point of view holds that such a requirement (1) encourages students to read books with large type print and no more than 100 pages in length, (2) encourages cynicism by emphasizing quantity, not quality, (3) boosts the sale of CLIFF NOTES, and (4) increases movie attendance or TV viewing when a book had been adapted for the screen.

Personally, I can see no reason for requiring students to read a specified number of books each year. If I had a high school student who wanted to read *War and Peace* or *Kristin Lavransdatter* or *Andersonville* —should I require this student to read a specific number of books? Further, if one student reads more slowly than another, should I discourage him or her from reading the aforementioned books in order to meet the assignment?

In addition to length as a consideration, the level of difficulty of a piece of work also warrants attention. Certainly, Joseph Conrad's *Heart of Darkness* makes more demands on the reader than does Jacqueline Susann's *Valley of the Dolls*.

Another point worthy of consideration is the parameters for writing the book report. (The sense of the question, as I read it, implies written reports.) How long should it be? Are the responses to be cognitive, affective aesthetic, or a combination of the three? The difficulty here becomes obvious when one considers *Heart of Darkness* and *Valley of the Dolls*.

Finally, one must ask the question: What is the purpose of a book report? If the function of individualized reading is to allow students to pursue reading that is of interest to them and at their own level of comprehension, then evaluation (which is what the book report is for) should not be based on numbers, but rather, on differentiated assignments.

This brings me to the second question: Are there any imaginative ways for students to approach book reports? It seems to me that giving differentiated assignments involves more than allowing students to choose their own reading. It frequently necessitates individualized assignments of varying degrees of complexity depending on the ability of the student. Here are some suggestions:

1. Keep a class "Reading File" and ask students to record their thoughts about individual titles. The file might help others in making a book selection. Often, as the file on a particular book grows, students will react not only to the book but also to others' responses.
2. Arrange a library reading period for the class and have conferences with individual students. Talk with each student about the book he or she is reading on a level that is appropriate for that student; discussion might center on plot, the implications of the book, its literary elements, or simply what the student accepts or rejects in the book.
3. If a number of students are reading or have read the same novel, invite them to share their ideas in small group discussions—with only occasional assistance from the teacher.
4. If a novel has been adapted for the movies or TV, a comparison of the two treatments might be in order. This can be done in individual conference with the teacher, in a written book report, in a debate, in small group discussions, or in a general class discussion. Using any of these approaches, it is possible for the teacher to direct students to focus on specific considerations. For example, in *The Old Man and the Sea*, the teacher might ask the students to consider how inference is conveyed in the novel and in the film.
5. If a student opts for the traditional written report, the teacher can suggest several questions and ask the student to respond to some or all of them. Questions might deal with the following: the student's feeling about the book; the definition of literary

elements; the discovery of relationships—between the book and the student's own experiences, between literary works, or between the book and another art form; what the student has generalized or abstracted from what he has read.

6. In small groups, or as a class, ask students to select a passage which they especially liked or found to be irritating and have them read it aloud. Let them comment on their reasons for making the selection. Again, the teacher can give direction to the discussion by asking students to focus on the author's style, description, characterization, etc.

The most a teacher can do is to help students create for themselves a natural pattern of reading, a pattern that, hopefully, will encourage them to value reading and want to continue reading for the rest of their lives. A specified number of book reports a year is a sure fire way of guaranteeing that this will never happen. A student so taught ". . . hath not fed of the dainties that are bred of a book; he hath not eat paper, as it were; he hath not drunk ink." (Shakespeare, *Love's Labour's Lost*, IV, ii, 25.)

Question II, 18

What kinds of research paper(s) should college bound students write in high school English courses?

Florence R. Roberson, Belton-Honea Path Senior High School, Honea Path, South Carolina

Answer by:

JOSEPH O. MILNER, Assistant Professor of English at Wake Forest University whose specialities are English Education and Contemporary Literature. Mr. Milner is the editor of *North Carolina English Teacher,* a teacher at North Carolina Governor's School, and a contributor to both English and English Education periodicals.

Perhaps it is necessary to ask first whether the research paper has a place in the high school English curriculum at all. It takes considerable looking to locate an article specifically directed to the research paper in either *English Journal* (an average of less than one per year in the last ten years, some of those primarily attacks)[1] or *College Composition and Communication* (only one in the last three years).[2] Two of the finest textbooks aimed at prospective English teachers, Stephen Judy's *Explorations in the Teaching of Secondary English*[3] and Dwight Burton's *Teaching English Today*[4]—both of which devote considerable space to writing—do not mention the research paper.

Such silence on this subject speaks loudly. Thomas Taylor's essay in *English Journal,* "Let's Get Rid of Research Papers," is more directly negative on the topic. Taylor says that "students are not equipped to carry on meaningful literary research" and that "reasonably correct and creative writing—the goal of instruction in composition—cannot be developed by teaching students to regurgitate the thoughts of others."[5] John Stevenson, in "The Illusion of Research," sees the research paper as "a *rite de passage*" which is in fact "an exercise in deception" brought about because of the woeful lack of emphasis on primary material.[6]

Nevetheless, much can be offered to substantiate the usefulness and worth of the term paper if its essential shape (investigation, evaluation) rather than its superficial form (notecards, footnote style) is kept in view. Its fundamental role in "encouraging critical thinking and the close examination of fact"[7] is surely compatible with the instructional design of any English classroom.

Fred Schroeder offers a slightly different focus in defining two primary components of the research paper as "*library research techniques and intellectual investigation of a subject.*"[8] He goes on to break down the development of the essential research skills into a four year continuum: ninth grade, library skills; tenth grade, paraphrasing and documentation; eleventh grade, controlled research; and twelfth grade, topic restriction and free research.[9] Beth Neman condenses the sequence of research skills into a six weeks' period of instruction in which she speaks of such matters as limiting the topic, taking an argumentative stance, and learning the art of documentation.[10] Other voices have suggested that tape cassettes [11] and mixed media [12] offer possible alternatives to the traditional research paper, but these appear to be manipulations of the surface aspects of research rather than suggestions of approaches which differ basically.

I can suggest five models for the research paper which I believe differ in kind and which might be appropriate for college-bound students: (1) Controlled Sources Research; (2) Textual Analysis Research; (3) Historical Synthesis Research; (4) Contemporary Issues Research; (5) Scholarly Research.

Controlled Sources Research is coming to be one of the most popular in English classrooms, for it allows the teacher to have a thorough survey of the source material and it insures that all students are exposed to a wide range of useable materials. This approach makes use of texts like the Norton Critical edition of *Moby Dick*, which contains raw historical material such as letters, analogues, sources, reviews and criticism, or more narrow casebooks like the Merrill text of *A Rose for Emily* or MacMillan's *Huck Finn and His Critics*, which contain critical essays without the other historical paraphernalia. To avoid the expense of buying sets of these books, many teachers make their own casebooks. No matter which of these approaches is employed, one encounters the disadvantage of the student's failing to get involved in original research. Yet in learning how to extract, evaluate, and synthesize materials, students engage in an essential and appropriate component of research.

Textual Analysis offers students the opportunity first to locate and then carefully examine a definable body of writing in order to recognize some differentiations, comparisons, or progressions within that material. Such dissections can be performed on both literary matter (a short story collection like Malamud's *The Magic Barrel*, selected poetry of the Harlem Renaissance, the fiction of *Esquire*) or non-literary material

(Franklin Roosevelt's inaugural addresses, William Buckley's editorials, Bob Dylan's lyrics). This analytical approach allows students' interests to be expressed in the research they select and without having access to huge library resources. Students in all but the most isolated locales can take part in the search part of research. The emphasis on primary materials and the student's ability to assess them is another attractive feature of this format.

Historical Synthesis demands an even more complete range of source materials, but it allows students to uncover both primary and secondary sources as a means of arriving at an informed answer to a prescribed question. Students for example might be asked to investigate the details (who, when, where, how, why) of a specific, isolated event in history, such as the death of Hitler. They might be asked to make use of varying kinds of sources and become involved in evaluating the reliability of those sources. Even when working with a limited supply of sources, a student has the chance to be confronted by the researcher's most essential task, locating and evaluating material.

Contemporary Issues Research offers some students an enticing subject matter to investigate, but it also broadens the scope of the research. Donald Larmouth offers a highly detailed outline for this approach to student research.[13] Students involved in research of this kind might probe local problems like zoning, child abuse, or allocation of funds by the school board, conducting interviews, examining records, and distributing questionnaires. Others might research more general problems such as no-fault insurance, gun laws, or sex roles in communes by consulting governmental reports, current periodicals, and recently published books. Both kinds of research consume much time and energy, but the resultant enthusiasm for and understanding of the research process can be considerable.

Scholarly Research earns the most prestige in the scholarly world because it seems the most pure, original kind of labyrinthian quest. Its free, uncontrolled search for relationships, connections, analogues, and influences can be directed toward non-literary as well as literary topics. Moreover, because this kind of activity demands a more comprehensive library and a greater measure of research sophistication than can be generally expected, students' time and energy can be saved by offering lists of possible productive investigations. Topics such as the influence of Eugene Zamiatin's *We* on George Orwell's *1984* or Hegel's place in German militarism offer solid potential and at the same time much room for student initiative.

References

[1]*English Journal*, 53–62 (1964–1973).
[2]*College Composition and Communication*, 22–24 (1971–1973).
[3]Stephen Judy. *Explorations in the Teaching of English.* New York: Dodd, Mead and Company, 1974, pp. 84–114.
[4]Dwight L. Burton, Kenneth L. Donelson, Bryant Fillon and Beverly Haley. *Teaching English Today.* Boston: Houghton Mifflin Company, 1975, pp. 109–166.

[5]Thomas E. Taylor. "Let's Get Rid of Research Papers." *English Journal,* 54 (1965), p. 126.

[6]John W. Stevenson. "The Illusion of Research." *English Journal,* 61 (1972), p. 1030.

[7]Glen A. Love and Michael Payne. "The Research Paper: Does It Belong in High School?" *English Journal,* 56 (1967), p. 741.

[8]Fred E. H. Schroeder. "How To Teach a Research Theme in Four Not-So-Easy Lessons." *English Journal,* 55 (1966), p. 898.

[9]Ibid. p. 899–901.

[10]Beth S. Neman. "A Handbook for the Teaching of the Research Paper." *English Journal,* 56 (1967), pp. 263–266.

[11]Marie O'Connor. "The Research Paper and the Tape Recorder." *English Journal,* 57 (1968), pp. 652–53.

[12]Sandy Johnson. "Sight and Sound and the Research Paper." *English Journal,* 58 (1969), pp. 1061–69.

[13]Donald W. Larmouth. "The Life Around Us: Design for a Community Research Component in English Composition." *College Composition and Communication,* 23 (1972), pp. 383–89.

SECTION III

READING

Question III, 1

What is the best way to instill in young people the desire to read?

Gladys Butler Prince, Smithfield-Selma Senior High School, Smithfield, North Carolina.

Answer by:

TERRY SANFORD, President of Duke University; former Governor of North Carolina, Attorney at Law, Educator. Author of: *But What about the People* and *Storm over the States.*

I have come to observe that reading, making out letters and words, is an almost insurmountable obstacle for some young children. Others pick it up rapidly. I am sure that there are scientific reasons to explain this, but I have also observed that the best way to get over that obstacle is a sympathetic, understanding teacher, who finds a way to build confidence along with comprehension, no matter how slow and painful the process. On the other hand, I have observed teachers who apparently figured that a certain percentage of first graders was not going to learn to read anyhow, and so that was that. There is, in my experience, no substitute for the teacher who cares, and there is no better way to instill in young people the desire to read, or for that matter to learn anything else. Those in official positions have an added responsibility of not only encouraging this kind of teaching, but also providing the right kinds of textbooks. Some are dreadful. Some express ideas and thoughts that carry the new reader along, eager to know what comes next. Those who select textbooks, and evaluate textbooks, can be careful to have in mind that most children are not going to find that reading comes naturally, and many are going to find that it is most unnatural. In a sentence, a good teacher with good books can be very successful in instilling in young people the desire to read.

Question III, 2

How can the English teacher help the reluctant reader develop the lifelong reading habit that will enrich his life?

Wanda Ann Watson, Jordan High School, Durham, North Carolina

Answer by:

SAUL BACHNER, Associate Professor of Education at the University of North Carolina at Wilmington, whose specialty is English Education. Mr. Bachner is the author of over thirty articles and two books. He is the author of the literature strand of Follett's *Success in Language: C,* a series designed to meet the needs of reluctant readers.

Developing the habit of reading which enriches the lives of all of us, reluctant readers and scholars alike, is inextricably bound up in making reading a means to pleasure of some kind. People who have developed the lifetime reading habit enjoy what they read. Reading is an essential part of their lives. They read because they love to read and because what they read provides both respite and sustenance in the day after day business of putting in one's seventy years. Both the desire for enjoyment and the need to satisfy an intermittent or consistent curiosity are the twin bases of one's reading regularly. It is my belief that all human beings have this desire for enjoyment and need to satisfy curiosity, and, further, virtually all human beings will *read* to satisfy that desire and to fulfill that need if the reading is in line with those motives.

How then do we develop the habit of reading? We do it simply by encouraging students to read. We encourage reading by broadening the reading base in our classroom and allowing students to read what they can read what they will read. If a youngster loves sports, for example, the chances are good that, no matter how reluctant to read he has been heretofore, he will read about sports. Capitalizing on a student's interest and providing reading material for it has made regular readers of reluctant ones again and again. Charles Spiegler[1] has demonstrated the success of this approach with both vocationally oriented readings and automotive themes from Gregor Felsen to motor magazines. When the reading program is built on the desire to satisfy student interests and to encourage reading for pleasure, it works. It develops readers. When the aim of the program is to use reading for performance, i.e., for recitation, test responses, critical interpretations, etc., it may develop students, but it may or may not develop readers. A reading program that is prescriptive, that forces all students into consistently common assignments, that emphasizes performance over enjoyment, will never turn reluctant readers into regular ones. There is a good chance it will never develop the lifetime habit of reading in not so reluctant readers as well. For, unfortunately, many of our college bound students never develop the lifetime reading habit either.

It is also my belief that there are very few reluctant readers. I have seen so-called reading improvement classes where all students were reading regularly—from periodicals to novels. Many years ago I taught such a class (I have had twenty years teaching experience in the public schools). Students in that group were reading from three to five years below grade level. They were eleventh graders. I used a healthy variety of materials with them—from periodicals to novels (but none, Heaven forbid, of the skill building, drill type matter). All students read and read regularly. A part of the course, Bantam's L.U.D. 600 Unit, was written up and appeared as an article in *The Journal of Reading*.[2] The point of the article was that even reluctant readers will read regularly if they are interested in the material and encouraged to read. And that, it seems to me, is the job of the teacher of such students. Given the materials, the creative, enthusiastic teacher can turn reluctant readers into regular ones—or at least make a start. More than that, perhaps, we just cannot do.

References

[1]Charles E. Spiegler. "Hit Them Where They Live," in *Improving English Skills of Culturally Different Youth in Large Cities.* Arno Jewett, J. Mersand, and D. Gunderson (eds.). U.S. Dept. of Health, Education, and Welfare, Office of Education Bulletin

no. 5, (1964), pp. 90-98; "If Only Dickens Had Written about Hot Rods." *English Journal*, 54 (April, 1965), 280-283.
[2]Saul Bachner. "The Portable Library in the Classroom." *Journal of Reading*, 10 (April, 1967), 473-475.

Question III, 3

Is there any fool-proof way of teaching basic reading skills to high school students? *I will try anything!*
Janet T. Davis, North Johnston High School, Selma, North Carolina

Answer by:
NORMA B. KAHN, Lecturer and Supervisor of the College Reading Program at the Graduate School of Education, University of Pennsylvania. Dr. Kahn holds a B.A. and M.A. in English and an Ed.D. in Reading/Language Arts. Prior to university teaching, Dr. Kahn taught English and Reading at the secondary level.

In my opinion, there *is* what may be called a "fool-proof" way for English teachers to teach basic reading skills to high school students. Before explaining the way, I should indicate what I believe to be the basic reading skills which most high school students need to learn:

1. critical and creative reading, beginning with the student's choice of material, primarily on the basis of its value and interest to him or her personally;
2. setting purposes for reading, and reading for those purposes;
3. adapting to the differences between factual and fictional materials.

Each of these three basic skills can increase motivation, comprehension, retention, and versatility in reading, and each can develop positive attitudes and habits which are essential for effective lifetime reading.

If the term "basic reading skills" is considered to mean decoding or "word attack" skills, I submit that the reading specialist should review these skills with the students who need it; the English teacher (with the reading specialist) should provide for the students' *caring* what the words say and mean.

The fool-proof way to teach basic reading skills is this:

(1) *Make available and accessible a wide variety of materials from which students may choose:*
   (a) Work with reading specialists, librarians, content-area teachers in addition to other English teachers, and administrators, to surround students with newspapers, magazines, paperbound books, and hardcover books—the "saturation and diffusion" which Daniel Fader and Elton McNeil reported to be uniquely successful in *Hooked on Books: Program and Proof.*[1] If a great variety of materials cannot be made available in every class-

room, several rooms can be fully furnished with reading materials, and classes can be scheduled to meet in these rooms several times a week.

(b) Provide a variety of annotated book lists, to aid students in their choice of non-periodical materials. Some of these lists can be purchased for or by students; for example, *Books for You,* edited by Jean A. Wilson, *High Interest-Easy Reading for Junior and Senior High School Students,* edited by Marion E. White, and *Reading Ladders for Human Relations,* edited by Virginia Reid. Other lists may be drawn up by the teacher, with the help of students, for particular subjects of study. A useful guide to teacher-made booklists, in addition to the lists named above, is *Books and the Teenage Reader,* by G. Robert Carlsen.[2] All four booklists are available through the National Council of Teachers of English.

(c) Include on the booklists, and among the materials gathered in classrooms, both non-fiction and fiction on similar subjects, so that students can become conscious of the relative values of each type of material, and so that they can be guided in developing versatility in turning from one type to the other.

(d) For the high school students who are least advanced in reading, gather materials developed for Adult Basic Education. ABE materials are available from publishers such as New Readers Press and Steck-Vaughn Company and from public libraries.

(2) *Encourage personal purposes and personal responses to reading:*

(a) Invite comparison between fictional and factual material, especially regarding their relative values; guide students in drawing conclusions regarding the reading approaches most appropriate for different types of material and for different purposes in reading them. For non-fiction, students may discover the appropriateness of previewing organizational aids (table of contents, concluding or summary paragraphs, key sentences), to gain the equivalent of a map of the material; the map can serve first as a basis for choosing to read the material as a whole, and then as an aid in comprehending the material more rapidly and remembering it longer.

For fiction, students may discover the appropriateness of reading opening pages to determine whether the experiences which the fiction promises to convey are appealing to them, and if so to become involved in the fictional world created by the author.

(b) As one basis for choosing material, encourage students to consider whether enough words are familiar in the material previewed (non-fiction) or in the opening pages (fiction) to avoid frustration in reading further. If more than a word or two on each page is unfamiliar, another book may be more desirable

(c) Encourage personal response through questions which ask essentially, "What value does this material have for me?"

For non-fiction, initial questions should be, in effect, "What did the author say? What did he imply?" These initial questions should be followed by more critical and creative ones: "In what ways is the argument strong? In what ways is it weak? How does this information compare with other reading I have done or with experiences I have had? How could I apply the ideas in this material?"

For fiction, initial questions should invite "engagement-involvement"[3]; only after personal response to fiction should analysis, interpretation, or evaluation be expected. Basic questions, both initially and finally, should be, in effect, "How do I feel about specific experiences in this fiction?" and "How has this fiction changed me?"

The recent international study, *Literature Education in Ten Countries*,[4] indicated that literature education in schools affects most of all the patterns of questioning and response of students. To build basic reading skills which will be likely to lead to effective lifetime reading, students need to become aware of the values of fictional and factual reading for them personally and to read primarily with these values in mind.[5] We need to provide practice in setting personal purposes for reading, because "ample evidence is now available that students do not alter their reading pattern to achieve particular purposes unless they have had guided practice in doing so."[6]

(d) Personal response is likely to be freer and stronger if the teacher conveys a positive attitude to both oral and written responses of students: individual insights, quality of expression, and effort should be praised before comments are made regarding need for improvement in the mechanics of written or oral form.

Why is the way described here likely to be "fool-proof" for teaching basic reading skills to high school students? Primarily because it provides for maximum motivation of the learner and therefore makes more likely the transfer of skills to new reading situations and the development of lifetime interest in reading. According to humanistic psychologists, the motivational force behind significant learning is "the desire of each student to implement those purposes which have meaning for him."[7] If teachers provide for individual interests, needs, reading abilities and responses, students should develop a more positive attitude toward reading generally, which in turn should contribute to reading achievement. Recent research reveals that a negative attitude toward reading is "the primary problem associated with lack of achievement in reading at all levels." [8]

References
[1] New York: Berkley, 1968.
[2] New York: Bantam, 1971.
[3] Purves, Alan C., with Victoria Rippere. *Elements of Writing About a Literary Work: A Study of Response to Literature.* Champaign, Illinois: NCTE, 1968.
[4] Purves, Alan C. New York: Wiley, 1973, p. 315.
[5] Kahn, Norma B. "A Proposal for Motivating More Students to Lifetime Reading of Literature." *English Journal, 63* (February, 1974), 34–43.
[6] Farr, Roger. *Reading: What Can Be Measured?* Newark, Delaware: IRA, 1969.
[7] Rogers, Carl. *Freedom to Learn.* Columbus, Ohio: Merrill, 1969, p. 164.
[8] Weintraub, Samuel, et al. "Summary of Investigations Relating to Reading," *Reading Research Quarterly,* 4 (Winter, 1970), p. 273.

Question III, 4

What is my responsibility to a student reaching my high school English class who reads at about the fifth-grade level, has little capability for putting words into acceptable sentences, and has little desire to learn? What responsibility have teachers in other subject areas to such a student?

Carol P. Carter, Needham Broughton High School, Raleigh, North Carolina

Answer by:
DELWYN G. SCHUBERT, Reading Clinical Director and Professor of Education at California State University, Los Angeles. Mr. Schubert is author of more than 85 research studies and articles and five books, the most recent of which is *Improving the Reading Program.*

and

PHILIP D. VAIRO, Dean, School of Education, California State University, Los Angeles. Mr. Vairo is the author/co-author of over 50 articles and four books, the most recent of which is *Learning and Teaching in the Elementary School.*

It is not unusual for high school teachers to encounter severely retarded as well as markedly accelerated readers in their classes. One high school teacher gave a standardized reading test to her eleventh grade class and discovered a range of fourteen grade levels! [1] Pedagogically speaking, it seems as if individual differences, like death and taxes, are always with us.

There was a time in our nation's history when only a small percentage of the population attended high school. Standards were high and very few students were able to weather the demands of four years of Latin, mathematics, English, and science. But with the passage of laws requiring attendance until age 16, 17, or 18 coupled with the initiation of a nonfailure policy in many of our schools, the situation changed. Today's secondary school teachers are faced by a radically different school population.

Without realizing it, many high school teachers subconsciously cling to the old belief that the teaching of subject matter by way of textbook assignments is for the select few. They are shocked at the suggestion that they have a responsibility to teach reading skills as well as subject matter content. Nevertheless, the problem must be faced realistically. The need to extend the teaching of reading into the total high school curriculum is absolutely essential.

The problem of what to do with the mathematics student who cannot read the text or the English teacher attempting to introduce *Hamlet* and *Paradise Lost* or *Leaves of Grass* to a high school student lacking the necessary reading skills can no longer be ignored. What then can a high school teacher do to assist an unmotivated student who reads on the fifth grade level? What specific approaches will enable the teacher to help the student grow in his reading skill while he learns the subject matter of the course?

1. Spend some time alone with the student. Be warm, friendly, understanding and patient and genuinely interested in him as an individual. Do not publicly reprimand or ridicule a student. If praise is deserved, make sure it is given. Nothing is more basic to changing a student's attitude toward learning than a good relationship with the teacher. The student who likes his teacher tries harder. When questioned as to how she managed to earn a grade of "A" in a course in which she seemed destined to fail, a high school sophomore said, "Well, we got a new teacher and I liked him."

2. Try to gain an understanding of the poor reader by checking available cumulative records. Questions that can be answered by consulting them are as follows: What is the nature of his achievement record? What are the results of past and current standardized achievement tests? Has any remedial work been provided? Do data on the student's past and present physical status indicate the presence of any defects that are significant? Are there anecdotal records that might prove helpful?

3. Have the student read aloud. This is the quickest way to learn what kinds of difficulties he is experiencing. Mechanical errors and reactions to difficulties encountered are readily disclosed in an oral presentation. Oral reading is also valuable in locating reading material of the proper difficulty.

4. Look for any manifestations of a visual problem. Some students pass school survey tests in spite of a serious visual defect. Symp-

toms with which the teacher should be acquainted are bloodshot, swollen, teary, or discharging eyes; inflamed eyelids; complaints of sleepiness, fatigue, headache, nausea, dizziness, blurred, double or distorted vision, and pain, or feeling of dryness, itching, burning, or grittiness in the eyes; strained and tense facial expression; rapid blinking or twitching of the face; and such habits as holding a book very close or far away or holding the head on one side while reading.[2]

5. Determine the student's potential. Mental ability as measured by intelligence tests is widely used as an index of learning capacity. However, care must be exercised in interpreting intelligence test scores. Many intelligence tests above the third grade require a great deal of reading. This means that the intelligence of a poor reader is often underestimated. It is important [therefore] to secure a nonlanguage or performance assessment of a poor reader's intelligence. Another way to measure potential is to read aloud for the student and quiz him on what was heard. If a student can comprehend material at or above his reading grade level, the teacher can be assured that normal reading potential is present.

6. Seek remedial help for the student. If no remedial classes are offered at your school, check with the school psychologist or guidance specialist to find where special help is available. Often nearby colleges or universities have reading clinics which can provide needed assistance.

7. Provide the student with subject matter material on his reading grade level. This can be done by having on hand a variety of material relevant to activities and projects which stimulate and require reading. According to Newton,[3] certain subject matter areas lend themselves to multi-level unitary teaching procedure. Consider, for example, the English teacher who is teaching a unit on the short story. Instead of requiring all students to read the same short story, students are allowed to choose from a large number of short stories the particular ones that coincide with their interests and level of reading skill. Similarly, a social science teacher who is introducing a unit on the Civil War might begin a multilevel approach by exposing students to a large collection of related material. Included would be textbooks that vary in difficulty, trade books of all kinds, newspaper and magazine articles, pamphlets, encyclopedias, and even comic books. After an exploratory stage during which students decide on suitable activities, the class studies various aspects of the topic. Students work individually, in pairs, or in groups. The teacher moves about giving help and making suggestions whenever needed. When the work is completed, students "contribute their reports in a pooling and sharing period. The exchange of information may be made by tape recording, panel of experts, quiz games, bulletin-board displays, debates, and the more formal committee report."[4]

8. Individualize assignments in a carefully selected class text by asking the poor reader to respond to factual questions of the *what, when,* and *where* variety. Better readers can be exposed to *why* and *how* questions which involve varying degrees of critical thinking. Different levels of interpretation can also be encouraged. In this connection, Ruth Strang [5] has said that while a teacher may

> . . . . . be content to have Helen enjoy a given story as a simple boy meets girl romance, he will expect Betty to discover its deeper social significance, perhaps in relation to an understanding of some adolescent problem. The teacher may induce Tony, who rejects the story as a whole, to improve his oral reading by taking part in a dramatization of a single scene that appeals to him.

9. Allow the poor reader to skip parts of an assignment in the class text as a way of compensating for his slow and laborious reading. On other occasions, parts of the text may not be assigned because the material is too difficult for the poor reader to comprehend.

10. Use a tape recorder to assist the student who cannot read the assignment. To do this, a recorded version of the text is made. The voice recorded may be that of the teacher or an able student who is accepted by the poor reader. Once the troubled reader hears the textbook assignment read out loud, it is easier for him to study it on his own.

11. Clearly, there is a need to build on the foundation which the student brings to school. Overnight success cannot be expected. In teaching pupils with below standard reading skills, use must be made of the vocabulary which they already have. At the same time that we attempt to upgrade a student's ability and provide the appropriate learning environment, we cannot ignore the words and situations which are already part of his culture in favor of words and situations foreign to his experience. To do this would make education irrelevant and meaningless to the student.

12. One final recommendation for beginning teachers: Simply said, take one day at a time. If a student in your English or social studies class learns one or two new vocabulary words a lesson, he will have added somewhere between 200–300 new words to his arsenal of communication for the academic year. Should all subject matter teachers concern themselves with this reading skill, each student will have been introduced to over 1000 new words in a variety of subjects fields.* There is great strength in concerted action. All teachers can play an important role as vocabulary builders. Why not you?

---

* See Harold Herber, *Success with Words,* New York: Scholastic Book Services, 1964. This paperback book is of inestimable value to teachers of English, social studies, science and mathematics who wish to develop students' meaning vocabulary.

For much too long we have discussed the need for all teachers to be concerned with student reading skills. The time has come for us to accept and implement the concepts which we have supported but have not integrated in our respective subject fields. If and as we do, we shall witness the breakthrough in reading appreciation and comprehension too long coming.

References
[1]Ruth Strang and Dorothy Bracken, *Making Better Readers*, Boston: D. C. Heath and Company, 1957, p. 60.
[2]Albert Harris, *How to Increase Reading Ability*, 5th edition. New York: David McKay Company, Inc., 1970, p. 255.
[3]J. Roy Newton, *Reading In Your School*, New York: McGraw Hill Book Company, Inc., 1960.
[4]*Ibid.*, p. 138.
[5]Ruth Strang, *Meeting Individual Differences in Reading*, Supplementary Educational Monograph No. 94, "Effective Use of Classroom Organization in Meeting Individual Differences." University of Chicago Press, 1964.

Question III, 5

What can one teacher do to help three non-readers in a high school class of 30 students? Some differential materials are available. The class meets five days a week for fifty minutes.
Ruth E. Bertsch, North Central High School, Indianapolis, Indiana

Answer by:
BARBARA A. BLISS, counselor for Barneveld Public Schools, Barneveld, Wisconsin. Mrs. Bliss has been working with junior and senior high non-readers (or reluctant readers), providing them with successful daily recorded reading practice in order to stimulate their interest in Reading.

Innovative materials and teaching techniques may fail to change non-readers into readers. Although skills are carefully taught, unless the non-reader begins to read much more than he has in the past, little improvement takes place from one semester to the next. The non-reader remains at the bottom of his class, falling farther behind each year.

Levine reminds us that it takes "thousands of words read daily in school before the below average reader will take his rightful place in the world of written communication."[1] If the non-reader were to read as much and as often as the proficient reader, perhaps the efforts of the teacher would stand a better chance of getting results.

In the second semester of 1974, forty-five non-readers among 7th through 12th graders in our school were invited to take part in an audio-visual reading practice program. The immediate goal was to get non-readers reading and enjoying it. Over a period of nine to eighteen weeks we hoped daily practice would also bring about an increase in rate of reading, because the prerecorded materials we employed were made at a faster rate than our students could read, 150 to 200 words per minute. Both goals were accomplished. Self-concept improved, and attitude toward school work changed for the better.

There are many advantages to audio-visual reading:

1. It is easy to explain to students that reading must be practiced, just as the piano or the game of golf must be practiced, if they expect to improve.
2. Recorded reading is enjoyable.
3. It can be completely individualized as to interests, style, and/or sophistication.
4. The classroom teacher can work with other class members without neglecting the non-readers, since the latter are better able to comprehend with audio input.
5. Non-readers once again are able to learn new words through context as they did when very young, before they were supposed to read.
6. The exact timing possible when using tapes or records makes lesson plans simple to construct.
7. Students gain a new sense of time, and tend to read longer books, rather than short ones with many pictures.
8. Students can test their reading rate at any time merely by turning down the volume, reading ahead, and turning it up again to see who is ahead, they or the narrator.
9. Weaning is a natural result of improved reading and self-confidence.
10. Taping a book only as far as an exciting episode may encourage some students to take the book home to be finished without its recording.

We must not overlook the possibility that we may have in our classes a small number of students who try but cannot read. (Four of our forty-five students were thus handicapped.) While their vision may be 20/20, their inability to read is as frustrating as if they were blind. Following the printed text is extremely difficult for them, and of dubious benefit. They should have access to recordings made for the blind, and be taught listening skills which will help them to learn. While maturation seems to improve the situation, despair and loss of confidence may cause the child to become disruptive or just tune out. It is possible Bryant's method of using materials taped at only 127 words per minute might help such severely handicapped readers, although he found the slow speed inhibited learning with subjects who were able to read faster than the tapes.[2] Thames and Rossiter increased the speed of their recordings by electronically altering them, a process called compressed speech. Their non-readers were exposed to a gradual increase in speed to 350 words per minute.[3]

While there are many innovative materials on the market for non-readers, experiencing success in reading through recordings and daily practice will do much to change non-readers into daily readers. Once they grasp that reading is possible and worth doing, they will be less inclined to avoid it.

References

[1]Isidore Levine. "Quantity Reading, an Introduction," *Journal of Reading*, 15 (May 1972), p. 583.

[2]Antusa S. Bryant, et al. "Effectiveness of Taped Reading Instruction in Increasing Reading Rate and Comprehension of Uneducated Adults." *Adult Education*, 21 (Summer 1971), p. 250.

[3] Kenneth H. Thames and Rossiter, Charles M. "Effects of Reading Practice with Compressed Speech on Reading Rate and Listening Comprehension," *A.V. Communication Review*, 20 (Spring 1972), p. 35-42.

[4]Barbara Bliss. "Recorded Reading Practice, A Daily Activity for the Non-Reader," *Reading Horizons*, 16 (Summer 1976), pp. 272-273.

Question III, 6

What role should phonics have in the teaching of reading at the secondary school level?

Jackie Hill, Cherryville Senior High School, Cherryville, North Carolina

Answer by:

WILLIAM S. PALMER, Chairman, Reading and Language Arts, The University of North Carolina at Chapel Hill. Dr. Palmer has written several articles on the teaching of reading and English. He is the author of a soon to be published textbook, *Teaching Reading to High School Students.*

In recent years, the question of reading instruction in phonics has been of much concern to both the elementary and secondary school teacher. Jeanne Chall had much influence in generating interest in this one aspect of reading after the publication of her book *Learning to Read: The Great Debate.*[1] However, Chall was concerned with the question of phonics from the viewpoint of beginning reading instruction, not the teaching of phonics to high school students. High school teachers interested in improving instruction in reading, then, must put the question of phonics in a different perspective.

A pitfall for the high school teacher to avoid is the assumption that the best place to begin reading instruction is with extensive training in phonics. Phonics does have its place in reading, but it is principally in the beginning reading stages through grade 6 where instruction in this area must be emphasized. Heavy code emphasis should begin as the child is first learning to read, and gradually diminish in intensity of treatment as the child progresses through the grades. A good example of phonics in this perspective is illustrated in the *Holt Basic Reading System.*[2]

Arthur Heilman[3] has warned that the history of reading instruction in America is a chronicle of frustration which stems in part from our predilection to make reading consist exclusively of letter-sound analysis. For the high school student, such instruction is not only unwarranted, but it is also deadly. Such instruction is unwarranted because phonics is only *one* of many ways to the analysis of words. Instruction in phonics at all levels, especially high school, can beome deadly for the students if it consists of meaningless, dull drills.

The discerning high school teacher, then, does not teach phonic skills *per se*. Rather, he combines phonics skills with context clues and sight vocabulary because he realizes that those skills in reading are tasks that live within one another. Moreover, he realizes that at the high school level, the study of phonics is only one of many ways to the analysis of polysyllabic words. Of course, there are words the high school student will meet in print that divide themselves phonetically into syllables. But the high school student constantly comes across many non-phonetic words. He will be making use, for example, of compound words. He will also discover, more than likely he already has, that many words share similar roots. Olive Niles[4] over her magnificent career in the field of secondary reading has consistently and continuously shown the need for more than mere phonetic ways to word recognition. Among her additional suggestions are the use of context clues and structural analysis.

Thus, the high school teacher must constantly remember that the reading act is multifaceted. Decoding is a part of reading, and instruction in phonics is only one way a student learns to decode. Reading instruction, however, is also concerned with the concepts behind the words, with the way the words sequence themselves in sentences, with the meaning the reader brings to these larger units of print. Reading also involves the student and the relationship between his oral language and his ability to read.

Although it is still not known exactly what constitutes the reading process, recent research in psycholinguistics using information-processing models offers even more promise for a clearer understanding of this complex activity. Moreover, the implications of these recent models supply a strong rationale for developing teaching strategies in reading that enable the reader to decode directly to meaning, without the use of phonics. The implications are of much significance for improving the teaching of reading at all levels—especially in the upper grades. Instead of beginning instruction in reading with a set of discrete and fragmented phonic skills, the discerning teacher makes use of skills involved in reading in a different way. He does—to repeat—put certain reading skills to work, but they are those reading skills that go to work within the framework of meaning-getting strategies. Thus, the student, instead of becoming a passive identifier of letters and words, becomes an active searcher for meaning. But to succeed in reading, the student must make use of both visual and non-visual information.

According to Frank Smith,[5] the most recent and prominent reading theorist, non-visual information transcends the text or printed materials being studied. First, non-visual information involves the student's ability to conceptualize and his previous experiences and reading, particularly in relation to the topics of the material at hand. Second, non-visual information involves the student's prior knowledge of language and familiarity with the structures and patterns within forms of written discourse. Visual information, on the other hand, involves similar yet other complex strategies of information-processing. The redundancies within printed language greatly influence the student's task of correctly making decoding responses. Redundancy in print occurs at a number of levels. There is featural redundancy in individual letters. For example, some letters are curved while others are straight. The same kind of featural redundancy occurs in words. There is also much redundancy within the structure of words because in the English language patterns of features tend to occur only in certain combinations. These highly consistent patterns of features are examples of orthographic redundancy. Redundancy also extends across sequences of words and thus involves syntactic and semantic constraints.

Reading instruction in the high school, then, must go beyond phonics, for it is an activity often done to obtain information—or, in other words, to reduce uncertainty. However, teachers must remember that the student who is a skilled reader minimizes his use of feature analysis and maximizes his use of graphic redundancy to reduce uncertainty. Like Smith, Goodman[6] theorizes that this kind of student uses the most direct route and as few cues as necessary to arrive at his goal—reading comprehension. He does not need to make use of all the information available to him for reading comprehension to occur. His understanding of language structures and his understanding that every bit of information may be conveyed by several cues make it possible for him to predict and analyze the printed grammatical patterns on the basis of identifying a few elements within them. The context in which the language occurs, created by the previous meanings he has gathered, allows him to predict the meaning that will follow. To comprehend in reading, then, the proficient reader predicts as he reads, selects only the most predictive cues, and samples the graphic cues as he tests out his predictions. When his predictions are not confirmed, then he engages at this time in greater visual analysis. Even with poor readers in high school, we must give them many opportunities to make much use of both predictive and graphic cues.

Teaching reading to the high school student, then, must go beyond the meeting of superficial phonic instruction that is in isolation of more meaningful reading experiences. Otherwise, the curriculum itself is likely to be of little importance to the student's life and the school, in short, will continue to ignore the realities of reading and life surrounding the student. Hence, reading, as William Gray[7] suggested years ago, must be perceived as an activity that permits students to find meaning in what otherwise would be mere phonic skills, mere facts about phonics.

References
[1]Jeanne Chall, *Learning to Read: The Great Debate*, New York: McGraw Hill, Inc., 1967.
[2]*The Holt Basic Reading System*, New York: Holt, Rinehart and Winston, Inc., 1973.
[3]Arthur Heilman, *Phonics in Proper Perspective*, Columbus, Ohio: Charles Merrill and Co., 1968.
[4]Olive Niles. Speech presented at a Lancaster, Pennsylvania Workshop on "Reading in the Content Areas," Nov. 30, 1974.

[5]Frank Smith, *Psycholinguistics and Reading*, New York: Holt, Rinehart and Winston, Inc., 1973, pp. 6–7.

[6]Goodman, Kenneth, "Behind the Eye—What Happens in Reading," *Reading: Process and Program*, Urbana, Illinois: National Council of Teachers of English, 1970.

[7]Arthur Gates. "Reading in the Elementary School," *Forty-Eighth Yearbook of the National Society for the Study of Education, Part II*, Chicago: University of Chicago Press, 1949.

Question III, 7

I teach two senior high school classes of developmental reading and have not been able to find a suitable text or suitable materials. Do you have any suggestions?
Erminia D. Creech, Smithfield-Selma Senior High School, Smithfield, North Carolina

Answer by:

JAMES M. SAWYER, Director, Membership and Council Relations, International Reading Association, 800 Barksdale Road, Newark, Delaware. Mr. Sawyer has conducted reading classes at the junior and senior high school levels.

In considering materials for developmental reading programs, ask if such materials develop the following in a realistic way: (1) comprehension, including critical reading, (2) vocabulary, (3) study skills, and (4) flexibility of rate. Select materials that provide for the continuous and sequential development of skills and for increased independence on the part of the learner. Consider the relationship to assignments and expectations of the school as well as how relevant the materials are to the student. The chief criterion should be whether the materials enable the student to become a more adequate learner.

In choosing materials for the program, variety and range are key factors. Resources for the development of skill areas can be drawn from workbooks, both elementary and secondary; textbooks, from all content areas and levels; paperbacks, newspapers and magazines as well as commercially prepared kits and instructional aids. Nonprint material such as audio tapes, films, filmstrips, slides, pictures, maps, graphs, charts, and cartoons can greatly strengthen the program, especially in the areas of critical thinking, interpretation, and study skills. In the selection of books and workbooks, five copies of any one title are usually sufficient to meet the needs at any one skill level within a particular class. This is especially true if the workbooks are torn apart and filed according to skill level—a color code is helpful. Other resources include:

- a paperback library (seek donations from teachers, students, parents and the PTA);
- popular magazines and trade journals (let the student come in contact with the types of reading that will be demanded in later life);

- audio tapes (have them made by teachers in various content areas for use in developing listening skills and note taking; this also provides a means of relating what is done in other classes to the reading program);
- mail order catalogs;
- do-it-yourself books;
- a library of textbooks (use as a reference library); and
- games.

Resources

Annotated bibliographies are available to aid teachers in the search for instructional material. Compilations such as *Good Reading for Poor Readers* by Spache,[1] *Sources of Good Books for Poor Readers,*[2] and *What We Know About High School Reading*[3] provide an excellent starting point and should be consulted. Books focusing on the use of specific materials such as Fader and McNeil's *Hooked on Books*[4] and *Teaching Reading Skills Through the Newspaper*[5] demonstrate how the reading program can be expanded through the effective use of these resources.

Professional journals such as the *English Journal*[6] and the *Journal of Reading*[7] contain reviews of recent publications and instructional materials.

Is there a textbook suitable for all students in a developmental studies progam? No, but numerous resources are available to the teacher to meet the individual needs of students.

References

[1] George D. Spache. *Good Reading for Poor Readers*, (9th edition). Champaign, Illinois: Garrard Publishing Company, 1974.
[2] George D. Spache. *Sources of Good Books for Poor Readers.* Newark, Delaware: International Reading Association, 1969.
[3] Thomas G. Devine. *What We Know About High School Reading.* Urbana, Illinois: National Council of Teachers of English, 1969.
[4] Daniel Fader and Elton B. McNeil. *Hooked on Books.* New York: Berkley, 1968.
[5] Arnold B. Cheyney. *Teaching Reading Skills Through the Newspaper.* Newark, Delaware: International Reading Association, 1971.
[6] National Council of Teachers of English, Urbana, Illinois.
[7] International Reading Association, Newark, Delaware.

Question III, 8

What are the advantages and disadvantages of using teacher-made reading lists with junior high school students?

Garry Leonhardt, Cherryville Junior High School, Cherryville, North Carolina

Answer by:
MORTON BOTEL, Professor of Education and Director of the Reading
Clinic of the Graduate School of Education at the University of Penn-
sylvania.

The teacher who is a reader, who keeps up with contemporary
literature for young adults, and who knows the community of young
people in her/his class is the one most capable of developing an appropriate starter list for the independent and self-selected reading of students.
Any such list, no matter who prepares it, is best thought of as a minimal
and suggested list and should lead to all the options available in the
library. The notion of a "right group of books" which limit choice
severely is myopic in failing to recognize the universal themes, value
focuses, etc. found in literature in general.

Many fine sources are available to teachers in developing such a
reading list—from NCTE and ALA through their book lists and journals,
from paperback book publishers, from the avid, discriminating readers in
one's classrooms and even from the reluctant readers who, given choice,
have found readable, appealing books for a largely ignored segment of
our pupil population.

Question III, 9

**Do students tend to learn more and show more significant improvement
in their reading skills when they are tracked according to their reading
levels?**

Lois L. Crowder, Fortier High School, New Orleans, Louisiana

Answer by:
NICHOLAS P. CRISCUOLO, Supervisor of Reading, New Haven, Connecticut Public School System. Dr. Criscuolo is author of more than 150
articles and six books, the most recent of which is *100 Individualized
Activities for Reading.*

By the time the student reaches high school, differences in reading abilities and mastery of reading skills are quite marked. A completely heterogeneous class poses many problems for teachers at the middle and high school levels where the range of reading ability may be as
much as six or seven years.[1] A variety of techniques, materials and grouping procedures need to be used to accommodate these differences.

One major concern of teachers is the exploration of ways to reduce the wide ability range found within a given classroom or section.
The need for differentiated instruction is quite apparent and further
grouping within these sections is often desirable.[2] Consequently, it is
common in schools to group students homogeneously for reading instruction. This is accomplished by placing students in various reading sections
or classes according to standardized test scores and the results of tests
which indicate strengths and weaknesses of specific reading skills.

Moorhouse[3] reports on a study conducted with 380 intermediate
grade children in two public schools in Laramie, Wyoming to determine

whether interclass grouping for reading would produce readers superior to those grouped conventionally by grade levels for reading instruction. The study was evaluated at the end of one semester, at the end of three semesters, and again after five semesters. The results of this study indicated that, although the initial results favored interclass grouping, these results appeared to diminish and became statistically non-significant. The lack of significant differences occurred at a time when pupils were reaching maturity in the development of reading skills.

At the secondary level, a two year experiment was conducted in 1967 in the junior and senior high schools in Berkeley, California to determine the effect of homogeneous versus hetereogeneous grouping on achievement.[4] At the conclusion of the study, it was determined that differences in achievement over the two-grade span did not support the common wisdom that narrowing the ability range or separating extreme groups from the intermediate groups enables teachers to be more effective in raising the pupils' achievement level. Further, simply narrowing the ability range in the classroom does not result in a greater differentiation of content or method and is not associated with greater academic achievement for any ability level.

These findings support those of Esposito[5] who discovered that homogeneous ability grouping as currently practiced shows no consistent positive value for helping students generally, or particular groups of students specifically, to achieve more academically or to experience more effective learning conditions.

Recent research suggests that track systems produce detrimental effects upon a substantial portion of high school students. It appears that low track students, when compared with the high track, exhibit high rates of school failure, school misconduct, expressive alienation, dropout, and delinquency. Evidence also suggests it can have a damaging effect on the self-image of students.[6]

It is evident, then, that students do not tend to learn more when tracked according to their reading levels. Although this is so, teachers report that tracking increases pupil interest and motivation and adds variety to the school day for pupils and teachers. Teachers report that they had more time to assist individual pupils because the problem of selecting reading materials on the basis of reading level was reduced.

Despite the enthusiasm of teachers for this type of grouping procedure, it must be pointed out that reading tends to become a discrete rather than an integrated subject. This is a serious flaw and must be recognized as such.

Tracking is not the answer to increasing achievement in reading. Rather, emphasis should be placed on viable in-service programs for teachers and on seeking alternative strategies. In any reading program, the teacher is the key. This was demonstrated quite convincingly in twenty-seven cooperative reading studies in 1964–65.[7] Supported by the U.S. Office of Education, those studies showed almost unanimously that difference in results were far greater among the classes of teachers using the same method than were the differences between the averages resulting from contrasting methods of instruction.

In terms of alternate strategies, it seems wise to concentrate on the following:

1. Provide opportunities for frequent teacher-student contacts which will facilitate planning for individual pupil success.
2. Although students are heterogeneously grouped, allow for flexibility in grouping which will permit individual students to work and plan in a variety of situations which involve other students, materials and teachers.
3. Provide opportunities for small groups of teachers who are jointly responsible for the development of the reading program to plan together regularly in order to facilitate learning for students who present reading problems.

In summary, changing the type of grouping but not the level of teacher competence or the content of the reading program does not result in more significant gains in reading for students. Tracking is not an effective grouping procedure and does not result in reading improvement for students. It appears the reverse is true. If improvement is to be effected, flexibility, program individualization and emphasis on improving teacher competence and expectation levels appear to be the cornerstones on which a solid, effective reading program are based.

References

[1] Mary C. Austin and Coleman Morrison. *The First R.* New York: Macmillan, 1963, p. 75.

[2] Robert Karlin. *Teaching Reading In High School.* New York: Bobbs-Merrill Company, Inc., 1972, p. 330.

[3] William F. Moorhouse. "Interclass Grouping for Reading Instruction." *Elementary School Journal,* 64 (1964), pp. 280–286.

[4] Leonard A. Marascuilo and Mary Ellen McSweeney. "Tracking and Minority Student Attitudes and Performance." *Urban Education,* 6 (1972), pp. 303–319.

[5] Domenick Esposito. "Homogeneous and Heterogeneous Ability Grouping: Principal Findings and Implications for Evaluating and Designing More Effective Educational Environments." *Review of Educational Research,* 43 (1973), pp. 163–179.

[6] Delos H. Kelly. "Track Assignments and Student Mobility Patterns as Barriers to Equality of Educational Opportunity: A Review of Recent Research." *Contemporary Education,* 45 (1973), pp. 27–30.

[7] Nicholas P. Criscuolo. *Improving Classroom Reading Instruction.* Worthington, Ohio: Charles A. Jones Publishing Company, 1973, p. 29.

SECTION IV

LITERATURE

Question IV, 1

In a world of drugs, abortion, threat of nuclear war, etc., what emphasis should be placed on reading the classics in secondary schools?

Dorothy Williams, Smithfield-Selma High School, Smithfield, North Carolina

Answer by:

DWIGHT L. BURTON, Professor of English Education at the Florida State University. Mr. Burton, a past chairman of the Conference on English Education and a former editor of the *English Journal*, is the author of a number of publications including *Literature Study in the High Schools*.

A first answer to the question is that the classics *should be* included in the secondary school literature program. (I assume a definition of "the classics" as being works commonly considered great from any historical period of literature, not any one particular list of works.) An answer to what should be the relative emphasis on classics must develop from a brief examination of the probable assumptions underlying the question.

The question implies a relationship between the evils and horrors of the present and the reading of great literature in the high schools. The assumption seems to be, and it is a common one among teachers of literature, that the present—with its first-hand evils and corruptions along with its beauty and nobility—can be given perspective by the reading of great literature, because evil and corruption as well as nobility and beauty have always been with us, and that from such perspective comes understanding and that "stay against confusion" to which Robert Frost referred. Suffering, by becoming understandable, becomes more bearable. In other words, though literature is read for enjoyment and for esthetic experience, it is a particular way to knowledge, a "felt" knowledge about human experience. The belief that literature is a way to a certain kind of knowledge provides, in fact, the major rationale for the teaching of literature.

Literature as knowledge seems to interest teachers of literature in the secondary schools more than literature as esthetic experience or literature as study of a form of art, though these latter functions are by no means ignored. Now relating reading of classics to literature as knowledge makes necessary two key observations. The first is that the classics of the past have stood the test of time because they have made the greatest continuing impact on readers, particularly those who are looked to for judgments of the significance and worth of literature. These works undoubtedly represent the most penetrating insights into human experience in the context of mature literary art. The second observation, though, is that a "classic" is only really a "classic" to its individual reader. The significance or beauty of any given great work of literature may not register on the majority of high school students.

The potential for felt knowledge through literature or for esthetic experience or enjoyment does not reside alone with great works. Some high school students find their most rewarding literary experiences in relatively ephemeral contemporary works or in novels, for example, written expressly for adolescents. Hopefully, some of these students will progess to enjoyment of more mature works, as they develop appropriate understandings and motivations, but rewarding experiences with great works of literature may never be the legacy, for varied reasons, of some people.

Classics of literature, then, should be emphasized with those students who can profit from them. Literature programs in the secondary schools should be flexible enough and individualized enough, ideally, so that each student can find rewarding experiences at his level of attainment. Whether works studied are "classics" or not, I would recommend some emphasis on long selections of literature, particularly novels, which can furnish the student a series of sustained engagements in assessing how characters change and develop as a result of their total experience. Regarding this matter, Robert Heilman states the case:

> If literature is a form of knowledge, then that knowledge ought in some part to come through the large work that comprehends more of life, in its duration, with its variations of tone, its diversities of incident, its conflicts of thought, its multiple patterns of feeling and conduct—with all the roughness and contradictions of actuality concretely present, and yet in the end surmounted by a formal power that, in its long tension with chaos, has neither a factitious triumph nor a failure that invalidates art. Hence I like to think that the formed long work may act through the imagination to contribute to the formed life. Or alternatively, the long exercise, the one that goes on, with whatever inevitable intermissions, from one reading to another, may itself enhance the competence of the imagination—to be discontented with the facile stimulation of the hasty conclusion, to endure the succession of contradictions, to embrace the more readily those whole representations in which dualities and inconsistencies are ever present but never finally obscure the ordering vision of human breadth and depth. This is one way of saying that reading maketh a full man, and of trying to define the fullness.*

Literature, classic or otherwise, then, with its power to distill away the irrelevancies in experience, can be an aid to every student in negotiating his own separate peace.

Question IV, 2

With increased emphasis on the thematic teaching of literature, is there a danger that secondary school students will not develop an appreciation for historical setting and background?

Margaret Dixon, Bessemer City Senior High School, Bessemer City, North Carolina

---

* "The Full Man and The Fullness Thereof," *College Composition and Communication*, 21 (October 1970), p. 243.

Answer I by:

RICHARD BEACH, Assistant Professor of English Education, University of Minnesota, who is co-author with Alan C. Purves of *Literature and the Reader: Research in Response to Literature, Reading Interests, and Teaching of Literature.*

Assessing the relative merits of different approaches to literature instruction requires some understanding of the desired goals of the instruction. If literature is conceived of as a body of knowledge—a vast storehouse of facts about authors, periods, historical backgrounds, works —and the goal of instruction is that students should assimilate that body of knowledge, then studying historical background and setting is a worthwhile approach. If the goal of literature instruction is to develop enjoyment or appreciation of literature, then the thematic approach may be more appropriate than studying historical background or setting. As participants at the Dartmouth Conference argued (Squire, 1968), literature is not a body of knowledge but rather an experience which should be enjoyed.

It could be argued that knowing the historical background and setting does enhance enjoyment and appreciation for certain works; knowing about life in Puritan New England may enhance one's enjoyment of Hawthorne, knowing Indian history may help one appreciate Indian legends. However, one can still read and enjoy Hawthorne and Indian legends without knowing about the historical background. Moreover, many of the works that students read—adolescent novels, science fiction, fantasy, poetry—have familiar contemporary settings.

The problem with devoting an excessive amount of time to studying historical background is that students will learn "incidentally" certain attitudes toward literature study: that if studying literature involves doing "background research" in the encyclopedia or memorizing names and dates, then reading literature is a chore. Classroom discussions of works may also center on the teacher's imparting facts or checking on students' knowledge of the facts, undermining students' opportunities to formulate their own personal responses to their reading. There is also a danger that students, assuming that some works are simply historical tracts, will fail to appreciate the imaginative nature of these works.

The question of whether studying historical background is incompatible with the thematic approach depends upon the type of thematic approach employed. The traditional thematic approach often emphasized global, didactic themes which were deductively imposed on works. Students were given prepackaged units based on themes such as "man versus society"; the essential focus of such units was learning how the works illustrated the theme, shifting attention away from the students' own personal, unique responses to the work. Defining the theme often consisted of deciding on the "correct interpretation"—an interpretation already defined in the teacher's mind or teacher's manual.

A more recent approach is based on a far broader conception of theme. Instead of global, didactic themes, it focuses on adolescent problems, concerns, and needs. "Theme" could be defined as those "identity themes" (Holland, 1973) that are apparent in the student's responses.

For example, in his responses to a short story, a student may recognize that he is identifying with certain characters, reflecting his own need for power.

This more recent thematic approach encourages students to formulate and develop their own responses so that they learn to trust their own ability to respond and learn to recognize similarities and differences between their own responses and those of others (Purves, 1972). Thus, if a student were able to develop his own perceptions of a relationship between historical background and a work, then that response would certainly not be incompatible with a thematic approach. The student's willingness to talk about his own understanding of history as related to a work depends to some extent on establishing a classroom atmosphere in which students can respond openly and actively and respect the validity of each other's perspectives, whether these responses are based on emotions, aesthetic criteria, background experience, personal interpretations, or, in this case, knowledge of history.

An option to responding with information about historical background is that of responses based on the students' recalling their own autobiographical experiences, a form of "personal history" that allows them to relate their own lives to their reading. There has also been much interest in cultural background in courses on women in literature, minority literature, sports literature; students can discuss their own experiences with certain cultural values, their experience with sex-role stereotyping, hero-worship, and hours and hours of television commercials, a vast realm of personal history that is not only expressed in their reading but also is reflected in and influences their own responses.

Bibliography

Holland, Norman, *Poems in Persons,* New York: W.W. Norton & Co., 1973.

Purves, Alan C., *How Porcupines Make Love,* Boston: Ginn & Co., 1972.

Squire, James, ed., *Response to Literature,* Urbana, Illinois: National Council of Teachers of English, 1968.

Answer II by:

SHEILA SCHWARTZ, who teaches English Education at the State University of New York, New Paltz. Ms. Schwartz is editor of *Teaching the Humanities* (1970) and is a frequent contributor to professional journals.

Lack of an appreciation of the historical background, development, and setting of literature does not constitute a clear and present danger.

To begin with, most students never had that knowledge. And most teachers haven't either. And the reason is that this kind of knowledge has been nonessential for life for a long time. On my desk are a number of reference books. One of them, the inexpensive Mentor *Guide to World Literature,* contains necessary information of this kind. That need rarely arises unless it is teacher induced.

The above question states that there is increased emphasis on "the thematic teaching of literature." I'm not sure of what this means, exactly. Does the questioner refer to the movement toward electives? I will assume that she does because "thematic teaching of literature" is not new. It is old. I identify it with the way we used to contort material to conform to the man-against-man, man-against-God, man-against-nature, and man-against-self themes. I found this approach as pointless as the historical approach.

So I will assume the writer is referring to the electives movement, and I will deal with this aspect of the contemporary scene. The electives movement isn't perfect. Among the problems that have arisen in connection with it are teacher inadequacy, omission of the so-called basic skills, superficiality, lack of sequence, etc. All criticisms may be true. Education is a most imperfect institution. But the electives movement has one built-in plus that is of incalculable value to the learner. That is the existence of choice. And choice is related to interest and motivation, without which there can be no learning.

When students have the illusion of freedom through choice, discipline problems diminish. John Dewey High School in Brooklyn, New York, is based completely on choice. In addition to a complete electives progam, they have three other alternative programs, including an independent study one, and, despite the fact that their student and racial composition is similar to that of other public New York City high schools, they have few discipline problems and a waiting list of 1,000 students who would like to be admitted. They also have a long waiting list of teachers who would like to work there.

Teachers want to work there because the school not only capitalizes on student interest and choice, but does the same for its teachers. To illustrate, Brian McCarthy, a fine English teacher, teaches only science fiction, one of the most popular electives in the school. His students are in communication with science fiction buffs across the state. They publish a fine science fiction newsletter, have built up an outstanding book collection, and attend science fiction conferences with their teacher. When they visited my college to explain their work, I was most impressed by their maturity, articulateness, and social ease. These skills are far more important to me than are the needs about which the questioner expresses concern. These students are developing depth and competency in a field that interests them.

I have similar feelings about the field of Adolescent Literature. Most adolescent literature is set in the present. Students won't get an understanding of historical background from it, but they will get help in understanding such contemporary problems as boy-girl relationships, parent-child relationships, social and psychological ills, and the meaning of ethics and morality in a technological society.

In closing, I would like to tell the questioner that she is asking curriculum questions which have decreased in relevancy and usefulness to students. To be of greater help to students, teachers must become knowledgeable about contemporary needs, problems, and issues, and use the English classroom to give students a better understanding of themselves and the world, as well as the skills with which to confront the world.

Question IV, 3

How can one in teaching literature in an English class lead the discussion so that simple facts and necessary details are brought out without insulting the students' intelligence and without stifling further discussion?

Carole L. France, Phillips Exeter Academy, Exeter, New Hampshire

Answer by:

JAMES S. MULLICAN, Professor of English at Indiana State University (Terre Haute). Mr. Mullican is the editor of *Indiana English Journal* and the author of numerous articles on literature, rhetoric, and pedagogy.

If we proceed Socratically toward instilling knowledge, understanding, and appreciation of literature in our students, we have at our disposal at least two possible strategies. We may proceed from the simple to the complex, from the concrete to the abstract, from the lesser known to the better known, or we may do the opposite. The former procedure is probably preferable toward the beginning of a term or unit, while the students are gaining confidence. At this time we may ask a number of low-risk questions, as Cross and Nagle recommend.[1] Low-risk questions, which "do not require students to risk much if they attempt to answer,"[2] elicit opinion or simple facts. Opinion questions, in my view, may even take place before the literary work is read. The teacher may, for example, ask students how they would feel if their father, whom they love, is about to commit some crime. Students may even be asked to improvise a situation in which one student-as-son tries to convince another student-as-father not to burn down a neighbor's barn. Only then would Faulkner's "Barn Burning" be assigned.

After students have read a literary work, simple recall questions may be used to elicit donnée, to give students an opportunity to answer successfully, and to inform the teacher on what level to pitch the discussion. While this approach can be overdone—and indeed has been overdone for more than fifty years[3]—it has its usefulness. The procedure becomes stultifying only when it is used excessively or when it is continued after a majority of students have demonstrated that they know the facts of the literature.

As the course proceeds and the students gain some confidence in answering questions, the teacher might begin a discussion with more difficult, more abstract questions. In answering these questions, students supply details incidentally in substantiating their answers. If students are not able to handle the more complex question, the teacher can always slip back a step on the abstraction ladder. For example, adapting a technique recommended by Edward J. Gordon,[4] the teacher might ask students to generalize about the character of Faulkner's barn burner: "What is there in him that makes him seek revenge, and to seek it in this way?" If students are unable to make such a generalization, the teacher may make a generalization for them and ask them to supply details that would support the generalization. In this way details are elicited without rote questioning.

Geraldine Murphy makes an analogous suggestion in *The Study of Literature in High School.*[5] To make questions only as factual and directive as necessary, she recommends that the teacher prepare both main (general, abstract) questions and auxiliary (specific, directive) questions. Auxiliary questions are held in reserve in case students cannot answer main questions: "In each instance, where auxiliary questions are used they become increasingly directive; but each successive question prods only as much as it must; the questions make the students do, at all times, as much as they can—on their own."[6] In my own experience in the classroom, I have frequently written out the main questions, perhaps five for a class period and then improvised the auxiliary questions to lead students to the answers of the main questions. In this way only those directive, factual questions that are actually needed must be asked.

There are other types of discussion that lead beyond the trail marked out by the teacher. Some students may even resent being led to fore-ordained conclusions by carefully-worded questions; they do not wish to be asked questions for which there are pre-conceived answers. The polarized question, recommended by Abraham Bernstein in his *Teaching English in High School*,[7] encourages the student to arrive at his own conclusion and argue his point cogently. Mr. Bernstein's student teachers report much success with such polarized questions as "Who was more vengeful, Madam DeFarge or her husband?" and "Which reveals more about the main character in each poem, the raven or the albatross?"[8] Bernstein concludes, ". . . I know no better questions than those that drive students to one alternative or another, with no possible compromise in between, questions that exact a polarizing effect on the class, that present two sides, only one of which you can take."[9] Even though we must be on guard against reinforcing the two-valued orientation (Hayakawa's term), polarized questions encourage drawing inferences and making judgments. They also require that students supply evidence, factual material in the literature.

By asking questions that stimulate argument and debate, teachers encourage students to draw inferences, make judgments, and speculate on the meaning of literary works. As they devise and defend their own interpretations,[19] they present as evidence specific data in and about the literature. Students and teachers are thus spared catechism-like questions and answers too prevalent in English classrooms.

References
[1]Janet S. Cross and John M. Nagle. "Teachers Talk Too Much!" *English Journal*, 58 (December 1969), p. 1363.
[2]*Ibid.*
[3]See James Hoetker's "Teacher Questioning Behavior in Nine Junior High School English Classes." *Research in The Teaching of English*, 2 (Fall 1968), pp. 99–106.
[4]"Levels of Teaching and Testing." *English Journal*, 44 (September 1955), pp. 330–334, 342.
[5]Waltham, Massachusetts, Toronto: Ginn and Company, 1968, pp. 3–14.
[6]*Ibid.*, p. 12.
[7]New York: Random House, 1961, pp. 345–352.

8Ibid., 346.
9Ibid., pp. 345-346.
10For guidelines in conducting such debate, see Laurence Perrine's "The Nature of Proof in the Interpretation of Poetry." *English Journal*, 51 (September 1962), pp. 393-398.

Question IV, 4

How can one avoid asking leading questions about literature in secondary school classes? Should we not be teaching the students to ask the questions themselves?

Carole L. France, Phillips Exeter Academy, Exeter, New Hampshire

Answer by:

GEORGE H. HENRY, Professor of Education and English (Emeritus), University of Delaware. He has served on many committees of the NCTE, the last two being *English and Accountability* and *English and the National Interest*.

i

The real aim of instruction is to aid the student to instruct himself, eventually to be free from the mediation of the teacher's questions. Because many teachers mistakenly think they are asking questions of the student when in reality they are asking questions of the literary work by way of the student, they seldom cut the apron strings of instruction. The student, of course, does not know what questions to ask, even of himself, and thus very often cannot become engaged in the work though he may answer a list of prepared questions on a worksheet. The traditional recitation nearly always commits the student to the teacher's direction of the reading, while the free, open discussion, with the teacher as observer or guide, usually becomes discursive and shallow. Generally, however, it is falsely assumed that if the teacher continues to question pupils over a period of time, the pupils, by imitation or contagion, will come to ask the right questions of another work, in a different context, at a later time.

Instruction, therefore, should be such, first, that the students become aware of how one questions a literary work; and, second, that the students be practiced in the nature of the language of discussion; for the two are organic, in that no one knows what he has read unless he speaks or writes about what he believes he has read; even silent reading is interior dialogue—an implicit question and answer process.

For several years I have been conducting an empirical inquiry into teacher-pupil verbal interaction in the English classroom. So far, several findings bear directly upon the problem of the kind of teaching that induces students to ask questions of a work. From a sample of thirty lessons taught by A-rated veterans in academic suburban classes, this condition prevails: Eighty-nine percent of the word flow of the students falls within their responses to the teachers' questions about the work, leaving but eleven percent of student words for framing questions,

Literature 113

for reacting to others about the ideas being developed, and for structuring their thoughts. Of 2,195 utterances of all students, only two percent were questions, and none of these was directed explicitly toward the work being discussed. The average student utterance was thirteen words, hardly enough, seemingly, for a critical involvement with the work, or for answering a significant question of the teacher's. In no class was there a sense of responsibility toward the work among the students and in those classes where the teacher announced that they would be graded on "their taking part" in class discussion, no attempt was made to teach the nature of discussion, the teachers seemingly content with "just talk."

Being a teacher chiefly meant asking questions of one student at a time and expecting "an answer," not several from various students. After the student answers, the teacher ninety percent of the time reacts with some praise or repetition of the student's answer, then structures an outcome of the transaction, and finally frames *another* question. This sequence of teacher moves repeats itself with little variation. It is clear that this kind of teacher-pupil verbal interaction does not evoke student reaction or response in terms of the work being "discussed." It blots out pupils' questioning one another, sharing their responses, reacting to one another's responses, and exchanging interpretations. The lack of student questions, thus, is not so much "repaired" by the teacher's inviting more questions as by improving the verbal interplay in the classroom. A teacher's curtailment of his own questioning does not mean that students' utterances will rush in to fill the vacuum (the silence). From past conditioning, they will become silent too! There is no bestowed freedom that evokes questions.

ii

These measures may transform a traditional recitation into a discussion:

1. *The teacher should come to understand the nature of discourse.* Ironically, rarely is an English major skillful in the language of discussion. He should read an inquiry like Bellack's *The Language of the Classroom*, where he may examine an objective observation of the verbal interplay between teacher and pupils. The teacher will then soon see that he is the pedagogical culprit. Even the teacher who prides himself on his liberality and his humanity will often, to his chagrin, find himself employing most conventional and traditional patterns of discourse. The teacher must become sensitive to multiple student responses to a single question, student reaction to other students' responses, a student elaborating an answer into a structure of ideas, a student asking a question of another student, student reaction to the teacher's thought, strings of student utterances up to six, eight, even ten or more, before the teacher intervenes.

2. Once the teacher has become sensitized by noting these interactions or their absence, *he should initiate the students gradually into the full potential of discussion,* so that they too become conscious of good discourse, and the various roles they may play

in it. Instead of some vague solicitation to a "silent" student "to speak up" in class, the teacher may say to students who do speak up, "Why is it you never ask a question of another student?" Or, "You never react to another person's response. Why do you wait for me to call on you? Why don't you call on a classmate?" When both teacher and students become more aware of the quality of the verbal interaction, certain other aspects of discourse about a literary work may be examined.

3. Parallel with this "treatment" (the teacher must bear in mind that he is part of the "treatment") there may be on alternate days, or twice a week or so, a kind of gradual systematic study of how to attack or read a literary work. This should be the main ingredient of "appreciation." The emphasis here is that the student be taught not only to "know" a particular work—say, *Macbeth* or *We Are Seven* or *Catcher in the Rye*—but to use it as a means of learning to read another poem, play, or novel better.

A good model or paradigm for this is Alan Purves's, which was used in a comparative international study to measure students' writing about literature. Another, which is probably the original of this, is the model provided by the College Entrance Examination Board's *Freedom and Discipline*. Along with these in Guerin's *Handbook of Critical Approaches*. The suggestion is not that the students read these but that the teacher simplify them so that the students have some strategy for discussing and writing about a work. Care should be taken, however, to see that the model not be reduced to a formula. The ultimate goal is that by the end of the year some "noticeable" improvement in talking and reading about a work be perceived, particularly by the pupils.

Unless the above substantive criticism is done, those students who are "allowed" free, open, student-led discussion, as we observed, may turn loquacious, with plenty of verbal give and take, but little improvement either in talking about the reading or in framing significant questions about it. Since free, open, spontaneous talk about a work breaks down inhibition, and compels the teacher to a period of silence (part of the treatment), it is good to have such a "lesson" at times, though there be little development of thought, much digression, and inconclusiveness at the period's end. Actually, such lessons are tests of the students' skill in coming to terms with the literary work. This leads us, then, to a fourth set of procedures.

4. The beauty of the logic of application is that it is at once practice and evaluation. It points both ways; how well did we interact and how adequately did we use the several concepts by which to encounter the work?

   a. In this procedure, for about fifteen to twenty minutes, the teacher sets the stage in the conventional question-answer manner for the students, who are fully aware that they are to go it on their own for the remainder of the period. The teacher sits in the back of the room taking notes on the performance, and, later, perhaps the next day, offers his critique. A student, too, may be a critic/observer. The usual weaknesses are that in the heat of discussion the students ignore or "forget" to employ the concepts they can define on a test; or else the questions soon degenerate to random comments. Thus, for the first time, students are called upon to engage in a kind of discourse that was not their prerogative before— to ask questions, to react to responses, to leave and begin new topics, to decide when a topic is "finished."

b. A variation of the above is to permit the class to carry on alone, without the teacher's preparation for the event, and then later in a teacher-led discussion consider the merit of the discourse—always, of course, in two modes, the degree of interaction and the range in use of literary concepts. Radical manifestations of discourse would be (1) students reacting to a teacher's structure, (2) a student's attempt to synthesize several successive student structures, (3) a teacher's reaction to a student structure without diverting the discourse to himself via a new question, (4) several students running a full cycle (reacting to one's own response and organizing the two into a question to advance the topic). These are referents for the phrase "noticeable" results.

c. Here have the students conduct the entire class discussion, with the goal of the lesson set by themselves. They can then be video- or audio-taped, evaluation taking place during the playback. A look at the affective tone of the discussion may be such a goal. A lead question may be: Why does this poem, so obviously laden with emotion, stir neither the students nor the teacher. Especially when in the Purves model, engagement, empathy, involvement are considered necessary to participation in a work. Another goal: What kind of logic was being employed? Comparison, application, building up to a generalization, cause and effect, the value of a belief, the ground of an interpretation? In this respect the author suggests a look at his monograph *Teaching Reading as Concept Development*.

d. Then, too, student compositions on a work may be read to the class, which later debates the appropriateness and the richness of the student's response to the work, which means, what questions of the work implicitly guided the writing of the composition? Several compositions may be read, their differences argued, their adequacy in encountering the work compared. This could be done, as well, in small groups, each making its report to the class.

Readings
A. C. Purves and V. Rippere. *Elements of Writing About a Literary Work*. Champaign, Illinois: NCTE, 1968.

Arno A. Bellack. *The Language of the Classroom.* New York: Institute of Psychological Research, Teachers College, Columbia University, 1965.

George H. Henry. *Teaching Reading as Concept Development.* Newark, Delaware: International Reading Association, 1974.

George H. Henry. "Style of Teaching and Teacher Evaluation." *English Journal,* 59, October, 1970, pp. 921–27.

Wilfred L. Guerin. *Handbook of Critical Approaches in Literature.* New York: Harper & Row, 1966.

Question IV, 5

In literature classes, have you suggestions to help the teacher reinforce valid responses and discourage invalid ones without having every remark bounce back to the teacher for judgment?
Carole L. France, Phillips Exeter Academy, Exeter, New Hampshire

Answer by:
SAMUEL SCOVILLE, Professor of English and Dean, Warren Wilson College, Swannanoa, North Carolina. A 1973 recipient of a National Endowment for the Humanities Summer Fellowship to study the teaching of writing, Mr. Scoville has contributed articles to *English Journal* and *ESQ: a Journal of American Transcendentalism.* Presently, he is helping to develop an undergraduate program in Appalachian music and culture.

The question poses two problems: one, how is it possible to get students in a literature class to analyze and discuss literature without the instructor playing the central role of guide and arbiter; two, given a solution to the first problem, how can students become sensitive to their own responses—and to those of others—so that they can discriminate among the "pertinent" and the "not pertinent"? Can we encourage students to make independent judgments of literature in the first place, and of their own and their fellow students' responses in the second? In other words, can we help develop independent and intelligent thinkers?

A good reference on developing independent thinking in the classroom is Postman and Weingartner, *Teaching as a Subversive Activity* (a Delta paperback, $2.25, first published in 1969). Most English teachers are aware of this book, and I won't re-tell it. But I recall two particular points: teachers should teach students how to ask questions; teachers should avoid manipulating (and summarizing) the discussions that come from good question-asking. How to accomplish both of these is, of course, the problem at hand.

I think a teacher must choose his emphasis. In a particular course, is he essentially interested in "process" (appreciative and critical skills), or "content" (literary heritage)? If the former, he will find ways that students can explore and use literature in acquiring interpretive and critical skills (perhaps some "content" too). If the latter, he will try to transmit a specific body of knowledge (hopefully, some skills as well). My initial preference is to emphasize "process"—to encourage skills that I believe can carry a student into whatever literary content he may eventually encounter.

In a current American Literature "survey course," for example, students are given several ways that they may "take" the course, one of which involves participation in discussion groups. Those students choosing such an option do so realizing that the success of the discussion throughout the course depends on their individual willingness to raise questions and discuss the literature from their own perspectives. Each class takes its own head, based on the assigned reading—the questions, objections, and observations of the participants providing the impetus for the class hour. If the students, from the start, understand their roles as critics and participants, and if the instructor avoids managing (even indirectly) the discussion, then the first part of our problem is met.

The second part of our problem concerns "validity." In a student-centered discussion, how are "valid" responses reinforced? First, we should admit to ourselves and our students that "invalid" remarks are necessary. Intellectual discussions always produce more chaff than wheat, and the whole process of creating good ideas involves working through bad ones. The problem of evaluation can be given students as an initial issue. "What analytical or interpretive procedures," they might be asked, "should be established as the basis for the semester's work? What is a 'valid' response to literature? What are the most effective ways for discovering (or creating, or expressing) meaning? What kinds of questions are worth raising about literature?"

Somewhere in past readings I learned of three questions that are useful in distinguishing among levels of meaning and response: "What happens *literally*? What is *implied*? What kinds of *associations* are provoked?" The questions are appropriate to any external situation, but they are especially effective in testing critical responses to a piece of literature. The first two deal with the work itself. Unless a work is particularly difficult, students usually agree on "literal" meanings—what actually happens, what actually is said. Getting at "implied" meaning offers a greater range for interpretation (and discussion), but at the same time forces the critic to consider objective evidence in the work itself. Understanding on this level depends on the kinds of critical tools the class accumulates through its experience and practice.

The third question distinguishes subjective associations from responses on other levels. Students quickly see that their individual associations are not debatable. Purely personal reactions to a poem may be interesting—and "valid" for the individual—but to the extent that they are private they cannot be accepted as part of the artist's literal or implied meaning. (Wallace Stevens' "The Emperor of Ice-Cream" might remind me of the Good Humor Man, but the association is personal—not implicit in the poem.)

These three areas of meaning (literal, implied, associated) help students examine their own responses and become their own arbiters. Given responsibility for the intellectual activity of the class, students soon realize that problem-solving, theorizing, criticizing, and evaluating are exciting and demanding processes. These processes may well elicit more "invalid" than "valid" responses, but they eventually enable most of us to tell the difference.

Question IV, 6

In an introductory nine-week poetry course for 10, 11, and 12 grade students, what and how much should be taught?

Annie Newell, Smithfield-Selma Senior High School, Smithfield, North Carolina

Answer by:

ALAN B. HOWES, Professor of English Language and Literature at the University of Michigan. Mr. Howes has directed and taught in a number of summer institutes for secondary teachers and currently is involved in the Professional Semester, a team-taught experimental program for preparing undergraduates to teach English. His most recent book, which he co-authored with Stephen Dunning, is *Literature for Adolescents*.

How much in nine weeks? Only enough to permit a leisurely absorption of what is read, leading to sufficient enjoyment for at least some of the students so that they will go on to read some poetry on their own. This means rejecting at the outset any notion that there is a body of "classics" which must be "covered." It means allowing enough time for related activities during the course—probably some writing and perhaps the study of certain aspects of language. It means time for extended talk in class about some of the poems students read, briefer talk about other poems, and little or no talk at all about some of the poems they read outside of class, as they extend the work of the class, perhaps in the direction of their own individual preferences.

The "what" of the question can be answered only with some rather general guidelines. The "what" should grow out of clear objectives for the course. Although, if I were teaching such a course, I might well ask students to collaborate with me in working out those objectives, the following list is perhaps not an unreasonable guess about what we might decide: (1) to give ourselves a chance to like poetry; (2) to develop some appreciation of the range of things that can be called poems; (3) to come to some understanding about the resources of language (form) and experience (content) available to the poet and the way he uses those resources when he writes poems; and (4) to come to some understanding about what happens to ourselves as readers when we read poems. Examining these objectives in turn should help to provide guidelines for the "what" to include in the poetry course.

1. *Giving students (and teachers!) a chance to like poetry:* This objective implies that the poetry course should contain a good deal of variety to have the best chance of appealing to different tastes; some of the poems to be studied might be chosen by the students themselves. It also means that there should be a significant amount of contemporary poetry, since this is most likely to win students' immediate liking and can then serve as a gateway to other periods and other kinds of poetry. It means, finally, a great deal of tact on the teacher's part in determining the amount of analysis for different poems: some should be presented without analytical comment, others may require or repay fairly

extensive analysis. Students should never be allowed to get the idea that poems are crossword puzzles to be "solved" by the teacher's elaborate explication (perhaps with a little student help), nor, on the other hand, should they come to feel that poems can't be talked about and analyzed on occasion. Above all, they should think of a poem as an experience in itself, not as an illustration of a particular poet's characteristic philosophy, or the sonnet form, or the Romantic Movement.

2. *Giving students an idea of the range of poetry:* This objective implies that the poetry course will be organized around the nature of poetry itself, rather than around the history of a particular poetic tradition. It implies variety, change of pace, eclecticism both in the poems selected for reading and in the varying approaches taken toward those poems. It means getting some sense of the limits of the genre (try printing a passage from *Moby Dick* as a poem and a passage from a narrative poem in blank or free verse as prose and see if the class can discover the similarities and differences)—not because definition is important but because rigid or narrow definitions can stand in the way of understanding and enjoyment. The one-sentence definition will inevitably falsify—try instead defining poetry as a cluster of characteristics, not all of which are present in every poem. Poems may differ from prose in their rhythm, meter, rhyme, imagery, compression, richness of connotation, and so on; but any single poem may not have rhyme or a definitive meter, nor illustrate compression of experience or richness of metaphor.

3. *Understanding the resources available to the poet and the ways he uses them:* This does *not* mean studying Wordsworth's biography in order to find out how much of his experience he put into his poems (though an occasional biographical footnote may be helpful); it *does* mean trying to see the way that a poet captures an experience in a poem and leaves it there for a reader to recapture. It also means understanding something about the way language works—connotation and denotation, metaphor, symbol. More than this, it means trying to come to grips with language in the same way the poet does. Have students write haiku or heroic couplets, even try their hands at a sonnet perhaps: only by actually coming to grips with language in the same way as the poet can one fully appreciate what the poet does.

4. *Understanding one's self as reader:* This means looking at the way a poem affects you, without letting that become the sole basis for judging the poem. It means helping students to learn to recognize their own strengths and limitations as readers and critics. It means helping students to broaden their tastes through exposing them to a variety of poems and helping them to assess their reactions. It does *not* mean letting the poem simply become a Rorschach test with each student saying "what it means to me." It *does* mean taking every student reader and his re-

action seriously and building upon it to improve his comprehension, taste, and pleasure.

At the end of such a poetry unit as I have sketched out, students should have some idea about what poetry is, some sense of the many different kinds of poetry, some appreciation of the way the poet uses language, some understanding of the experiences they themselves go through as readers and critics. But above all they should have been developing an easy familiarity with poetry that may lead to liking. Poetry without pleasure is not poetry at all. The teacher cannot produce an equal degree of interest and excitement in every student reader, but he can make pleasure in the reading of poetry one of his major goals. The paths to that pleasure are many. Tony Connor once gave this recipe for writing a poem: "Invent a jungle and then explore it." * For the student reader of poetry the jungle has already been invented, but the exploration should be endlessly exciting.

---

*Quoted in Robin Skelton, *The Practice of Poetry*. New York: Barnes and Noble Inc., 1971, p. 1.

SECTION V

DRAMA

Question V, 1

How is drama best approached in junior and senior high schools? Should plays be read aloud, acted out, read individually outside of class? Should drama study be a regular part of English courses or separate courses unto themselves?

Guy Boyd Lucas, Rogers-Herr Junior High School, Durham, North Carolina

Answer by:

JAMES R. RANKIN, Associate Professor of English and Secondary Education at the University of Arizona. Mr. Rankin has recently published articles in the *Arizona English Bulletin* and has written a chapter on English teaching and the Committee of Ten for a forthcoming book on the history of English teaching in the United States.

Drama exists on the page and on the stage. This distinction makes for advantages and disadvantages, as writers and researchers on drama reveal in their discussions and recommendations. Yet most agree solidly that "drama is far the easiest of all the literary forms to make exciting in the classroom" and that "it is also the most effective introduction to the pleasures of reading literature and the skills involved in enjoying it." [1] James Moffett reminds us: "Drama is the most accessible form of literature for young and uneducated people. It is made up of action; and the verbal action is of a sort we all practice all the time." [2]

The value of teaching drama is clear. But how can we best approach it? Most generally, we want our students to respond to drama sensitively, according to their abilities and the demands of the genre and the particular play. Most English teachers, because of their training and experience, probably emphasize drama as literature and work to improve close reading by students. These teachers hold to Geraldine Murphy's advice—to help students "learn to become an *armchair* audience by teaching them how to *read* plays *as plays* . . . . This means that with just the dialogue and stage directions in hand, the reader must simultaneously produce the play on the stage of his mind and respond to the performance. This is no small task." [3] Such an approach involves reading the lines *and* reading between the lines, tuning in to implications and nuances of meaning, becoming actor and director and playwright. · The teacher, of course, builds on the students' prior and current experiences with drama presented on stage, screen, and television.

More detailed recommendations for teaching drama receive attention in *Teaching a Literature-Centered English Program* by James Knapton and Bertrand Evans. [4] In discussing in-class reading of plays, the authors reject, with a variety of arguments, three popular formats: independent reading by students, oral reading by students, and the heavy use of professional recordings. Instead, they favor reading aloud by the teacher while students follow in their texts, with comments and discussion as needed. The emphasis here stays away from performance and zeroes in on the engagement of teacher and students in a "joint enterprise of discovery about the meanings in the play."

Parker and Daly assert the polar position: "Don't 'teach' plays until the class has done enough improvisation that the class members feel comfortable taking on roles in front of each other. . . . Plays should be acted out, or at least read aloud with students *out of their desks* and moving about. Textual analysis or literary study should come after the first acting of the play, and should help the class move from this stage to further acting."[5] Others make similar suggestions, although they are less adamant about *either* acting out by students *or* reading aloud solely by the teacher. Most call for reading aloud of some portions of the play at some point, and warn that reading aloud needs careful preparation and guidance before, during, and after the presentation.

A growing consensus maintains the central position of a "middle ground between close reading and public performance that is well worth a teacher's exploring." [6] As Gladys Veidemanis neatly summarizes: "By whatever method of organization, drama should be taught both as literature and as theater, not exclusively as one or the other. A play is language, rhythm, spectacle; and we do it injustice to act as though it were either permanently entombed on its pages or just as ephemeral as the life of a single production." [7]

In brief, it is the teacher's responsibility to establish and extend the transaction between the play and the reader, a two-way street that demands response *and* understanding. Keeping in mind the chemistry of the class and the needs of the students, the teacher will use a variety of approaches and activities to teach both one-act and full-length plays: reading aloud and silently, and rereading; improvising dramatic situations; discussing the movement of the play on the page and on the stage, stressing characterization and theme as they emerge from the action; listening to recordings after the play has been discussed. J. H. Walsh has outlined a helpful sequence for teaching drama.[8] Following a preliminary reading aloud, the study of the play proceeds in seven stages: (1) an introductory discussion of the story and the plot; (2) a brief consideration of each scene; (3) a closer examination of the play, act by act; (4) a study of some of the longer speeches; (5) consideration of the linguistic detail; (6) a discussion of the characters in relation to the play; (7) a reconsideration of the play as a whole.

The study of drama deserves a place in every English classroom. If the opportunity arises for an elective in drama, so much the better. In either arrangement, the basic questions remain the same. The teacher must choose the best answers he can to "bring off" his performance of engaging students in this productive and appealing art form. For the benefits to be derived from a stimulating study of drama should permeate the entire English program. As Irvin Poley remarked twenty years ago:

> Drama in the classroom—I am tempted to plead for classroom drama in a broader sense than for drama as a mere study of plays. The virtues that adorn a classroom are likely to be those of good drama—organization, good dialog, climax, variety, human understanding, proportion, humor, emotional warmth.[9]

References

[1]Maynard Mack, "Teaching Drama: *Julius Caesar*" in Edward J. Gordon and Edward S. Noyes, eds. *Essays on the Teaching of English.* New York: Appleton-Century-Crofts, 1960, p. 320.

[2]"Drama: What Is Happening." *Teaching the Universe of Discourse.* Boston: Houghton Mifflin Co., 1968, p. 63.

[3]*The Study of Literature in High School.* Waltham, Mass.: Blaisdell Publishing Co., 1968, p. 209. A valuable aid for teaching students how to visualize a production of a play is James Hoetker, "Reading a Play: An Essay for Students." *English Journal,* 57 (1968), pp. 1193–96. This article reprints one lesson from a series by the Central Midwestern Regional Educational Laboratory on reading drama: "The emphasis in the lessons is on providing the students with the sorts of experiences they must internalize before they can be expected to experience imaginatively a play they read—acting, improvising, observing, and discussing performances." (p. 1193).

[4]New York: Random House, 1967. These remarks occur in an extended discussion, pp. 142–152.

[5]Robert H. Parker, Jr. and Maxine E. Daly. *Teaching English in the Secondary School.* New York: The Free Press, 1973, pp. 135, 136. Two useful references for the teacher who wants to emphasize the "stage" approach are: Marianne P. Simon and Sidney B. Simon, "Dramatic Improvisation: Path to Discovery." *English Journal,* 54 (1965), pp. 323–27 and James Reeves and Norman Culpan, *Dialogue and Drama.* London: Heinemann Educational Books Ltd., 1950. The former deals with dramatic improvisation in the classroom and its benefits. The latter is concerned with promoting an intelligent and expressive oral reading faithful to the author's intention.

[6]Alan C. Purves (ed.). *How Porcupines Make Love: Notes on a Response-Centered Curriculum.* Lexington, Mass.: Xerox College Publishing, 1972, p. 147.

[7]"Drama in the English Classroom" in Dwight L. Burton. *Literature Study in the High Schools.* New York: Holt, Rinehart and Winston, 1964, p. 233.

[8]*Teaching English to Children of Eleven to Sixteen.* London: Heinemann Educational Books Ltd., 1965, p. 153. See also J. N. Hook. *The Teaching of High School English.* New York: The Ronald Press, 1965, p. 155, and Walter Loban, Margaret Ryan, and James R. Squire. *Teaching Language and Literature.* New York: Harcourt, Brace and World, 1969, pp. 479–488.

[9]"Drama in the Classroom." *English Journal,* 44 (1955), p. 148. See also James Hoetker. *Dramatics and the Teaching of Literature.* Urbana, Illinois: National Council of Teachers of English, 1969.

Question V, 2

How can we persuade the skeptics—among them many parents and administrators, and even some teachers—that improvisation and other types of creative drama are valuable learning experiences? Even when they are not openly critical—and they often are—their "body language" reveals how uncomfortable they are with having time diverted from what they have traditionally considered the "basic skills" of English.

Ida Mae Speeks, English Curriculum Specialist, K-12, Fairfax County Schools, Fairfax, Virginia

Answer by:

CHARLES R. DUKE, Associate Professor of English at Plymouth State College, Plymouth, New Hampshire, whose specialty is English Education. Mr. Duke is the editor of several anthologies of student writing, and the author of numerous articles and, most recently, the book *Creative Dramatics and English Teaching.*

Even though drama is an intuitive part of our everyday lives, many people view their lives as non-dramatic; they fail to see that everywhere they turn some form of dramatic activity engages them, whether it be trying to imagine how they will act in the next confrontation with the boss or trying to understand how a teenager acts when he is refused the use of the family car. Because dramatic activity is an integral part of human relations, it is not surprising to see that drama in many forms has made its way into our schools. However, because people continue to insist upon seeing their lives as lacking in drama, and because an absence of understanding exists about the difference between creative drama and theatrical drama, we raise questions about the propriety of dramatic activity in the classroom.

Like many experiences, drama is a subject for research and entertainment as well as a tool for personal development.[1] Few people will quarrel with the first two purposes, but they tend to squirm a bit when the third is mentioned. And it is here that creative drama takes the brunt of the criticism because it is directly involved with personal development. Siks,[2] a leader in the field of creative dramatics, underlines this personal growth by using creative drama as a group experience in which every child is guided to express himself as he works and plays with others for the joy of creating improvised drama.

Unlike theatrical drama, creative drama is not a spectator activity; it demands involvement and wide participation and this is what causes most of the misunderstanding. People have no objections if time is taken out of class to rehearse for a school musical or dramatic production; such activity is thought to be worthwhile, both educationally and socially, and in most cases it can be classified as extra-curricular. But when the dramatic activity begins and ends in the classroom, a basic myth about American education is threatened. Many Americans still cling to the notion that if you are going to learn anything in school it should be done with strict sit-down, hands-in-front-of-you attention; "play-acting" destroys that belief, seems frivolous, and does not appear to have any recognizable ends for learning.

The basic problem with creative drama, as with any other form of drama, is that teachers find it difficult to explain what they do to achieve their ends for a good dramatic experience often is spontaneous and as such can neither be preserved nor transferred easily. Most good elementary teachers, for example, are able to judge *when* they should join children at play, especially dramatic play, but most would be at a loss to explain *how* they judge.

Another problem in explaining the role of creative dramatics in education is that all too frequently no one has bothered to explain in any detail that dramatic activity does not have to exist outside the framework of learning "basic skills." It is true that creative drama can be a separate subject, particularly on the secondary level,[3] but it does not have to be handled in this way and will achieve better results, in most cases, if it becomes an integral part of all learning activity. No reliable evidence exists to suggest that the mere presentation of generalizations about language, literature and writing, regardless of the method, will hasten the development of thinking, speaking, listening, reading, and writing—and these are, presumably, recognized and desirable goals of most language arts curricula. Recognizing this problem, Moffett has devised a model curriculum which takes dramatic activity as one of the key parts of the entire learning process. He does this because drama "is that preverbal way of understanding, expressing, and representing that underpins not only literacy but oral speech as well." [4]

The most direct way to convince the skeptics, then, is to have a curriculum designed to reflect the role of creative dramatics in the learning process. Creative drama is not an end in itself; it is a means for accomplishing recognized and defensible goals in speaking, writing, reading, and listening. But for the success of such a curriculum to be realized, as Heathcote points out,[5] teachers must understand thoroughly the influence of dramatic activity upon the learning process, and they must be aware of what aims are sought through this activity and what assessments can be made to realize whether or not those aims have been achieved. Here is where we have been vulnerable to criticism and it is here that we need to educate ourselves and the public.

Toffler has warned us that unless educators begin to "systematically organize formal and informal activities that help the student define, explicate and test his values, whatever they are," [6] we may have a nation unable to cope with the future. Creative dramatics in the classroom provides one important way of preparing students to make future decisions and to engage in continuous learning. It would be too bad to see creative drama displaced simply because it *looks* too much like "play" and not enough like serious learning. Careful planning of the curriculum, a clear sense of sequential development, and a clear purpose for integrating dramatic activity with the learning of basic skills will relieve most of the skepticism about creative drama in the classroom.

References

[1]Charles R. Duke. "Drama," in R. Baird Shuman, ed. *Creative Approaches to the Teaching of English: Secondary*. Itasca, Illinois: F.E. Peacock Publishers, Inc., 1974, pp. 39-100.

[2]Geraldine Brain Siks. *Creative Dramatics: An Art for Children*. New York: Harper and Brothers, 1958.

[3]Charles R. Duke. "Creative Dramatics: A Natural for the Multiple Elective Program." *Virginia English Bulletin*, 21 (1971), pp. 9-12, 22.

[4]James Moffett. *A Student-Centered Language Arts Curriculum, Grades K-13: A Handbook for Teachers.* Boston: Houghton Mifflin Company, 1968, p. 33.

[5]Dorothy Heathcote. "Drama," in Arthur Daigon and Ronald LaConte, eds. *Challenge and Change in the Teaching of English.* Boston: Allyn and Bacon, Inc., 1971, pp. 138-146.

[6]Alvin Toffler. *Future Shock.* New York: Random House, 1970, p. 355.

Question V, 3

Shakespearean drama presents problems for many average and below average students in today's high schools. How can teachers best prepare their students to deal with Shakespearean drama?

Michael Tad Hippler, Alleghany County High School, Covington, Virginia

Answer by:

ROBERT W. BOYNTON, Editor, English Language and Literature, Hayden Book Company; former Principal, Senior High School and Chairman, English Department, Germantown Friends School, Philadelphia, Pa.; co-author with Maynard Mack, Yale University, of *Introduction to the Play* and co-editor with Maynard Mack of the Hayden Shakespeare Series.

There's no easy way to teach Shakespeare, and no easy way to determine whether one or more of his plays belong in a particular English program or class. I can't offer any clever ideas for making him palatable, any short cuts to understanding, any foolproof formulas for getting him across. I can suggest reasons for reading Shakespeare in high school classes and ground rules for approaching a given play.

It might be useful to suggest first some good reasons for *not* teaching Shakespeare: (1) if the emphasis is simply on familiarity with William Shakespeare, his hometown, his working town, his theater, and his collected works; (2) if some familiarity with his plays is seen as one of the exposures to culture and tradition that every child needs on the way to adulthood; (3) if plot summaries, famous lines, and scenic highlights are seen as better than no exposure at all, a kind of inoculation against total ignorance and total boredom; (4) if a misguided rigorous analysis, teacher-directed and teacher-dominated, drones its weary way week after week; and (5) if truncated, bowdlerized texts or jazzed-up idiomatic "translations" are substituted for the real thing.

If those are the wrong directions, what are some of the right ones? Foremost is the fact that Shakespeare is our greatest poet and our greatest playwright, probably the world's greatest both. That fact calls for neither smugness nor hero-worship but rather for simple thanksgiving that he spoke and wrote English and therefore is directly available to anyone whose native language is English—American students, for instance. To deny them a generous dose of Shakespeare's linguistic and dramatic genius because there are admitted difficulties to contend with is to deny them the delights of language greatly used and humanity greatly portrayed. This is not the same thing as saying that a dose of Shakespeare is good for them, or will make them better people, or will stamp them EDUCATED. It's a question of pleasure, not virtue.

Of all the writers in Modern English not working in the current idiom, Shakespeare is both the easiest and the most difficult to deal with. He's the easiest because he covers the whole complex range of human behavior, from the noblest to the meanest, the most tender to the most vulgar, the simplest to the most unfathomable. His characters are more alive, because more known, than the kid in the seat across the aisle or the adult running the school. His plots make the latest bombshell movie look like a one-reeler from the moviemaking class. His metaphorical baggage, packed with details of the everyday world, could serve a thousand less fertile artistic imaginations.

The things that make him easy to deal with also make him difficult. It's the density of it all—of imagery, of topical references, of ambiguity, of vocabulary, of syntactic shorthand—that discourages us, so we must be ready to meet it in a variety of ways, all of which require work on the parts of teachers and students, and none of which has any connection with short cuts or gimmicks. That variety of ways is suggested broadly in what follows.

First, it's imperative to get an overall view of the play before doing any kind of detailed work on language complexities or character interpretations or staging possibilities. Perhaps the best approach is seeing one of the better movies: Olivier's *Hamlet* or *Henry V*, the Brando and Mason *Julius Caesar*, Zefferelli's *Romeo and Juliet*, Polanski's *Macbeth* or the Evans/Anderson version. Of course, if a good live performance is available, so much the better; and obviously it makes good sense to plan to teach a play around an available performance. If neither play nor movie is available, a good recording will do (those of the Shakespeare Recording Society [Caedmon] or the Marlowe Society, for instance), having the students follow the text as they listen. It's important at this stage to get the plot line and the characters straight, so some filling-in or recapitulating may be necessary.

Next, deal with the play in detail as "a continuously unfolding conflict set in motion and seeking a resolution." [1] Reading Shakespeare is not a poor substitute for seeing the play performed, so long as "reading" does not mean treating the plays as if they were novels, or indigestible chunks of fancy to be gnawed over paraphrastically, or extended comprehension tests. The language should constantly be heard as well as seen on the page, and teachers should skill themselves in reading Shakespeare aloud, with students following along in their own texts to see how a skillful reader brings the lines to life. Students should also be encouraged to read aloud. "Contrary to popular belief," as Duke says, "this practice does not ruin the beauty of the play nor of the language." [2] The only danger is in asking them to do it with no chance to prepare or practice. Parts can be assigned ahead of time, and small groups can be asked to prepare a scene, perhaps several groups to do the same scene so that different interpretations can be assessed.

There's also no reason why whole scenes can't be prepared for simple production. There's no need for costuming, but there's no harm in it either if attention to it doesn't overshadow the acting. Again, small groups can prepare consecutive scenes or parts of scenes. Such a plan will make clear to students that the arbitrary scene divisions of modern texts are not part of Shakespeare's dramaturgy and that to treat them discretely distorts the sense of continuous flow that should characterize the plays. (In that sense, movie versions have a fidelity to Shakespeare's theater that modern proscenium stage can't match; the problem with movies is that the Shakespeare's language gets subordinated to visual richness, and not enough is left to the mind's ear and eye.)

At the center of it all must be a constant concern with what the language of the play tells us. Good readers stage the play, in a sense, in the theater of the mind, and all the direction they need is in the lines themselves. There's no sense in "staging" every scene in this way, but careful class attention to several of them will show what the possibilities are. In this connection it makes sense to spend a little time on Shakespeare's theater: its appearance, its conventions, its audience. More important is a text with unobtrusive but thorough notes. Shakespeare unfootnoted is very difficult for even well-educated adults, and close attention to annotations reveals the richness of a play's texture at no loss of immediacy or movement. Reading a play cannot be a once-over-lightly tour, and students should expect to savor and digest as well as taste. Only with familiarity comes pleasure, and we bamboozle them if we suggest otherwise.

A peripheral word about paraphrasing and about translating into some variety of current idiom. The former is a testing device that may have its uses with certain kinds of prose, but it shouldn't be used to deform poetry, least of all Shakespeare's. The latter may provide some idle fun and even show that certain images or attitudes can be approximated in different language uses, but it's no substitute for Shakespeare. It's like translating Nikki Giovanni's "Beautiful Black Men" into Standard Honky English and saying "Now, see what it means!" Ask students to read Shakespeare with the voice they grew up with and use every day, and don't worry if it doesn't sound like Received Standard. Shakespeare's voice didn't either.

What the foregoing suggests is that the play's the thing, as Shakespeare wrote it, and that the play lives through its language, its poetry. If a student, or a whole classful of students, has trouble reading the simplest stories or poems, there seems to me no sense in adding Shakespeare to the burden. But I would guess that the majority of students in high school are not so handicapped and can deal with Shakespeare's language—with help from a well-annotated text, a well-prepared and language-loving teacher, professionally done movies and records, and a willingness to work.

References
[1]Robert W. Boynton and Maynard Mack, *Introduction to the Play*, rev. 2nd edition, Rochelle Park, New Jersey, Hayden, 1976.
[2]Charles R. Duke, "Drama," in R. Baird Shuman, ed. *Creative Approaches to the Teaching of English*, Itasca, Ill.: F.E. Peacock

Publishers, 1974, p. 64. The article contains an excellent short bibliography and a list of audio-visual resources for teaching Shakespeare.

Question V, 4

My secondary school students seem to respond well to theater of the absurd. Where do you think it belongs in the high school English curriculum? What titles and/or authors would you stress?

Angela Raffel, Greenwich Senior High School, Greenwich, Connecticut

Answer by:

C. C. LIPSCOMB, consultant in English and Drama, North Carolina State Department of Public Instruction. Mr. Lipscomb taught English and Drama on both the high school and college levels before joining the State Department where he has involved schools, teachers, and students over the State in dramatic activities. Lipscomb was the recipient of the 1975 Frederick H. Koch award given by The Carolina Dramatic Association of UNC-Chapel Hill for distinguished service in drama.

The place of drama and especially theatre of the absurd is debatable for many teachers and adults alike; but for many students from the very bright to the slow, the absurdists offer a fascinating and challenging look at contemporary life. Peter J. Sheehan feels that studying plays of the absurdists helps to stimulate interest in drama while allowing teacher and student to achieve a common ground where both can communicate through collective learning experiences.[1]

According to Martin Esslin, the relevance of this kind of theatre is that it enables people to gain insights into the lives of other people. While the naturalist theatre, which had a realistic intention on the whole, shows the lives of people from the outside, the theatre of the absurd, which is non-realistic, looks a little bit deeper. We are not just looking into the room, we are also cutting a little window in the foreheads of the people concerned and looking into their minds, and the usual rules of ordinary life don't apply.[2]

The theatre of the absurd got off to a real start in 1950 when Ionesco's *Bald Soprano* opened in Paris. Some hailed this new movement as the theatre of the future, others felt that it represented a transitional period and that younger playwrights would, in the future, develop the style. Undoubtedly it is revolutionary, but the entire history of the theatre is marked by such changes in modes of expression.[3]

The leading characters in the plays of the absurd are in marked contrast to protagonists of old. Ibsen's heroes had goals to reach, or they wanted dignity; but the undignified characters of the absurd can find nothing to attain. Where other plays seek to free the spectator's mind of the petty or mean and elevate his thoughts by lofty themes and achievements, the absurd theory of playwrighting seems to depend on the element of shock and sensation rather than morality and human stature.

Many Americans are at present bewildered by the theatre of the absurd. Some feel that it presents just so much naive nonsense with pretensions of profundity. Characters appear to move in an atmosphere of futility . . . Americans expect plot and people with whom they can relate; these plays have only sequential development and deviates.

"Absurdist drama" is drama in which the theatre goer is confronted with the notion that life is without meaning and purpose, and that life will only have meaning and purpose when man faces up to the meaninglessness of his existence and his institutions . . . man leads a meaningless existence because his life and his world are dominated and controlled by meaningless institutions he has created.[4]

The theatre of the absurd is no longer considered by the general public as *avant-garde,* a term used loosely to cover all the controversial styles of theatrical techniques in recent decades. Many techniques accepted today as general theatre practices were considered *avant-garde* at their inception, but absurd drama introduced American audiences to a style of antiplay which goes nowhere from the standpoint of theme, plot or characterization.[5]

"High school students react to the whole theatre of the absurd," says Lenore Mussoff, "as they react to nothing else in literature. It works in the classroom because it's new, it's fresh, it's different, and most of all it communicates an immediate reality."[6] Edward Albee states:

> I have . . . discovered in my wanderings, that young people throng to what is new and fresh in the theatre . . . they are always questioning values, knocking the status quo about, considering shibboleths to see if they are pronounceable. In time, it is to be regretted, most of them—the kids will settle down to their own version of the easy, the standard; but in the meanwhile they are a wonderful, alert, alive, accepting audience.[7]

Young people crave excitement and involvement, not apathy. Theatre of the absurd demands their involvement though it offers no sustained narrative or character development, no pat answers, no absolutes. It remains tantalizingly open-ended and purposefully chaotic. The suspense that it offers is much different from our usual conception of suspense. In an absurdist play, then, when characters change their personalities, and events take senseless, unexpected turns, the audience must continually re-evaluate the character in terms of his conditions and vice versa. The theatre of the absurd presents a fluid world in which people and events interact continuously, each moment with a new reality.

As teachers of English and curriculum planners, our concerns must and ought to be to open the minds of students to the variables of human nature and to teach them to express their own natures intelligently and effectively; to comprehend their culture and to understand ours by finding a common ground where students and we can agree to share mutual points of interest, points whereon each of us has some meaningful things to communicate to the other; to realize that of the various literary genres, drama is the most instructive. Anyone doubting the universal power of drama should read the introduction to Martin Esslin's study, *The Theatre of the Absurd.*[2]

"Out of this complicated experience," says Sheehan, "they, the students, derive a great deal, mainly in the area of self-knowledge. Because almost everything in the play is debatable, students learn to listen to each other and to demand reasons for any and every opinion." Sheehan believes that there is far greater merit in teaching students the real lessons of life through the things they enjoy studying than there is in continuing to bore them with material they feel is irrelevant.

Theatre of the absurd rightly belongs in the English curriculum, preferably in senior high, with any level of students with inquiring minds and with those who are blessed to have a teacher who is not upset over good wholesome open-ended discussion and exchange of ideas contrary to his own philosophy or hangs-ups. The open-endedness of critical issues; the depth of thought and reason; the expansion of the imagination; the give-and-take in high level conversation and debate; the here-and-now innovative techniques; and the life-long experiences to be derived therefrom assures the absurdist an integral part of, and a most deserved place in the English curriculum for all times. If you have students who feel that the absurdist speaks to them and therefore can speak through them, the study can be a rare and beautiful experience. The following titles and authors are most appropriate for high school use:

Bibliography

Albee, Edward: *The American Dream; The Sandbox; The Death of Bessie Smith; Zoo Story; Who's Afraid of Virginia Woolf?*
Beckett, Samuel: *Waiting for Godot; Endgame*
Genet, Jean: *The Balcony; The Blacks; The Maid; Deathwatch*
Ionesco, Eugene: *The Bald Soprano; The Lesson; The Chairs*
Kopit, Arthur: *Oh Dad, Poor Dad*
Pinter, Harold: *The Birthday Party; The Dumb Waiter; A Slight Ache; The Collection; The Caretaker*

References

[1] Peter J. Sheehan. "Theatre of the Absurd: A Child Studies Himself." *English Journal*, 58 (1959) pp. 561–65.
[2] Martin Esslin. *The Theatre of the Absurd.* New York: Doubleday, 1961. "Youth and the Theatre of the Absurd" (an interview with Martin Esslin). *Dramatics*, 43 (1972) pp. 15–19.
[3] Hardie Albright. *Acting: The Creative Process.* Belmont, California: Dickerson, 1967, pp. 250–52.
[4] Julian M. Kaufman. *Appreciating the Theatre.* New York: McKay, Inc., 1971, pp. 258–9.
[5] Katherine Ommanney and Harry H. Schanker. *The Stage and School.* New York: McGraw Hill, 1972, p. 82.
[6] Lenore Mussoff. "The Medium Is The Absurd." *English Journal*, 58 (1969) pp. 566–70, 576.
[7] Edward Albee. "Which Theatre Is the Absurd One?" Horst Frenz, ed., *American Playwrights on Drama.* New York: Hill and Wang, 1965, p. 173.

SECTION VI

GRAMMAR

Question VI, 1

What should be taught in secondary schools under the broad designation of grammar? I am not asking necessarily *what* grammar(s) should be taught, but what areas should be covered in the teaching of grammar.
Robert Linblad, Atlantic City High School, Atlantic City, New Jersey

Answer by:

VERNON H. SMITH, Professor of Education and Head, English Education Program, Indiana University. Mr. Smith has been an English teacher, department chairman, and supervisor of English in the public schools. He has over a hundred publications in English and education, including a K-12 English language and composition textbook series.

What to teach secondary school students about their native language is a prickly problem. All secondary English teachers would like to have their students understand how language works and to have them use language effectively. Most English teachers would agree that their students should have a knowledge of the structure of language (grammar), the meaning of language and its effects upon the receiver (semantics), social, cultural, and regional variations in language (dialects), and appropriateness in a particular dialect—edited written English (usage and mechanics). Some would disagree with these four areas, and teachers would differ significantly in the priorities they would assign to these areas.

Beyond these four areas there is less agreement. Certainly the case can be made for including the history of language, lexicography, psycholinguistics, and sociolinguistics in the English curriculum because each of these can be a fascinating field of study that will appeal to the interests of some students. The study of the ubiquitous role of language in politics and in advertising provides a way to bridge the gap between the English classroom and the "real world" outside.

More and more today, secondary school English teachers have the responsibility for basic literacy. While we would all like to help our students to read and to write well, the role of grammar in the development of basic skills should not be overemphasized.

In 1948, Fred G. Walcott, in an article entitled "The Limitations of Grammar," wrote: "Within the subject of English . . . certain illusions have persisted for nearly half a century despite a good body of research to disprove them. One of these illusions is the supposed efficacy of grammar in improving oral and written composition and in preparing pupils for college."[1]

In 1963, in their report *Research in Written Composition,* Braddock, Lloyd-Jones, and Schoer reinforced Walcott's position:

> In view of the widespread agreement of research studies based upon many types of students and teachers, the conclusion can be stated in strong and unqualified terms: the teaching of formal grammar has a negligible or, because it usually displaces some instruction and practice in actual composition, even a harmful effect on the improvement of writing.[2]

From 1960 to 1970, the decade of curricular reform, the emphasis was on linguistics in the hope that more scientific approaches to grammar would be more effective in the English classroom. A few of the studies in transformational grammar showed promise. One study by John Mellon indicated a relationship between transformational sentence combining and syntactic fluency. But Mellon cautioned teachers not to conclude from his research that grammar study "improves" sentence structure, saying that it was the sentence combining practice associated with grammar study, not grammar study itself, which influenced the growth rate of syntactic fluency of students used in the research.[3]

The most promising study in this area to date is the grammar-free approach of Frank O'Hare described in *Sentence Combining: Improving Student Writing Without Formal Grammar Instruction.*[4] O'Hare's study showed a remarkable growth in syntactic maturity for an experimental group of seventh graders. Further, this approach may work with students of different abilities at all grade levels from the elementary school on.

One of the disappointing results of the "linguistics revolution" was that classroom instruction in language became more difficult and was geared more to academically talented students. While the National Study of High School English Programs was underway in 1966, Jim Squire, one of the directors of the study, wrote:

> One of the disturbing discoveries of the National Study was that the lower tracks—indeed, programs for as many as the middle 50 percent of our pupils—have received little thoughtful attention.[5]

Most English teachers want their students to be able to write in edited written English when the occasion demands it with appropriate usage and correct mechanics—punctuation, capitalization, and spelling. As teachers help students master the skills of edited written English, they must be careful not to disparage the natural dialect of any group or of any individual student. We must protect "the students' right to their own language." A resolution adopted by the Executive Committee of the Conference on College Composition and Communication in 1972 states:

> We affirm the students' right to their own patterns and varieties of language—the dialect of their nurture or whatever dialects in which they find their own identity and style. Language scholars long ago denied that the myth of a standard American dialect has any validity. The claim that any one dialect is unacceptable amounts to an attempt of one social group to exert its dominance over another. Such a claim leads to false advice for speakers and writers, and immoral advice for humans. A nation proud of its diverse heritage and its cultural and racial variety will preserve its heritage of dialects. We affirm strongly that teachers must have the experiences and training that will enable them to respect diversity and uphold the right of students to their own language.[6]

Rather than answering the question, I have tried to illustrate how complex the question and the problems related to it are. An English teacher spends a professional lifetime struggling with this question. What should be taught under the broad designation of grammar (or language)? That which will help students master the basic language skills. That which will be useful now and in the future. That which is interesting, stimulating, and satisfying for students and teachers alike.

References

[1]Fred G. Walcott, "The Limitations of Grammar," quoted in *Linguistics: A Revolution in Teaching* by Neil Postman and Charles Weingartner. New York: Delacorte, 1966. p. 64.

[2]Richard Braddock, Richard Lloyd-Jones, and Lowell Schoer. *Research in Written Composition*. Urbana, Illinois: National Council of Teachers of English, 1963. pp. 37–38.

[3]Nathan S. Blount. "Research on Teaching Literature, Language and Composition," in *Second Handbook of Research on Teaching*, Robert M. W. Travers, editor. Chicago, Illinois: Rand McNally, 1973, p. 1086.

[4]Frank O'Hare. *Sentence Combining: Improving Student Writing Without Formal Grammar Instruction*. Urbana, Illinois: National Council of Teachers of English, 1973.

[5]James R. Squire. "Evaluating High School English Programs," *North Central Association Quarterly*, 40:3, Winter, 1966, p. 251.

[6]*College Composition and Communication*, 25:3, Fall, 1974, *Special Issue: Students' Right to Their Own Language*. p. i.

Question VI, 2

Should we return to the teaching of more grammar in the junior and senior high school? What benefits might be derived from such a return?
Rachel Simon, Jordan High School, Durham, North Carolina

Answer by:
ALBERT H. MARCKWARDT*, Professor Emeritus of English and Linguistics, Princeton University, whose specialty is the English language. A *former President of NCTE*, Mr. Marckwardt has written extensively on the structure and history of English. One of his books is *Linguistics and the Teaching of English.*

This question in turn raises two others: (1) What kind of grammar is to be taught? (2) For what purpose will it be taught?

There are several kinds of grammars. They differ in the kind and degree of knowledge they contribute to an understanding of the structure and operation of the English language. The classically-based traditional grammars, typified by Goold Brown's *Grammar of English Grammars* [1] suffer from attempting to apply a descriptive mode well-

---

*Professor Marckwardt died on August 19, 1975. Ed.

suited to highly inflectional languages to one which uses word order and phrasal constructions to indicate grammatical function. They do rather well with the relationship of major sentence elements to each other.

The structural grammars, stemming from Trager and Smith's *Outlines of English Structure* [2] and Charles C. Fries's *Structure of English* [3] focus particularly upon the spoken language and are valuable for what they reveal about the grammatical functions of stress and intonation. They are weak in their treatment of English syntax, especially with respect to determining the nature of the relationship of sentence parts to each other.

Transformational grammar, heralded by Noam Chomsky's *Syntactic Structures*,[4] successfully clarifies syntactic relationships and accounts for ambiguities inherent in the structure of the language. Moreover, it makes an important distinction between language competence and language performance. It suffers from a murky concept of deep or underlying structure and places insufficient emphasis upon a firm body of data as a basis for grammatical analysis. In view of all that has happened in language study over the past fifty years, the existence of alternative approaches, each with its strengths and liabilities, cannot be disregarded.

There are two conceivable purposes for the teaching of grammar. One is as a subject in its own right; the other is to serve as a tool for language improvement. Presumably the teaching of grammar as an end in itself would display the way in which language, a characteristically human attribute, is put together and how it operates. It thus becomes a study of human beings in society and can be justified in the same terms as any other social activity, economic, political, historical, and so on.

One might also argue that a sound and well presented study of the way in which a language is structured would increase the students' awareness of its potential resources and enhance their manipulation of the medium. Many have believed it. So far, however, investigations of the matter have not borne this out. During the first half of the century, most of the studies had to be confined to the effect of a knowledge of traditional grammar upon the correctness and quality of student writing. In general, the findings were negative. They are conveniently summarized by Mellon.[5]

Three recent investigations have dealt with the effect of one aspect of transformational grammar, sentence combining, upon the ability of students to manipulate sentence structures. In the first of these, Bateman and Zidonis [6] concluded first that high school students can learn the principles of transformational grammar with relative ease, and second that a knowledge of it increases significantly the proportion of well-formed sentences and reduces the occurrence of error in what they write.

Mellon followed this with an experimental model which omitted the formal grammatical instruction but retained the sentence-combining exercises. He decided that it was the language practice thus provided rather than the overt grammatical learning which promoted the development of verbal facility. In the most recent investigation, O'Hare [7] omits even the grammar determined sentence-combining practice and is led to believe that it is communication-centered practice or experience with the language *per se* which accounts for whatever improvement will occur.

Thus conclusions based upon even the most recent research appear to be contradictory and uncertain. The difficulty lies not with the competence of the investigators but in the complexity of the problem. Because of the pervasiveness of language, it is difficult, if not impossible, to design controlled learning situations in which two variables may be isolated and a cause and effect relationship established between them.

This leaves us with three conclusions. As Sapir once trenchantly said, "All grammars leak." No one constitutes a wholly satisfactory mode of language analysis. Grammar does contribute to the understanding of language as a characteristically human activity. Whether a knowledge of it results in improved language use has been and is still moot.

References
[1] Goold Brown. *The Grammar of English Grammars.* New York: William Wood and Company, 1851.

[2] George Trager and Henry Lee Smith, Jr. *Outline of English Structure,* Washington, D.C.: American Council of Learned Societies, 1951.

[3] Charles C. Fries. *The Structure of English.* New York: Henry Holt and Company, 1952.

[4] Noam Chomsky. *Syntactic Structures.* The Hague: Mouton, 1957.

[5] John C. Mellon. *Transformational Sentence Combining.* Research Reports, #10. Urbana, Illinois: National Council of Teachers of English, 1969.

[6] Donald H. Bateman and Frank J. Zidonis. *The Effect of a Knowledge of Generative Grammar upon the Growth of Language Complexity.* Columbus: Ohio State University, 1964. Also, Research Reports, #6. Urbana, Illinois: National Council of Teachers of English, 1966.

[7] Frank O'Hare. *Sentence Combining: Improving Student Writing Without Formal Grammar Instruction.* Research Reports, #15. Urbana, Illinois: National Council of Teachers of English, 1973.

Question VI, 3

Is it more effective to teach grammar to high school students as a separate study (by units) or to incorporate the teaching of grammar into the teaching of literature and composition?
Jeanne T. Randall, Belton-Honea Path Senior High School, Honea Path, South Carolina

Answer by:
OSCAR M. HAUGH, Professor of Curriculum and Instruction at the University of Kansas, a specialist in methods of teaching the Language Arts and supervisor of student teachers in English, Speech, and Journalism in the secondary school. He was the first editor of *English Education* and is the author of a textbook series in high school English, seven standardized tests in composition and literature, and over 100 magazine articles.

History tells us that the teaching of grammar has passed through a series of definite stages. There was a time in American education when it was taught as a separate subject. Later it was united with composition, although to many teachers "Grammar and Composition" was a title only, for it was the study of grammar that consumed the major portion of class time. When the term "Language Arts" emerged, grammar was supposed to become a part of the writing and speaking portion of the curriculum; and the integration of all language arts was stressed to emphasize their interrelationship. Today, we are again witnessing the emergence of grammar as a course separate and by itself. In some schools English has been divided into a number of elective courses, some a semester in length with others of six or nine weeks duration. It is almost as if we have come full circle, since we now hear of courses labeled "Grammar" and others called "Grammar and Composition."

When questioned, those who defend grammar as a separate subject of study insist that it has very specific values. Some have defended it as a kind of mental discipline, since its neat classifications require the student to make many fine distinctions, and this has been looked upon as good training for the mind. However, this theory of mental discipline was questioned by William James [1] before the twentieth century, and it was shown to be false by Professor Briggs [2] in a well-designed experiment that was completed more than 60 years ago.

Some have argued that teaching grammar in the English class would improve a student's performance in a foreign language and vice versa. However, this assumed transfer of knowledge has not occurred, if we are to believe the results of research studies such as Werner's. [3] Furthermore, our modern grammarians are now telling us that the grammar of American English is so different from the grammars of highly inflected languages that transfer and facilitation of language proficiency to English would not only be unlikely but might cause confusion rather than clarity.

The most defensible argument for teaching grammar today is that it will assist the student in writing and speaking more effectively. Thirty years ago, Kaulfers [4] concluded from his research that a student's knowledge of grammar will transfer if the grammar is made functional and is applied to numerous speaking and writing situations. This is what Hatfield had in mind 10 years earlier when he demonstrated how grammar could be taught through use. [5]

A recent study in Florida has provided an opportunity to compare the results of teaching secondary school youth by several curriculum patterns. One was designed as a "tri-component" curriculum in which a series of units were taught in literature, composition and language, and another as a "literature-centered" curriculum in which the language study was partially related and the written and oral composition were exclusively related to the study of literature. Burton's observations of these approaches are particularly pertinent here:

> Students in the literature-centered program tended to rate higher than the others rather consistently on the writing samples, though there was less formal teaching of composition in their curriculum than in the other two. Perhaps the thematic unit, with literature, provides built-in motivation in writing.

Students in the tri-component curriculum which featured more formal and elaborate study of syntax than the other programs, did better than the others on the Sentence Relationships Test and the Sentence Combining Test, but not on the writing samples. The implication here is not new: grammar teaches grammar, not writing.[6]

Why is it that teachers hesitate to teach grammar as part of the writing and speaking process? Many reasons may be given. First and foremost is that this is the hardest way to teach grammar. The teacher must be not only a master of the subject, knowing when to teach what, but also a master of pedagogy, knowing how best to present it so that it functions in speaking and writing situations. Such an approach is further complicated by the fact that a textbook cannot be followed easily, for one will have to use the text as a kind of reference or source book, skipping about as remedial and developmental needs of the class arise. To complicate matters, if the teacher has several heterogeneous sections of a class, the order of presentation may well be different in each of them. Thus, five sections of sophomore English might require five different preparations! In contrast, teachers have found that it is much easier to teach and to manage the activities of a class if one proceeds from one part of speech to another, then to the study of phrases, and on to clauses, and even to the types of sentences without having written any of them.

Some teachers who have tried to teach grammar with speaking and writing report that it is most discouraging to teach an item of grammar only to find that the same problem again arises in the writing and speaking of the students six weeks later. As a result, some have given up in despair and conclude that there must be a better way. It is thus that many have turned to the teaching of grammar as a series of individual entities, rationalizing themselves into believing that this sounds like a good idea and ought to work because one "cleans up" the items one by one.

But research has shown us otherwise. We probably have not yet discovered the best way to teach the grammar of the English language, but of the alternatives mentioned in the opening question, the body of evidence clearly supports incorporating the teaching of grammar into the study of literature and composition rather than teaching it as a separate subject of study.

References

[1]William James. *Principles of Psychology.* Henry Holt and Co., Inc., N.Y., 1890, Vol. 1, pp. 666–668.

[2]Thomas H. Briggs. "Formal English Grammar as a Discipline." *Teachers College Record*, 14 (Sept., 1913) pp. 251–343.

[3]Oscar H. Werner. "The Influence of the Study of Modern Foreign Languages on the Development of Desirable Abilities in English." *Studies in Modern Foreign Language Teaching*, The Macmillan Co., New York, 1930, pp. 99–145.

[4]Walter V. Kaulfers. *Four Studies in Teaching Grammar from the Socio-Psychological Viewpoint.* Stanford Univ., California: Stanford Univ. Press, 1945.

[5]W. Wilbur Hatfield. "Instrumental Grammar." *An Experience Curriculum in English.* D. Appleton-Century, New York, 1935, pp. 228–38.
[6]Dwight L. Burton. "English in No Man's Land: Some Suggestions for the Middle Years." *English Journal,* 60 (January 1971), p. 27.

Question VI, 4

Is there any advantage really in teaching high school students modern or transformational grammar rather than traditional grammar?

Bonnie B. Barefoot, Reid Ross High School, Fayetteville, North Carolina

Answer by:

RONALD R. BUTTERS, Associate Professor of English at Duke University, who teaches courses in linguistics and in grammar for English teachers. His specialty is American dialects.

The question of what sort of grammar to teach to high school students depends upon our motives and goals. Do we wish to improve the students' writing? Do we hope to make them better speakers? Or are we interested in teaching them about language for its own sake, divorced from any immediate, practical goals—the way that we teach literature or algebra?

"Modern" grammar has decided advantages over "traditional" grammar in both the practical and nonpractical domains. But a word of caution at the outset: to expect that the detailed study of the theory of transformational grammar will improve many students' writing or speaking abilities is as ridiculous as to expect that advanced knowledge of organic chemistry will do much for the professional skills of the short-order cook. Transformational grammar should be taught as a subject in its own right—an important new theory of human language. It may even serve as a convenient framework through which the teacher may approach practical problems. However, any but the most elementary aspects of *any* grammatical theory, including the traditional approaches, are simply too abstract and indirect and remote from actual language use to affect behavior very much. One need know little about the muscles and the nervous system to learn to swim.

Still, many of the insights of modern linguistics have a direct bearing upon the improvement of the student's language skills; modern grammar for high school students—even when it is taught with purely practical results in mind—ought to differ from traditional approaches in several significant ways. Perhaps the most important insight of modern grammarians with respect to the high school English class is the important notion that grammar must be *descriptive,* not rigidly *prescriptive.* This does *not* mean what it is sometimes taken to mean: that the high school English teacher should not focus heavily on what is acceptable and what is unacceptable in writing and, to a lesser extent, speaking. But it does mean that "right" vs. "wrong" cannot be taught in a vacuum, divorced from the social, psychological, and historical reasons why certain linguistic features have made it into respectability, while others have not. Modern grammar means talking about *why* as well as *what:* the student who writes *She say* rather than *She says* must be made to know that the *-s* belongs there in Standard English, but he or she might find that fact more interesting and more easily remembered—or at least less demeaning—if the teacher also pointed out that the student's version reflects the continuation of a very old process in the history of English (in the linguist's terms, the simplification of the verb "morphology") that took out, in relatively recent times, such quaint old constructions as *thou lovest* and *they loven.* Almost without exception, student "errors" reflect ongoing historical processes, as natural and inevitable as anything in chemistry or physics, and just as susceptible to human control. Standard English is not more logical nor more pure nor in general less unclear than other dialects. It is simply a kind of lowest common denominator for all English dialects. It lets us keep our individuality, but lets us communicate with those from linguistic backgrounds quite different from our own. All of this the student, as well as the teacher, needs to know.

Modern linguistics also offers to high school English two very useful concepts, *phoneme* and *morpheme,* which are unknown in traditional grammar, but which have at the very least heuristic value in comparing English with other languages, and (more significantly from the English teacher) in comparing the language of the student with the language of Standard English. The student who writes or says *des* for *desk, birfday* for *birthday, pride* for *proud, dem* for *them, showa* for *shower, beg* for *bag* is not stupid or contrary; rather, he or she is merely reflecting the *phonemic* (i.e. sound) structure of the student's dialect. Likewise, students writing (or saying) *Jack's Johnson's car* or *Jack Johnson car* for the possessive, or *a whole nother potato* for *another whole potato,* or who overuse the *-wise* construction (*happinesswise*), reflect *morphemic* differences between their speech and acceptable usage. Even fry cooks have useful terms unique to the trade; the swimming instructor will talk about arms and legs and palms and mouths (if not *pectoralis major*). At the very least, language studies cast into the framework of phonemes and morphemes give to the learning situation a structure and organization not available before the advent of modern grammar.

Finally, there is a third contribution of modern grammar—the transformational variety, at any rate—to the study of grammar for practical purposes. This has to do with the vocabulary of grammatical studies, especially with respect to syntax: nouns, verbs, adjectives, adverbs, relative clauses, etc. Certainly, the teacher needs such a vocabulary in common with students in order even to discuss many of the issues that may arise. But isn't that traditional grammar? Yes, but in a very real sense transformational grammar here *is* traditional grammar. Historically, the work of Chomsky[1] and his followers is firmly grounded in the classical work of such early figures as Descartes and von Humboldt,[2] and more recent traditional grammarians such as Jespersen.[3] Transformationalists work unabashedly with the vocabulary of the tradition: even much of the more recondite earlier terminology has been preserved, for example, in the many current syntactical studies involving the notion of *case* to describe English in terms of such "universal" categories as *instrumental, dative, accusative,* etc.[4] It is true that modern linguistics before transformationalism turned for a while—especially in the 30's, 40's, and 50's—from this traditional vocabulary. Transformational grammar is in part a rebellion against these disruptions, a return to traditional grammar.

The question thus becomes how much transformational grammar should be taught at the high school level. It certainly seems that many of the less technical aspects and insights of transformational theory might well be of use to the English teacher and student in establishing their mutual vocabulary. If sentence diagrams, for instance, have any practical use, then transformational diagramming should be the method of choice simply because of its precise nature: one needs merely follow the explicit rules! Or take the difference between restrictive and non-restrictive relative clauses—so simply and elegantly described in transformational terms. Or the fact that transformational grammar is particularly concerned with two very important aspects of writing, ambiguity and paraphrase relationships. One might even suggest that there are students who might enjoy transformational analysis who do not find other approaches appealing.

But how much transformational grammar can be of practical benefit to the high school teacher will also depend on the teacher's own knowledge and interest. Instruction in phonology and morphology is vital; teaching descriptively as well as prescriptively is crucial; traditional grammatical terminology is important. Transformational grammar, however, though potentially useful at the practical level for the instructor who enjoys and has mastered the subject, becomes *vital* only where grammar is taught for its own sake; here its explicitness, comprehensiveness, elegance, and range make it superior to other theories. Viewed in the light of the goals of liberal education—learning for its own sake—modern grammar has much to offer. It is an exciting and rewarding pursuit in its own right.

References

[1] Noam Chomsky, the founder of transformational grammar, is best known for his books *Syntactic Structures*. The Hague: Mouton, 1957, and *Aspects of the Theory of Syntax*. Cambridge: M.I.T. Press, 1965.

[2] Chomsky's book, *Cartesian Linguistics*. New York: Harper & Row, 1966, demonstrates his heavy debt to Descartes. Similarly, the philosophical influence of Wilhelm von Humboldt (1767–1835) is seen in such works as Chomsky's *Current Issues in Linguistic Theory*, The Hague: Mouton, 1964.

[3] Otto Jespersen (1860–1943), the Danish grammarian, known for such works as *Growth and Structure of the English Language* (1905), and *Philosophy of Grammar* (1924).

[4] Charles J. Fillmore, "The Case for Case," in *Universals of Linguistic Theory*, Emmon Bach and Robert T. Harms, eds. New York: Holt, Rinehart and Winston, 1965, pp. 1–90.

Question VI, 5

Can a transformational program be implemented effectively in a high school curriculum after students have been taught traditional grammar through elementary school and junior high school?

Raymond R. Viverette, Jr., Smithfield-Selma Senior High School, Smithfield, North Carolina

Answer by:

ROBERT S. WACHAL, Professor and Chairman of the Department of Linguistics at the University of Iowa. Professor Wachal has written and spoken widely on the subject of transformational grammar and has made a major contribution in the field of computer aided studies.

A gadfly was winging down a path in the grove of academe when he met a centipede. "What do you do?" said the gadfly. "I'm a traditional grammarian," said the centipede. "Don't be an idiot!" said the gadfly. The centipede punched him in the nose and scuttled off. Next the gadfly met a millipede. "What do you do?" said the gadfly. "I'm a transformational grammarian," said the millipede. "Don't be an idiot!" said the gadfly. The millipede punched him in the nose and scuttled off. Next the gadfly met a grasshopper. "What do you do?" said the gadfly. "I'm a structural grammarian," said the grasshopper. "'Don't be an idiot!" said the gadfly. The grasshopper hopped in circles, smiling vacantly. He didn't understand an understood subject.

As Robert B. Lees, Chomsky's first disciple, put it almost a decade and a half ago: "The goals of traditional grammatical studies were high, in the sense that the classical grammarian attempted sincerely to account for what kind of knowledge the mature user of a language must have in order to construct correctly formed sentences and to interpret new sentences which he hears."[1] These are, of course, precisely the goals of transformational grammar, which differs from traditional grammar primarily in being explicit, in replacing the vague, but useful, commonsense definitions of the traditionalist with a precise characterization. The structural grammarian also was concerned with the need for explicitness but was willing to throw out all notions of understanding that would, for example, account for missing elements of sentences. The fact that structuralists were also extreme behaviorists made this easy to do. But as Lees put it: "This welcome gain in precision has been purchased at an inappropriate price."[2] The price is illustrated by the anecdote above.

Whereas the transformationalist, like the traditionalist and in contrast to the structuralist, believes in the understood subject of sentences like *Go home!*, he finds more explicit ways to argue for its existence. He notes that there are sentences like *You go home!* but not sentences like *He go home!* He also notes the existence of sentences like *Do it yourself!* He knows that the rule of reflexive object formation requires subject-object agreement, i.e. there are sentences like *He did it himself* but not like *She did it himself*. This leads him to posit that imperative sentences are derived from deep (understood) sentences with explicit second person subjects which may be deleted before the sentence is uttered and which can be supplied (i.e., understood) by the hearer.

Transformationalists have, in fact, posited an understood level of sentence formation (deep structure) and an apparent level of sentence formation (surface structure). Transformations mediate between these two levels. It is necessary to posit these two levels in order to account for many things which are understood but which may not appear in the sentence as uttered or written, to account for differences in understood order of elements versus their apparent order, and to account for the change in part-of-speech role from the deep to the surface level. Let's consider each of these accountings in turn.

Transformational grammarians posit a deletion process to account for the many noun phrases that do not appear on the surface. Consider a sentence like *John is eager to please* and its deep counterpart *John is eager for John to please someone* (the deep version is not, of course, a permissible surface [utterable] sentence). We can see that an indefinite noun phrase, *someone*, can be deleted or not as we please and that if deleted it is nonetheless understood. But what about the second *John* in the deep sentence? Its deletion is required for reasons not understood, but there is also a condition on its deletion: that it refer to the same entity mentioned earlier in the sentence. Note that if the deep sentence were *John is eager for Mary to please Sam* neither *Mary* nor *Sam* would be deletable because they would not be recoverable (i.e., the intended sentence would not be understood). We know as speakers of our language that deleted noun phrases are either referential copies of noun phrases to the left or they are indefinites.

The deletion of referential copies can occur in other types of construction too. In the case of conjunction reduction such deletion can apply to nouns, adjectives or verbs. Thus *John went home and John had a beer* becomes *John went home and had a beer, little old men and little old women* can become *little old men and women, John likes crab and Mary likes lobster* may reduce to *John likes crab and Mary lobster*.

There are also reordering transformations in all languages. A surface sentence like *John is easy to please* (which is superficially like the *eager* sentence of the last paragaph) is understood as *For someone to please John is easy*. Indefinite deletion and two movement transformations derive the surface form from the deep form. The same two movement transformations derive *John seems to like avocados* from *For John to like avocados seems*. In this instance the deep form is not utterable.

The case of part-of-speech change is exemplified by gerunds and participial adjectives. Traditional grammarians knew full well that these played a superficial role as nouns and adjectives but were in some deeper sense verbs. For the transformationalist they are verbs in deep structure and nouns and adjectives in the surface structure. A surface form like *the interrupted speech* is transformationally derived from *the speech which someone interrupted*. Deletion of the indefinite, passivization, and adjective formation are the transformations needed to derive the surface form.

Even such traditional rules as the one which states that a preposition should not end a sentence can be explicated more satisfactorily in a transformational grammar. At the deep level a true preposition never ends a sentence, because at that level all prepositions are followed by their objects. Two transformational operations take care of leftward movement. One of these moves the entire prepositional phrase, e.g., *To what do I owe this?* The other moves only the object: *What do I owe this to?* The second of these can be marked "rhetorically undesirable" or "nonstandard" depending on one's point of view. Thus transformations may be regarded as explicit descriptions of whole ranges of usage that we may wish to consider in a normative or prescriptive light.

A complaint frequently voiced by teachers of introductory linguistics courses is that students have to be taught (or retaught) the large vocabulary that traditional and transformational grammar have in common. The student who knows his traditional grammar has a head start. The commonality of vocabulary and of goals makes traditional grammar a useful background. Transformational grammar, in effect, extends the tradition. The answer to the question: Can a transformational program be implemented effectively after students have been taught traditional grammar is a resounding "Yes!"

References

[1] Robert B. Lees, "Transformation Grammars and the Fries Framework," in Harold B. Allen, ed. *Readings in Applied English Linguistics*, 2nd ed. New York: Appleton-Century-Crofts, 1958, p. 137.

[2] *Ibid.*

Question VI, 6

Has any one method of grammatical instruction proved itself more successful than the others in aiding students in their writing?

Patsy Johnson, Smithfield-Selma Senior High School, Smithfield, North Carolina

Answer by:

CHARLES WEINGARTNER, an employee of the College of Education at the University of South Florida.

Implicit in this question is the assumption that there is a correlation between "grammatical instruction" and writing ability. Various attempts to find such a correlation, especially between "traditional" grammar instruction and writing ability, have been fruitless. See the *Encyclopedia of Educational Research* for representative reports. One of the problems embedded in this question is largely ignored, to wit: "How is 'writing ability' judged?"

If conventional spelling, punctuation, and usage are used as criteria in arriving at a judgment, it is worth noting that *editorial ability,* not "writing ability," is being judged. The distinction between these two *quite different* abilities is not usually made in "composition classes."

There is no more of a consensus about what "good writing" is than about anything else.

Claims have been advanced that some forms of transformational grammar have enabled students to produce "well-formed sentences" with greater frequency than might otherwise be the case, but this too is more complicated than it might seem.

Apart from the problem of who is to judge (and how) what a "well-formed sentence" is, there is the (perhaps naive) question: "Why shouldn't students who have been drilled in the writing of what are essentially *formulas* not be better at writing such formulas after intensive drill than students who have not been so drilled?"

Having something one really wants to write about to or for someone for some particular reason (and the more urgent the better) is probably a necessary pre-existing condition for the production of any kind of good writing. This may be a result of the fact that one of the primary features of writing that grammatical approaches ignore or obscure is that in real life situations (which usually do not include classrooms) it is an attempt at human communication.

Question VI, 7

Is there any relationship between the teaching of grammar and the teaching of composition or speaking?

Bonnie B. Barefoot, Reid Ross High School, Fayetteville, North Carolina

Answer by:

MARY JANE COOK, Associate Professor of English and Linguistics, University of Arizona. Author of articles on teaching English as a second language and materials for teaching English to Navajo children.

The question of whether there is any relationship between the teaching of grammar—I think that we must immediately interpret this to mean the *formal* teaching of grammar—and the teaching of composition or speaking is a highly controversial one about which teachers of English usually feel quite strongly. There are those who firmly say yes, others who firmly say no. On the part of both sides, there have been attempts to demonstrate the validity of their points of view through various research projects. None of the reports on such research projects which I have read has seemed to me convincing or conclusive. My own point of view is that the relationship between the teaching of grammar and the teaching of composition or speaking depends on the kind of grammar the teacher presents and the use to which he puts it in his teaching.

We must first, of course, consider the meaning of "grammar" in this context. For our purposes it consists of two parts: *structure*—names of parts of speech, phrases, clauses, sentence types, and so on; and *usage*—choices between items of structure. Points of usage arise whenever two items of structure exist side by side in the same linguistic situation and where one structure is preferred to the other in standard usage or on a particular level of usage. An example in present-day English is "Everybody clapped *their* hands," as opposed to "Everybody clapped *his* hands." Both are commonly used by speakers of English, but the former is now accepted on the spoken level only, whereas the latter is accepted on both the spoken and the written levels and is required on the written level. The total of such instances and the choices made between them comprise our "standards of usage" at any given time. It is, of course, the concern of the English teacher to enable students to produce written and spoken English which conforms to these standards. In our discussion, the difference between grammar in relation to composition and grammar in relation to speaking is one of level of usage only.

We must next consider how we know what these standards are—what are the conflicts and the preferred forms. Most readily, we find out by consulting handbooks of usage and dictionaries. If we wish to know about current standards in American English, we must consult current editions of handbooks and dictionaries, because standards of usage change. Changes in languages come about in various ways, and the changes always make sense in terms of the structures of the languages themselves. In terms of present-day English, we may say that whenever there is an instance of conflict such as that given above—the simultaneous existence of *everybody-his* and *everybody-their*—it indicates that a formerly unaccepted form is coming into use in the language in competition with an accepted form, and that we may normally expect the new usage to replace the older one. It is these conflicts, changes in the language going on in the usage of speakers of English, which are recorded in handbooks of usage and dictionaries, in the form of what we might consider "predictable problems" of native speakers. The "predictable problems" are not "illiteracies"; they are predictable in the English of all native speakers, from grade school children through graduate students of English and even teachers of English.

In the many handbooks of usage currently published in the United States, we find almost universal agreement in the "predictable problems" listed. We find, for example, "dangling modifiers," "misplaced modifiers," "faulty pronoun reference," "lack of agreement between subject and verb," and so on. In each instance, we find a name for the predictable problem, a description of it in terms of structure, examples of the unacceptable usage, possible revisions to conform to standard usage, a comment on the levels of usage at which it is acceptable, and exercises for the student to practice on. The only point on which we occasionally find disagreement among handbook authors at any given time is on the degree of acceptability of a given form, for some handbook authors are more conservative than others in accepting changes in usage.

Now to relate these points to the teaching of grammar and its relationship to the teaching of composition and speaking. We may assume, I think, that teachers of composition generally recognize instances in their students' usage which they feel are not acceptable and regard as poor writing. I think, too, that teachers of composition generally agree on what these instances are. But there is a difference in the way in which teachers who do not believe in teaching grammar, and the way in which those who do, identify and explain such instances to their students. Teachers who do not believe in teaching grammar often use such terms as "vague," "awkward," "faulty sentence structure," "poor style," and the like. I cannot believe that such terms are meaningful or useful to students in improving their English, either in writing or in speaking. Also, it has been my observation in training classes of English teachers for more than ten years that nearly always when such a term has been used, the problem was not that the student's writing was merely "vague," "awkward," and so on, but rather was an instance of a specific predictable problem which could be defined structurally and found in a handbook of usage, such as a "dangling modifier," "faulty reference of pronoun," or other. I feel strongly that when a student's unacceptable usage can be demonstrated to him first in terms of structure, with the use of such terms as, for example, "participle," "subject of the clause," and so on, and then in terms of the point of usage, using such terms as "agreement," surely the student can understand his writing problem much better and work toward correcting it much more effectively than if he has been told simply that it is "vague" or "awkward."

What kind of grammar should be taught? First, students must be taught enough structure—that is, names of parts of speech, phrases, clauses, sentence types, and so on—that they can understand problems of usage. Second, they must be made aware of standards of usage in present-day English and of the predictable problems of usage which occur in their own writing and speaking.

Question VI, 8

What value, if any, can junior high school students derive from learning to diagram sentences?

Hilda Parker, Cherryville Junior High School, Cherryville, North Carolina

Answer by:

RALPH W. FASOLD, Associate Professor of Linguistics at Georgetown University, specializing in sociolinguistics. Mr. Fasold has written a number of articles on socially induced language variation and its implications for languauge arts education. He is co-author (with Walt Wolfram) of *The Study of Social Dialects in American English* and co-editor (with Roger W. Shuy) of *Teaching Standard English in the Inner City.*

Whether or not learning to diagram sentences is of any value depends on what the teacher hopes to accomplish by having students do the exercise. If it is considered a means for improving the students' writing or speaking ability, diagramming sentences is of negligible value. Simply knowing a system for representing the components of a sentence is very unlikely to have much effect in improving the student's ability to use sentences of that type more effectively.

Nevertheless, diagramming exercises can be worthwhile. One of the goals of general education it seems to me, should be to have students gain an understanding of the phenomena in the world that are part of their experience. Few things are more a part of human experience than language and it is important for people to have a good understanding of how language works.

Perhaps the distinction I am trying to make between learning something to improve a skill (like writing) and learning something to understand life better will be clearer with an analogy. In physics, youngsters are taught about fulcrums, levers and centers of gravity. Now it is possible that this kind of information could have a bearing on tasks an individual might have to do. Loading and pushing a wheelbarrow might be an example. The wheel point of a wheelbarrow, of course, is a fulcrum, the handles are a type of lever and the wheelbarrow is easier to push if the load is centered at the center of gravity. But it seems doubtful that the study of fulcrums and the rest would really make a person a better user of wheelbarrows. The most efficient way to become proficient at using a wheelbarrow is to practice using one. But this would hardly be considered a good reason for leaving the unit on mechanics out of the physics curriculum. We want kids to *understand* why a wheelbarrow is a good tool for certain jobs and to understand that the same principles apply in other situations, even if it has no effect on their actual ability to use a tool. Similarly, although diagramming might not have much to do with developing writing or speaking skills, it may well be useful in developing an *understanding* of how grammar works. If the best way to learn to use a wheelbarrow is to practice using one, then perhaps the best way to learn to write is to practice writing. Incidentally, by "understanding how grammar works" I mean how speakers use language in natural situations, rather than learning grammar rules, like the difference between "shall" and "will," that appear in grammar books but do not actually operate very much, even in the speech of educated people.

A teacher with some knowledge of modern grammar would be in a position to design "diagramming" exercises that would be both more fun and more valuable than the traditional type (although the traditional type is not without its usefulness). I am referring to the distinction between "deep" and "surface" grammar; a distinction which an increasing number of teachers is likely to have encountered in their preservice or in-service training. Take the example of a pair of sentences linguists are fond of discussing: "John is eager to please" versus "John is easy to please." The two sentences are very similar in "surface" grammar, that is, the structure of the sentences as they appear on paper. The "surface" grammar is what a student would be asked to diagram in the traditional format. The diagrams (unless I have forgotten how it goes, myself!) would be something like:

But these diagrams miss an important fact about the main difference between the two sentences. In "John is easy to please," "John" is not the one who is "easy"; rather, "pleasing John" is easy. In "John is eager to please," "John" *is* the one who is eager. A diagram of the "deep" grammar of the two sentences (it is in "deep" grammar where meaning differences are captured) would reveal these differences. The diagrams might look like: *

(Someone) || pleases	John ||| is	easy John || is	eager

ﾖ please | (people)

It is not important to teach the details of the "correct" diagram of such sentences (linguists argue with each other about such details anyway) but to get students to understand that there are differences in the two sentences that do not appear in the "surface" diagram. In fact, it might be just as good to dispense with the "deep" diagrams entirely and simply get students to realize that "John is easy to please" is related to a sentence like "It is easy to please John" and "John is eager to please" to "John is eager to please people." It is possible that it would take students with exceptional ability to profit from the teaching of "deep" grammar relationships, but I would not be surprised to learn that even average or below average students can be taught to match up "surface" sentences with other, more elaborate, sentences that show their meaning in a more obvious way. All speakers of English have a "feel" for this sort of thing and need only learn to make it explicit.

Exercises in English grammar, whether actual diagramming or more simply matching shorter sentences with longer ones that reflect their meaning more completely, can be of considerable value in developing an understanding and appreciation for the intricacies of English. These exercises may not lead to a more effective use of English in speaking or writing, but the insights that would result are worth a lot in themselves.

Question VI, 9

Has sentence diagramming proved useful to high school students? Should it be taught to all students? If so, at what age?

Martha Sofley, Holbrook Junior High School, Gastonia, North Carolina

Answer by:

JOHN R. SEARLES, Professor Emeritus of English and of Curriculum and Instruction, University of Wisconsin. Formerly editor or co-editor of the Teaching Materials Department, *English Journal;* annual bibliography of free and inexpensive materials, *English Journal,* 1955-1974.

* Unfortunately, there are no materials a teacher can use that would give guidance in deep grammar diagramming. This need not be too serious a disadvantage for several reasons. First, a teacher can use her "feel" for English to figure out adequate diagrams. Second, the diagrams need not be exactly what a linguist would call "correct" as long as they express the meaning distinctions involved. Third, since the idea is to give students insight into English grammar in general, the sentences diagrammed need only be examples rather than an attempt to cover English grammar as a whole. Teaching the diagramming of "deep" grammar would of course be easier for a teacher who has been exposed to the basic concepts.

The answer to this question must be a qualified *yes*. Diagramming, if not over-elaborate, can be of real but limited usefulness to some high school students in improving their own writing. First, it should be acknowledged that people learn language by "feel" and by trial-and-error experimentation rather than by linguistic analysis. Some students, through experiences in reading, speaking, and listening increase their language powers with little or no need for technical diagnosis. Others struggle with pronounced incoherence in their efforts to express meaning. Teachers who write "K," "awk," or "coher" in the margins of student themes have indeed shown that the student has language problems, but have done nothing to help him solve them.

Sometimes the teacher is unable to pinpoint the problems exactly: he recognizes a messy, unclear statement, but cannot precisely explain the cause and the cure. If he has faith that the study of grammar may somehow help, he begins to teach the parts of speech and a system of diagramming. He may use some variation of the traditional system used by many high school language textbooks with its horizontal base line with diagonals, dotted lines, and tripod platforms. A few years ago, IC (immediate constituent) analysis was sometimes used;[1] in this plan, successive strata of structure were cut off, beginning at the outside and proceeding to the core, rather like removing successive layers of an onion. Somewhat later, the transformational-generative system had some vogue, resulting in a proliferation of branching tree diagrams.[2]

Whatever the merits of the respective systems, each attempted a rather complete analysis of sentence-structures, and each became more difficult to manage as the sentences described became more complicated. The notion that grammatical analysis *per se* has any automatic carryover into the language skills of students has long ago been discredited by articles in professional journals and in successive editions of the *Encyclopedia of Educational Research*. If a technique of studying sentence structure is to be placed within the reach of many students, a simpler method than those just mentioned must be found, and its application to writing made clear.

Any system of diagramming, however simple, must reflect a certain minimum of grammatical knowledge on the part of the student. The so-called *form classes* of words—nouns, verbs, adjectives, and adverbs —are essential and can be recognized by their potential for adding suffixes as they perform various functions (plurality, tense, comparison). They are also recognizable by certain positions which they regularly occupy and by the markers which often accompany them. For example, in the test frame "He was very . . .",[3] the addition of an adjective is guaranteed by the pronoun-linking verb opening, and by the presence of the intensifier "very."

Subject and finite verb, as constituting the core of nearly all predications, deserve the emphasis traditionally given to them, and must be recognized if diagramming is to be done. As to adjectives and adverbs, it is more valuable to understand the importance of modification and the levels (word phrase, clause) on which it can occur than to label individual modifiers. A simple way to achieve this end is to begin with a basic clause pattern such as subject-verb-object and call on the class to supply details which will give a clearer picture. The teacher may limit the game by calling for elaboration which will make the resulting picture as attractive or unattractive as possible: "A child chewed biscuits" may be amplified into "A delicate, blue-eyed child chewed some golden, delicious biscuits." At this point, it might be suggested that "chewed" seems a bit crass for so ethereal a creature, and "nibbled daintily" may shortly be forthcoming. From here on, further expansion is easy, and phrase and clause modifiers can be attached at will: "child with long, golden hair which hung down nearly to her waist." No call for analysis is made; students merely supply modifying structures with which they are entirely familiar.[4] Later, for purposes of diagramming, it suffices to use parentheses around phrases and brackets around clauses. Similar techniques, calling upon students for things they already know, may be used to clarify essential grammatical concepts other than modification.

For designating subjects and finite verbs, single and double underlining may be used; objects may be given a wavy underline. Or one might prefer the markings used by George G. Gates: capital SVO for main clauses and lower-case svo for dependent clauses.[5] Subordinators whether relative pronouns or subordinating conjunctions, may be encircled or written in caps. Gates further suggests that other structural groups may be designated by numerals:

1 for prepositional and infinitive phrases; 2 for -ing constructions, whether participial or gerundial; 3 for past participle constructions. Experimentation with moving these groups in relation to the SVO elements will show the possibility of altering meaning or emphasis. Compare, for example,
$$\overset{s}{\text{"The book}} \overset{1}{\text{of old poems}} \overset{v}{\text{brought}} \overset{1}{\text{for a moment}} \overset{o}{\text{memories}} \overset{1}{\text{of his childhood"}}$$
and $\overset{s}{\text{"The book}} \overset{v}{\text{brought}} \overset{1}{\text{for a moment}} \overset{o}{\text{memories}} \overset{1}{\text{of old poems}} \overset{1}{\text{of his}}$ childhood."

Addition of the 1,2,3 elements to the SVO frame shows the possibility of expansion and elaboration of meanings. Other suggestions for experimental manipulation may be found in two other publications whose usefulness has not diminished with age.[6]

Let us consider briefly a few remedial uses for the diagramming techniques suggested here. Students often fail to achieve agreement between subject and verb because of intervening phrasal or clausal constructions which attract the verb into the wrong number:
$$\overset{s}{\text{"Shakespeare's use}} \text{(of fantastic plots and unusual characters)} \overset{v}{\text{cause}} \text{the}$$
reader. . . ." Cutting off the modifying element shows the problem clearly. Or consider the situation where the writer forgets how he began his sentence: "(By swallowing a great deal of water) (in his struggle) $\overset{s}{\text{(toward the shore)}}$ made him violently ill."

At once it appears that the verb has no eligible subject. Finally, here is a sprawling, cumbersome, and repetitive sentence written by a student: "The reason that I gave for doing this job which needed to be done was that the workman who usually did this job was prevented from doing it by circumstances over which he had no control." A simple diagram of the structural makeup of the sentence will show the source of the problem:

"The reason [THAT I gave] (for doing this job) [WHICH needed to be done] was [THAT the workman [WHO usually did this job] was prevented] (from doing it) (by circumstances) [over WHICH he had no control.]"[7]

The analysis shows graphically that the relatively simple main statement has been cluttered with heavy phrase and clause modifiers; the cure is to change them to less weighty ones: "My reason for doing this necessary job was that the regular workman was unavoidably prevented from doing it." Or, even more simply, "I did this necessary job because. . . ."

Illustrations could be multiplied, but perhaps those already given will indicate the usefulness of the diagram in showing up some structural weaknesses. Now, when should these diagramming techniques be taught and used? Unfortunately, chronological age gives us little guidance, although analytical powers generally improve as students mature. At any specified age, however, the range of linguistic skills within a student group is likely to be great. As previously suggested, some students will not need to use diagramming at all, though they could profit from the kinds of sentence-experimentation suggested by Gates, Ward, and Stageberg and Goodrich. A few others may prove impervious to grammatical knowledge of any kind. For the considerable body of students lying between these extremes, diagramming is worth a try. At least it will help to demonstrate that clear, straightforward sentences are not produced by black magic, but by the application of a few ascertainable grammatical principles which should be applied to one's own writing, rather than to textbook exercises.

References

[1]Paul Roberts, *Patterns of English,* New York: Harcourt, Brace and World, 1956.

[2]Paul Roberts, *English Syntax,* New York: Harcourt, Brace & World, 1964; also Owen Thomas, *Transformational Grammar and the Teacher of English,* New York: Holt, Rinehart, and Winston, 1965.

[3]Again, see Roberts, *Patterns of English;* also John R. Searles, *Structural and Traditional Grammar: Some Uses and Limitations,* Wisconsin Council of Teachers of English, 1965.

[4]Robert C. Pooley, *Teaching English Grammar,* New York: Appleton-Century-Crofts, 1957; "Steps in Concept Building in Grammar," p. 140.

[5]George G. Gates, "Let's Teach Grammar Too!" *College English,* Vol. 17, No. 5, February, 1956.

[6]C. H. Ward, *Grammar for Composition,* Scott, Foresman, 1933; Norman C. Stageberg and Ruth Goodrich, *Using Grammar to Improve Writing,* Iowa State Teachers College, 1953.

[7]Searles, *op. cit.,* p. 10; also *Parts of Speech and Sentence Building,* a series of transparencies, 3M Company, 1965.

Question VI, 10

How should a teacher approach the teaching of grammar when his classes are divided between those students who have vocational interests and feel that grammar is of no importance and those students who are college-bound and who see the need to master certain aspects of grammar?

Angela H. Thompson, Belton-Honea Path Senior High School, Honea Path, South Carolina

Answer by:

CONSTANCE WEAVER, Associate Professor of English at Western Michigan University, whose specialties are Applied Linguistics and English Education. Dr. Weaver is coauthor of *Transgrammar: English Structure, Style, and Dialects.*

The obvious, easy, and perhaps best answer to the above question is to teach grammar to those who feel a need for it, and to find other, more meaningful activities for those who feel no such need. But perhaps the teacher can *create* a need, or at least an interest, by engaging students in deciding for themselves the answers to such questions as: (1) What's the difference between "My sick friend became green" and "My green friend became sick"? Would "borf" or "riffled" fit better in the sentence "She _____ him by the water fountain yesterday"? Do two negatives make a positive in "He was not unhappy" or in "He ain't got no money"? (2) Which is more "normal" and more effective, "John got hit by a car" or "A car hit John"? Which is more effective, "Tom, his face purple as a grape, stood in the doorway" or "Tom stood in the doorway, his face purple as a grape"? (3) Should you reply "No, he doesn't," "No, he don't," or "You're right," if the father of your new boyfriend/girlfriend says "That fella sure don't have no trouble gettin' around on the court"? Are employers *really* more likely to hire someone who avoids "ain't" and "he don't"?

Of course not all of these questions will be equally interesting to students (college-bound *or* vocationally-oriented), but generally their interest can be aroused if *they* instead of the teacher or the textbook are required to carry the burden of intellectual inquiry. Students should not *learn* grammar, the definitions, descriptions, generalizations, and often the pronouncements of others; rather, they should *do* grammar, should themselves observe and classify data, define terms, and generalize about their own observations.

Before engaging students in such investigations, however, the teacher should have clearly in mind what he or she means by "grammar" and what this exploration of grammar is expected to accomplish. Does *grammar* mean the parts of speech, sentence types, transformations—the kinds of things associated with the formal study of traditional, structural, and/or transformational grammar and illustrated by the questions in group 1 above? If so, what is the reason/justification for such study? In general, research shows that the formal study of grammar (of whatever kind) has, in and of itself, little effect upon usage or upon the communicative processes of listening, speaking, reading, and writing.[1] Why, then, study grammar?

One possible reason is simply that language is a uniquely human achievement and, as such, deserves to be studied. This seems to be the motivation in, for example, William Rutherford's *Sentence Sense* (Harcourt's Domains Series, 1973): "Our ultimate aim is to gain a deeper appreciation of what it means for us, as fluent speakers, to know English" (p. 8). Rutherford's book is an excellent inductive, transformationally-oriented book for high school students, and Mark Lester's *Words and Sentences* (Random House English Series, 1973) is a fine inductive introduction to parts of speech for junior high students. Even more innovative are the suggestions in the grammar chapter of Neil Postman and Charles Weingartner's *Linguistics: A Revolution in Teaching* (Dell, 1966). Indeed, this book is a must for those interested in the inductive "discovery" approach to language. With texts and resources such as these, the teacher may well be able to interest students in deciding for themselves such matters as what the major parts of speech are and how they can be characterized, what makes a sentence grammatical or ungrammatical, what the difference is between surface structure and deep structure, how a "kernel" sentence can be transformed into related sentences, and so forth.

Many English teachers, though, teach grammar not for its own sake but in the hope of helping students write sentences that are grammatically (syntactically) more mature and rhetorically more effective. Recent research has shown, however, that students can increase the syntactic maturity and rhetorical effectiveness of their sentences without the formal study of grammar; all they need are well-designed exercises in sentence-combining and an opportunity to discuss the relative effectiveness of the various syntactic options.[1] In how many ways, for example, can you combine "The evergreens stood by the creekside" with "Their branches were cradling snow"? Which combinations do you like best? A useful source of such exercises is William Strong's *Sentence Combining* (Random House, 1973); another useful resource is Victor Gould's *Experiments in Effective Writing* (Harcourt's Domains Series, 1972). A helpful book that takes the reader beyond sentence-combining to other aspects of style is Walker Gibson's *Persona* (Random House, 1969). It will require the ingenuity of the teacher to create inductive explorations and exercises from most of these materials, but the results should be well worth the effort. Even the vocationally-oriented students may find limited amounts of such activity interesting, provided the teacher finds ways of encouraging *them* to decide what is stylistically appropriate and effective.

But what about *usage,* the kind of "grammar" illustrated by the questions in group 3 above? Perhaps this is what the teacher meant in asking how to approach grammar when some students are vocationally-oriented and see no value in grammar, while some are college-bound and see the need to master some aspects of grammar. Once again, the answer may be to try to arouse the interest of *all* students by having them actively investigate actual usage and usage attitudes instead of passively learning usage "rules," many of which may be outdated anyhow. The vocationally-oriented students might survey local businessmen as to how they react to job applicants who say "he ain't" and "he don't," while the college-bound students might survey (by mail, if necessary) college professors to find out what they think of the split infinitive, the dangling participle, the comma splice, and so forth. Again, interesting suggestions can be found in Postman and Weingartner. Such investigations would logically broaden to include dialects.[2] Indeed, the National Council of Teachers of English considers it vital to expose students to the various dialects of American English, so that students will come to respect all dialects. Furthermore, the NCTE has denounced the new usage section of the Scholastic Aptitude Test because "this superficial concept of 'correctness' ignores the students' ability to produce logical, thoughtful, imaginative language." Also, "In setting forth a single dialect standard as the norm, this part of the test is racially and socially biased and excludes the dialects of millions of students."[3] Thus in encouraging students to investigate current usage and usage attitudes, the teacher may well find it necessary to investigate and re-evaluate his or her own attitude toward usage (dialects included). And what could be more exciting than the genuine involvement of *both* teacher and students?

In summary, then, formal grammar has little if any practical value in and of itself and should probably be taught only insofar as it can be made interesting and challenging to students. Further, most of the time in an English "grammar" class might best be devoted to an exploration of the social and communicative aspects of language use, to an investigation of style and rhetoric, of dialects, and of such relatively recent concerns as public doublespeak and sexism in language (write to the NCTE* for ideas). But whatever the teacher does about teaching the English language, a crucial point is this: the most important task of our schools is to help students discover how to think and how to learn by and for themselves. By using an inductive "discovery" approach to language and thus placing the burden of intellectual inquiry upon the student, the English teacher can help in the attainment of this goal for *all* students, the vocationally oriented as well as the college-bound.

References
[1] See *Encyclopedia of Educational Research,* 1950, pp. 392-393; 1960, pp. 459-463; 1969, pp. 451-453. The transformational sen-

---

*1111 Kenyon Road, Urbana, Illinois 61801.

tence-combining study by John Mellon at first seemed to show that the formal study of transformational grammar increases the syntactic maturity of students' sentences. However, Frank O'Hare's later investigation showed that formal grammatical study was not necessary; the sentence-combining exercises were sufficient in themselves to increase students' syntactic maturity. See John C. Mellon, *Transformational Sentence-Combining: A Method for Enhancing the Development of Syntactic Fluency in English Composition* (1969) and Frank O'Hare, *Sentence Combining: Improving Student Writing without Formal Grammar Instruction* (1973); both are published by the National Council of Teachers of English. A useful summary is Charles R. Cooper, "An Outline for Writing Sentence-Combining Problems," *English Journal*, 62 (Jan. 1973), 96-102, 108. The teacher should also be aware of Francis Christensen's views on syntactic maturity. See, for example, his article "The Problem of Defining a Mature Style," *English Journal*, 57 (April 1968), 572-579; for teaching ideas, see Philip H. Cook, "Putting Grammar to Work: The Generative Grammar in the Generative Rhetoric," *English Journal*, 57 (Nov. 1968), 1168-1175.

[2]Practical teaching suggestions are offered again in Postman and Weingartner, in Janet Johnston's article in the January 1974 issue of *Elementary English*, and in Jesse Colquit's article in the December 1974 issue of *English Journal*. Although all of the following texts give inadequate attention to Black English, each is useful: William Reynolds's *Dialects in America* (Random House English Series, 1973), a highly inductive text for junior high; and, for high school, J. N. Hook's *The Story of American English* (Harcourt's Domains Series, 1972) and his *People Say Things Different Ways* (Scott, Foresman, 1974), both of which are more informative and less inductive than Reynolds's book: and Joseph Littell's *Dialects and Levels of Language* (McDougal, Littell, 1971), an interesting collection of articles for high school.

[3]The statement about teaching an understanding of dialects is from a resolution passed at the 1974 convention of the National Council of Teachers of English; the quotes are from the background statement to a related resolution. For the background statements and full texts of both resolutions, see *English Journal*, 64 (Feb. 1975), 28-30.

Question VI, 11

What is the most effective method of teaching basic grammar to a group of slow learners?

Judy C. Wiggs, Smithfield-Selma High School, Smithfield, North Carolina

Answer by:

WILLIAM W. WEST, Professor of Education at the University of South Florida, Tampa, who teaches courses on methods of teaching elementary language arts and secondary English. Dr. West concentrates on the teaching of writing and has written or co-authored fifteen high school textbooks on writing.

The question cannot be answered until at least two preliminary questions are first considered: (1) What does the word *grammar* mean in this question? and (2) For what purpose or purposes is grammar being taught to the slow learner?

The word *grammar* is commonly used in at least three different senses. A linguist uses the word to refer to the "structure" of a language,[1] and a serious grammarian aims at identifying and describing all of the accepted kinds of utterances (sentences) possible in a given language. He may work by locating the "items" (parts of words, words, and groups of words) and describing their possible "arrangements" or he may work by attempting to describe the pre-speech thinking processes that lead to accepted expressions. In either case, he is trying to describe all of the accepted sentences possible in a language.

A second use of the word *grammar*[2]—and the use probably intended by most parents when they are criticizing the schools ("They don't teach no grammar no more!")—refers to both "usage" and "mechanics." *Usage* has to do with the selection of certain words, forms, and grammatical structures which will identify the speaker or writer with a particular social class. Making these choices may be important socially and economically, but in the technical sense they have little to do with grammar as the linguist uses the term. Since he is interested in describing all of the sentences of a language, he will describe the sentence "He don't know no grammar" (and note the kind of person who uses it) as well as "He knows little grammar" (and note the kind of person who uses that form.) *Mechanics,* which also is sometimes considered as "grammar" by lay people, is simply the set of conventions which people follow in order to make their writing intelligible to others. These conventions include spelling, capitalization, and punctuation. They are, of course, important to anyone who reads or writes, but classifying them as "grammar" leads to confusion.

A third use of the word *grammar* is more subtle and leads to additional confusion: it refers to the ability to use the subtleties of effective grammatical structure to achieve precision of meaning and variety and beauty of style—perhaps without being conscious of the names of the structures and the arrangements or processes involved. Certainly the ability to *use* grammatical structures effectively is important, but *using* grammatical structures and *knowing about* them are two very different things.

Having considered some of the possible meanings of the word *grammar,* we can move to a consideration of reasons for teaching it. Postman and Weingartner[3] have listed and demolished (with excerpts from the *Encyclopedia of Educational Research*) most of the more prominent claims made in behalf of the study of grammar in the sense of "structure of the language." Studying grammar does not (1) discipline the mind, (2) aid in the study of foreign languages, (3) help one to use better English, (4) help one to read better, or (5) aid in the interpretation of literature. Though isolated individuals may remember occasional insights or increased abilities as a result of studying the structure of English, the preponderance of research evidence indicates that such growth is not common with most students.

Perhaps the one defensible reason for giving students some insight into the structure of English (grammar in the first sense) is that such insights may impress them with the intricate beauty and complexity and power of language and thus interest them in learning more about and being sensitive to language. To accomplish this purpose, the best teaching method is to show students, incidentally, in connection with any effective communication, how grammatical structure has been used. Show them, for example, that a rapid-action fight scene is described with short sentences; that a single-word modifier (*heavy* snow) precedes a noun, but that a multiple-word modifier follows it (heavy snow *to shovel*); that an unusual arrangement, such as an inversion, brings emphasis (Into the hall came the elephant). But point these out briefly, interestingly, and move on. There is no reason to believe that slow learners have any need whatsoever to learn more about grammar in the first sense. There is every reason to believe that they cannot and will not learn more and that attempting to force them to do so will develop in them a resistance to becoming sensitive to language—the primary reason for studying grammar at all. Richard Meade,[4] for example, after studying test scores of Virginia students who had studied grammar for four years, concluded ". . . those of average or below average intelligence had very little chance of learning the abstract principles of grammar with which they had been presented during their high school years."

The obvious purpose of teaching *grammar* in the second sense—that is, the mechanics of capitalization, punctuation, and spelling—is to enable students to handle the conventions of writing effectively. If this is what is intended by the term *grammar*, then the obvious method should be to sensitize students to the importance of these conventions, to increase their awareness of the presence of the devices in their reading, to develop pride and responsibility in their personal use of conventions, to devise activities involving team- and group-work for pleasurable drills, to provide frequent opportunities to use the conventions purposefully, and to reward growth. (Perhaps another concept to develop is that the term *grammar* should not be used in the sense of "conventions" and "mechanics.")

The third meaning of the word *grammar* concerns the ability to use grammatical structures effectively. Oddly enough, the worst way to teach *grammar* in this sense is "to teach grammar." Instead, Moffett[5] suggests that as students use language for any meaningful purpose, growth in language naturally occurs, and all grammatical structures necessary for the students' thoughts and expressions emerge. A second approach is suggested by Bateman and Zidonis,[6] O'Hare,[7] and Mellon.[8] These researchers suggest ignoring "formal" grammar instruction and taking students through interesting, terminology-free, sentence-combining practice. As students talk through and re-write numerous short sentences into longer, more precise, more pleasing expressions, they grow in this kind of grammar.

Briefly, then, to teach grammar to slow learners or to any other students, clarify what you mean by the term and what your purpose is. Then select your method.

References
[1]Robert C. Pooley. *Teaching English Grammar*. New York: Appleton-Century-Crofts, Inc., 1957, p. 5.
[2]Walter Loban, Margaret Ryan, and James R. Squire. *Teaching Language and Literature, Grades 7–12*. New York: Harcourt, Brace & World, Inc., 1961, p. 543.
[3]Neil Postman and Charles Weingartner, *Linguistics: A Revolution in Teaching*. New York: Delacorte Press, 1966.
[4]Richard A. Meade, "Who Can Learn Grammar?" *English Journal,* 50 (1961), p. 91.
[5]James Moffett. *Teaching the Universe of Discourse*. Boston: Houghton Mifflin Company, 1968.
[6]Donald Bateman and Frank Zidonis. *The Effect of a Study of Transformational Grammar on the Writing of Ninth and Tenth Graders*. Urbana, Illinois: NCTE, 1966.
[7]Frank O'Hare. *Sentence Combining: Improving Student Writing without Formal Grammar Instruction*. Urbana, Illinois: NCTE, 1973.
[8]John C. Mellon. *Transformational Sentence-Combining: A Method for Enhancing the Development of Syntactic Fluency in English Composition*, Urbana, Illinois: NCTE, 1969.

Question VI, 12

What justification can I give for teaching grammar to secondary students who are not highly motivated or school-oriented?

Dennis L. Jackson, Emmerich Manual High School, Greenwood, Indiana

Answer by:

MICHAEL G. CROWELL, Associate Professor of English at Knox College. Dr. Crowell has written a number of articles on language attitudes and English teaching and is co-author with J. N. Hook of *Modern English Grammar for Teachers*.

The question can be taken two ways: What justification is there for teaching grammar to unmotivated studnts? and What reasons can we give those students for subjecting them to the rigors of secondary school grammar? Both interpretations are important; both are difficult to answer. My own response to them is simply stated: If we can't explain to our *students,* motivated or not, *why* they are studying grammar, if we can't, that is, give them some kind of meaningful framework into which to fit the details they are asked to learn, then we can't justify grammar study to ourselves or anyone else, because without that framework students won't learn much or be able to put what they do learn to use. But I believe that justification can be provided to our students and thus to ourselves. Let me try to indicate how I reach this conclusion.

There are three basic viewpoints on the value of teaching grammar: (1) Formal grammar is not valuable in any way, so don't teach it, and instead give your students plenty of talking and writing to do; (2) We have always had grammar in the curriculum and many persons feel it has been of great value to them, so keep it as is; and (3) studying formal grammar *can* be valuable, but its value depends on how you do it. My own answer belongs under (3), and I'll work up to it by dealing with (1) and (2) first.

Probably the best known exponent of the first viewpoint is James Moffett, who defends his position in *Teaching the Universe of Discourse*.[1] Moffett here emphasizes what linguists have been telling us for years, that all norman human beings have unconsciously constructed a very complicated internal grammar of their native language by the time they get to our classes. Linguists have some idea (though hardly a clear one) of how complex this linguistic *competence,* as it is called, must be; and they are currently trying to understand more fully the means by which it is acquired. But we know that it *is* acquired, and Moffett would say that the job of the English teacher is to provide an environment in which the essentially *unconscious* process of acquisition can flourish. Teaching formal grammar (trying to direct a conscious process of language learning) won't work. As Moffett says, "To hope, by means of grammatical formulations, to shortcut through the deep, cumulative learning that comes from speaking is to indulge in wishful dreaming. These formulations cannot seriously compete with the profound conditioning of speech habits acquired in the learner's native environment. For children who learned a non-standard grammar at home, description and analysis remain a little body of intellectual knowledge powerless to permeate the automatic process that generates their utterances." [2]

In answering this view, most teachers, at least in my experience, say that *they* learned to write and speak more "correctly" (more in accordance with Standard English) and more clearly from studying grammar, and while the values of grammar may not be measurable by tests, questionnaires, and statistics, they are very real nonetheless. And it *does* seem to be true that most college students who studied formal grammar in secondary school are glad they did. What *are* the benefits, if any?

First let's agree that the unconscious processes Moffett speaks of do account for almost all of one's language learning. And let's admit it's true that some good speakers and writers have never studied formal grammar. We can still leave room for the possibility that *some* improvement in writing and/or speaking can result from formal grammar study. The kinds of improvement, I believe, include "correctness" (ability in Standard English as opposed to other dialects), complexity of sentence structure, and clarity in sentence structure.

Improvement in the use of standard English, in so far as it is attributable to grammar study, will be very minimal and will proceed largely from comparative grammatical description of the two or more dialects involved. Complexity in sentence structure can probably best be achieved *consciously* (there is always, as we have seen, the *unconscious* language learning mechanism) by carefully worked out and extensively used drills such as those developed and tested by John C. Mellon. Mellon, although he emphasizes that his research does *not* prove "that grammar study should remain a component subject in English," [3] demonstrated that a system of sentence-combining exercises like those he tested can lead to increased sentence complexity and thus a more mature style.

But Mellon's exercises, though clearly related to grammar study, are not the things with which our question is really concerned. That leaves clarity in sentence structure as a major benefit of the study of formal grammar. Bateman and Zidonis [4] have offered evidence, though their research is inconclusive, that teaching *transformational* grammar, at least, does lead to greater clarity. By this they mean avoidance of the kinds of sentence confusion that we call *dangling* or *misplaced modifiers, run-on sentences,* and the like. How does this work?

Bateman and Zidonis used an early version of transformational grammar in their study, and were thus able to emphasize the sentence-combining quality of many transformational rules. To make a long story very short, transformational grammars have given us, as traditional grammars tremble on the verge of giving us, a means of talking about the ways in which many statements, represented as simple sentences, can be combined into longer sentences. Such combination is obviously desirable, but human beings often misapply the rules for such combination and the result is the lack of clarity I've mentioned. Getting the combinations straight, through a study of the ways in which they occur in Standard (or not-so-standard for that matter) English is probably the major result of a study of formal grammar. Recent proposals for a generative semantics, if they ever get into the textbooks, will, I believe, provide the best means yet of achieving this result.

Now, finally, we can get to the question of justifying grammar study to our students. I would say to them that the study of grammar will not produce miracles; but that we can, if we look at it the right way, get insight into something we already know *unconsciously,* can increase our awareness of what we already do. To make good on this promise, though, we teachers will have to emphasize insight and the general structure of the sentence and de-emphasize detached drills, exercises, and the little details, at least until we have explained a general theory. This point is crucial, for if we are going to go at grammar in bits and pieces, we had better not go at it at all. Transformational theory, with its emphasis on deep and surface structure, its many attempts to create models of linguistic competence, can help us here, since such models provide a framework that will organize the bits and pieces. To emphasize this point, I'll end with something Jerome Bruner wrote some time ago: ". . . the curriculum of a subject should be determined by the most fundamental understanding that can be achieved of the underlying principles that give structure to that subject. Teaching specific topics or skills without making clear their context in the broader

fundamental structure of a field of knowledge is uneconomical . . ."
Surely grammar must be included in this general prescription. Taught as
a series of unrelated details, it can never be justified, I believe, to anyone.

References
[1]New York: Houghton Mifflin, 1968.
[2]*Ibid.*, p. 168.
[3]*Transformational Sentence-Combining, A Method of Enhancing
the Development of Syntactic Fluency in English Composition,*
Cambridge, Mass.: Harvard University, Project 5–8418, Cooperative Research Bureau, U.S. Office of Education.
[4]Donald Bateman and Frank Zidonis, *The Effect of A Study of
Transformational Grammar on the Writing of Ninth and Tenth
Graders,* Champaign, Illinois: National Council of Teachers of
English, 1966.

Question VI, 13

How can one teach punctuation to secondary school English students
who do not have enough background in grammar to understand rules
governing punctuation? Can it be taught without rules? For example,
can terms like *introductory participial phrase, non-restrictive clause, and
appositive* be bypassed?

Miriam R. Jones, South Point High School, Belmont, North Carolina

Answer by:

K. WAYNE PRUITT, Assistant Professor of Education at Francis Marion
College, Florence, South Carolina. Dr. Pruitt taught English at all grade
levels (9-12) for six years prior to his present position where he works
closely with English coordinators in school districts in South Carolina.

A perusal of the literature in English education regarding punctuation tends to support the notion that the traditional "rules approach" to
teaching punctuation is ineffective. Inherent in this approach is a strong
dependency on knowledge of the elements of grammatical language such
as restrictive clause, parenthetical phrase, introductory participial phrase
and the like. Crews points out that under the rules approach, "Punctuation, in the eyes of some students, amounts to a dreary question-and-
answer game. . . . Understandably, the students come to regard an
interest in punctuation as mere fussiness, or at best as something to be
faked for the duration of a writing course."[1]

Willis reminds the secondary English teacher that the student
does not need too much formal grammar to know how to punctuate effectively. Comma usage, for example, can be taught by merely stating
a general rule and following it with clear, concise examples. The rule,
"Commas are used to set off non-essential and essential constituents," is
used in place of numerous rules governing appositives, non-restrictive
clauses and introductory participial phrases, just to name a few. Of
course, sentences containing these grammatical constituents are given to
the student.[2] Willis' point is well taken. Too often, students are blinded

by the highly technical language of punctuation rules. Many times, a general rule, followed by clear examples, serves a better purpose.

For the English teacher who feels that more precise rules are necessary, Meyers suggests a more extensive rule system.[3] The rule for commas, for example, is: "Commas are used to set off introductory and apposite elements and separate elements in a series." Under this system, although a more extensive knowledge of the language of grammar is required, the student is not lost in an avalanche of terminology which has little meaning for him. Like Willis, Meyers suggests the use of clear examples of introductory elements (introductory participial phrases, etc.), elements in a series, and appositives, rather than a heavy reliance on technical definitions.

Backscheider recommends a very useful method for teaching punctuation. To avoid the usually anesthetic rules approach, he says, "We first create a need [for punctuation], and, second, develop a product to meet the need. . . . Developing a product to meet this newly recognized need is not so quickly done. The student who has memorized rule after rule and exception after exception has little desire to tackle the morass again. However, a two-pronged attack which is different, direct, and individualized, can largely overcome the students' feelings of helplessness and frustration." [4]

Under Backscheider's plan, students are asked to write themes or "working papers." The teacher evaluates each paper and, without comment or penalty, simply strikes out or adds commas and semicolons where necessary. Other punctuation problems are circled and explained in as non-technical language as possible. The teacher then asks the student to correct his "circled mistakes." Recurring punctuation problems in the latter category may require the teacher to give the student sentences which show the proper use of the mark of punctuation in question. From these sample sentences, the student is asked to formulate a rule governing the mark(s) of punctuation which gave him trouble.

The second prong of the attack calls for the students to work in small groups at first. Using the class's earlier papers on which comma and semicolon errors have been recorded, each group tries to list and classify the use of commas and semicolons. From this list, rules for usage can be derived. Each group compares its "list of rules" with lists from other groups in the class. A final list of comma and semicolon rules from the entire class is then presented to the teacher.[5]

Backscheider's plan is basically inductive. Rather than the teacher's presenting a long list of meaningless rules, the student writes his own punctuation rules. This method creates a need on the student's part to improve his punctuation. By using student prepared themes as a "framework for study," the teacher avoids the detachment that is often felt by the student when he is given a set of rules merely to memorize. Also, by writing his own punctuation rules, the student is more likely to internalize and correctly use marks of punctuation in his future work.

The question, "Can punctuation be taught to students who do not have enough background in grammar to understand rules governing punctuation?" cannot be answered entirely in the affirmative if the teacher insists on using rules which are packed with highly technical language. Obviously, the teacher cannot expect the student to place a comma after an introductory participial phrase if the student cannot identify a participial phrase. On the other hand, many experts feel that punctuation can and should be taught by the use of clear, concise examples of usage. Giving examples in context lessens the teacher's dependency on the technical language of the grammarian.

Can punctuation be taught without rules? Kierzek and Gibson say, "The conventions of punctuation have to be learned."[6] In support of this thesis, Whitehall reminds the English teacher that punctuation in the English language is a superficial coding system designed to aid the reader in understanding the written word. Man has been speaking for over 700,000 years, writing (using the alphabet) for only about 3,450 years, and punctuating for less than 250 years.[7]

How these rules are taught and learned, however, is the crucial question. In many cases, the English teacher starts with the complex rule and then teaches the particular mark of punctuation governed by that rule. Some teachers, on the other hand, give students broad, non-technical, and functional rules for punctuation. Others give contextual examples and allow students to derive their own rules from the examples. Each of these approaches requires the student to memorize rules, whether they be non-technical, general rules given by the teacher or "vernacular rules" written by the student. In the latter examples, however, memorization is not merely a rote process. It is a meaningful part of inductive learning.

Punctuation can be taught to students who have poor backgrounds in grammar if the technical languauge of grammar can be avoided. Rules governing punctuation are necessary, but, they too, must be non-technical. Constant practice with general, non-technical rules and the use of clear contextual examples from student writing appear to have some proved in combating problems with punctuation.

References

[1]Frederick Crews, *The Random House Handbook*, New York: Random House, 1974, p. 268.
[2]Hulon Willis, *Basic Usage, Vocabulary, and Composition*, New York: Holt, Rinehart and Winston, Inc., 1975, pp. 63–72.
[3]Walter E. Meyers, *Handbook of Contemporary English*, New York: Harcourt Brace Jovanovich, Inc., 1974, pp. 312–315.
[4]Paula Backscheider, "Punctuation for the Reader—A Teaching Approach," *English Journal*, 62 (1972), pp. 874–875.
[5]*Ibid.*, pp. 874–877.
[6]John Kierzek and Walker Gibson, *The Macmillan Handbook of English*, New York: The Macmillan Company, 1965, p. 290.
[7]Harold Whitehall, "The System of Punctuation," in Leonard F. Dean and Kenneth G. Wilson (eds.), *Essays on Language and Usage*, New York: Oxford University Press, 1963, pp. 223–224.

SECTION VII

DIALECTS

Question VII, 1

What are some ways that junior high students can be introduced to dialect study in English classes? How can English teachers involve students directly in this?

Guy Boyd Lucas, Rogers-Herr Junior High School, Durham, North Carolina

Answer by:

STEPHEN D. CHENNAULT, Assistant Director of Center for Black Studies and Assistant Professor in Department of English, Wayne State University. The major thrust of Dr. Chennault's work deals with "social forces that influence attitudes toward the linguistics of Black folks" and implications for language arts educators of Black students.

An effective approach to introducing *any* student to dialect study in language arts classes is through honest discussion that begins with explanation of the fact that *all American dialects are equal!* Such discussion should be followed by teaching approaches which focus on what encourages comfortable language usage—linguistic self-respect—among nonstandard dialect speakers. The first consideration, it seems, should recognize the fact that nonstandard dialects are forms of American English with systematic grammatical and phonological structures of their own. It should also be understood that learning mainstream English[1] is not an easy carry-over process that nonstandard dialect-speaking students can grasp automatically. Because of this phenomenon, the Black student (the model I will use for illustration in the discussion of this paper) who speaks so-called Black dialect[2] must be taught in a way that will enable him to grasp mainstream English (when and if he needs to) by using the rules of the language he is used to thinking in—his own. This can perhaps best be explained in the words of Walker (1971):

> The [Black] child must be made to understand, by concrete examples, why he must learn this new way of speaking. He must have the opportunity to use [his own language] in the classroom in dialogues, skits, reading aloud, and recitations. Praise and encouragement must reward his progress . . . Standard English should not be imposed as the only correct way of speaking.[3]

In order, then, to provide a comfortable learning environment for Black dialect-speaking students, the teacher must first of all recognize that his students speak a language that is well ordered and logical. He then must teach his students accordingly. The University of Michigan's Professor Jay Robinson asserts:

> The concept of dialect equality does not decrease the complexity in the task of teaching effective language use; perhaps it increases it. Once we grant that nonstandard speakers have the linguistic competence to do what we will ask them, we place the burden on ourselves as teachers for helping them develop that competence.[4]

I will remember an incident that illustrates just how successful teaching based on this belief can be. When I was teaching English in a Detroit high school several years ago, one of my white co-workers, after having had very little success teaching *Julius Caesar* to her tenth graders, decided to take a different approach: have the students interpret the play through their own language—Black dialect. The students, under the teacher's careful direction, produced a short film of their own version of Shakespeare's drama. The great difference here was the language: Black dialect and slang flowed from the mouths of the student characters. Imagine how baffled and shocked the faculty members were when they saw the film in the auditorium. Imagine further, though, how "turned on" the student viewers were, for they had no problem following the action and understanding the "hip" dialogue—language they were used to hearing and using daily, especially away from school.

This illustration, a desirable approach to acquainting Black students with the dramatic arts through their own control of language, was an exciting experience for the students, and it provided some knowledge about many things: Shakespeare, himself; drama as a literary genre; film production; and acting devices. Isn't that what teaching is all about? That is, shouldn't the teacher dig into the student and shovel out all of what he comes into the classroom with, all of what helps produce *willing literacy* and *human development?*

When I taught in a Black community college a few years ago, one of my students who had always had writing difficulty seemed "turned on" suddenly at the start of the school semester after reading a short story of mine filled with Black dialect. Her immediate reaction was: "I didn't know it was okay to write that way!" I told her that what she had read is considered Black dialect, Black folks' English with its own grammatical construction.

After giving my explanation some thought, the student decided she would like to write "freely" in her own tongue. She did so, turning out many voluntary pieces of writing that seemed logically developed in her easy expression of Black dialect. And I was pleased with her efforts.

It must be fully understood that an appreciative understanding of and a genuine respect for nonstandard dialects are the primary requisites for teaching nonstandard dialect-speaking students. Labov (1970) underscores this assertion even more when he stresses that ". . . the teacher will . . . need to know a great deal about the social forces which affect linguistic behavior if he is to interpret his students' language."[5] For it is not the student who is wrong when he expresses himself; it is the teacher who is wrong for not recognizing and respecting the language that that student uses to express himself.

References
[1]The term "mainstream English" is used in this paper to make reference to speakers who strive to fit into, or who are a part of, the American mainstream, the so-called middle class. In contrast to a Black dialect speaker, a mainstream (or standard) English speaker would likely say, "He is on Joe and their team."

[2]The term "Black dialect" refers to Black speakers who retain their native phonology and do not attempt to avoid usage of the grammatical shibboleths of their linguistic system. An example

is a Black speaker's systematic deletion or contraction of certain verbs: for example, "He on Joe nem team." Here there is no verb after the subject *He,* and the word *nem* implies the same as what *and them* suggests in mainstream English.

[3]Sheila Walker, "Black English: Expression of the Afro-American Experience," *Black World* 20 (1971): 12.

[4]Jay Robinson, "Voices in the Classroom: Unity or Diversity?" Unpublished manuscript, p. 24. University of Michigan, Department of English, 1971.

[5]William Labov, *The Study of Nonstandard English,* Urbana, Illinois: NCTE, 1970, p. 11.

Question VII, 2

Much has been written about the problems of colloquial and/or regional speech. How important is it to insist that Blacks be *made* to say "birthday" rather than "birfday?" Should they be permitted to omit part of the verb, as in "I going to town" rather than " I *am* going to town"

Herbert L. Krause, The Pennington School, Pennington, New Jersey

Answer by:

KENNETH R. JOHNSON, Associate Professor of Education, University of California, Berkeley, who is an authority on the language of Black children and its effect on learning. He is the author of numerous publications on Black English, and he has lectured extensively on it.

The dialect of English many Black children speak contains certain pronunciation variations from standard English such as the substitution of /f/ for the final voiceless /th/ in words that end like *birth;* the substitution of /d/ for the initial voiced /th/ in words that begin like *there;* the omission of final consonant stops—/d/, /k/, /p/, and /t/ in particular linguistic environments—*col* for *cold, des* for *desk, clas* for *clasp* and *tes* for *test.* Black children omit the final consonant stop /d/ if it is preceded by a voiced consonant, and they omit the final consonant stops /k/, /p/, and /t/ if these consonant stops are preceded by a voiceless consonant—these final consonant stops are pronounced if they are preceded by a vowel, however, if the following word does not begin with a consonant. The dialect of many Black children also contains certain grammatical variations from standard English such as substitution of *done* for *have,* omission of the copula verb *is* or *are* in present and present progressive tense, the reversal of the past tense and the past participle forms of irregular verbs—i.e., "I *taken* a pencil"; or "I have *took* a pencil"; or "I *done took* a pencil." The important point for teachers to know is that these variations from standard English are not *individual* errors of *random variations or deviations* from standard English; instead, these are examples of features that comprise that dialect of English called "Black English" or "Black dialect." The phonological and grammatical features of Black English and its historical development have been described (Dillard, 1972). Black English is *not* "sloppy"

English spoken by children with "lazy lips and lazy tongues"; it is a structured, functional variety of English, and it should not be stigmatized.

When Black children who speak Black English begin school, they are required to learn a different variety of dialect of English, and their own dialect "interferes" with their learning. The Black English-speaking child has difficulty in learning those standard English features which are not included in his dialect. Thus, when the teacher insists that he say "birthday," he actually *hears* "birfday," because his dialect does not contain the voiceless /th/ at the end of *birth*.

Interference also occurs when these children attempt to learn to read standard English (Johnson, 1971, pp. 136-147). Obviously, the difficulty occurs because these children are required to read a variety of English they don't speak, and they attempt to impose the phonological and grammatical features of Black English on the standard English text (Johnson, 1975, pp. 535–540).

Yet, these children need to learn standard English for academic, vocational and social success. Young children, however, don't recognize the need for learning standard English. Children do not become aware of the social and vocational significance of their dialect until adolescence. Thus, this is the time when the Black child should be "made" to say "birthday" and include the copula verb in the sentence, "I *am* going to town." The language program for Black English-speaking children, in summary, should be as follows:

1. In the primary grades, they should be given many experiences of hearing standard English, with the emphasis on those features their dialect does not contain; they should not be required to *reproduce* standard English.

2. In the intermediate grades, they should begin to receive formal, highly structured lessons in *reproducing* the sounds and grammatical features of standard English. The instructional approach should be an adaptation of the approach used in teaching English as a second language to speakers of other languages. Essentially, this approach involves five steps: (1) recognizing that there are two dialects of English which differ somewhat in particular features; (2) hearing those standard English features that differ or are not features of Black English; (3) discriminating between the features that are interference points between the two dialects; (4) reproducing standard English; and, (5) drilling in standard English sentences.

3. In the secondary grades, they should be "made" to reproduce standard English in sustained speech and recognize situations in which standard English is used as an alternate dialect. (Standard English should be taught as an *alternate* dialect rather than a *replacement* dialect.)

As long as the Black children live in a cultural environment where Black English is functional, they will not stop speaking it. Teachers must recognize and accept this. Thus, teachers must permit these children to communicate in their own linguistic system. The only time these children should be "made" to reproduce standard English is during the period when it is formally taught (and during this period, the emphasis should be on learning another variety of English, and not on replacing "good" English for "bad" English). During all other periods of instruction (i.e. social studies, science, etc.) the instructional emphasis pertaining to language should be on getting children to express concepts and ideas in whatever linguistic system they are competent in using. Finally, the suggestion here is not that Black English be taught to Black children (they already know how to speak it); the goal of the language arts program must be to teach Black children standard English—the problem is *when* and *how*. Presently, the school is failing to do this, because the instructional approach used is wrong: the instructional approach is, "Don't say it like that, say it like this" without giving these children the necessary sequential instruction procedures to "say it like this." This approach will perpetuate the failure of the schools in teaching standard English to Black children who speak Black English.

References

Dillard, J. L. *Black English.* New York: Random House, 1972.
Johnson, Kenneth R. "Black Dialect Shift in Oral Reading." *Journal of Reading*, 18 (April, 1975), pp. 535-540.
——————. "The Influence of Nonstandard Negro Dialect on Reading Achievement." *English Record*, 21 (April, 1971) pp. 136-147.

Question VII, 3

In trying to teach standard usage to high school students, I get the comment, "That's not the way we talk." What can I answer, and how can I proceed to make students aware of the need for them to use the language in a more standard way?
   Margaret C. Shirer, Belton-Honea Path Senior High School, Honea Path, South Carolina

Answer by:

J.N. HOOK, formerly professor of English, University of Illinois at Urbana, whose specialties are English Education and the English language. Mr. Hook is a past executive secretary of the NCTE, and is author or co-author of over thirty books, including the recent *People Say Things Different Ways.*

A teacher owes it to his students to be reasonably certain that he himself knows what "standard usage" is. To avoid prescribing usages that indeed are not "the way we talk" (or the way anybody else really talks), the teacher needs to be familiar with one or more modern, scholarly books on usage, such as the Evanses' *Dictionary of Contemporary American Usage,*[1] Bryant's *Current American Usage,*[2] and Copperud's *American Usage: The Consensus.*[3] Too many teachers for too many years have taught "standard" usage that isn't standard with anyone—sometimes not even with themselves in unguarded moments. I remember, for instance, the teacher who told her class, "Today we will be discussing *shall* and *will.* We will find out that with the first person we should always use *shall* unless we are expressing determination or promise."

Robert Pooley, whose *Teaching of English Usage* (1974 edition) should be on every English teacher's bookshelf, says:

A general, common, widely used dialect known as standard English serves as an agreed-upon standard medium of spoken and written communication in all parts of the United States. This dialect incorporates a wide range of functional variety, having sufficient breadth to permit the shades of difference in language use appropriate to specific occasions. The standard dialect is in no way intrinsically superior to any other dialect. Rather, its value lies in its role as a national standard of commonly accepted form. With minor variations, it has international value as well, for it shares in substance the major part of British standard English, Australian standard English, South African standard English, and the standard English of many other parts of the world. To those students who wish to expand the range of alternatives available to them in their professional lives, the value of attaining proficiency in this dialect must be obvious.[4]

V. Louise Higgins would agree with Pooley's emphasis on standard English as a medium of communication outside our own neighborhood, but would add that we need as teachers to teach the concept of levels of usage—that, for instance, the language used with close school friends isn't quite the same as that used *en famille*, which in turn isn't quite suitable for the classroom, and so on. Ms. Higgins elaborates:

. . . in taking up levels of usage, the first big distinction I make is that between public and private utterance. This clears the ground of dear old Dad and all the other parental ghosts, or don't your students ever say, "Well, my father says that at home all the time!" The hallmarks of private utterance are that it is definitely limited and that the emphasis is on content, not form. It is language in most pragmatic form and we all use it with our families, our friends, in our notes to the milkman. Public communication differs in that it is meant for a wider audience and that both form and content are considered. In our classrooms we are dealing primarily with usage as it pertains to public utterance.[5]

Students should be shown that they themselves already shift gears in their speech according to the situation, just as they drive their cars in accordance with conditions. They don't talk to a three-year-old as they talk to their grandfather, and they don't talk to Mom and Dad as they talk to the principal. They constantly adapt their language (its vocabulary, its tone, its degree of formality, its "correctness") to the circumstances in which they find themselves.

When we instruct them in standard English, we are not criticizing their "natural" language or the language they hear at home or in the street. Rather, we are illustrating the type of language that is generally heard on TV news broadcasts and on college campuses, that is expected in most school and college writing, that is the norm in business writing and much business speaking, and that on some occasions most likely will be expected of them. (Not inevitably and not of everyone, we should honestly admit. Some people live in such a narrow world that they never find out what lies outside it. But anyone who does venture outside his own neighborhood will probably have to transcend private utterance occasionally.)

Standard usage, it should be emphasized, is not pompous and stiff. It is most often, in fact, easy and informal and fluid. Illustrations abound: e.g., in many television and radio interviews, in most newspaper and magazine articles. Standard English, in fact, does not call attention to itself at all: nobody notices when we say "we were," but somebody may notice and be critical if we say "we was" outside the neighborhood where it may be expected.

One further comment. Students tend to be aggressively modern; they want to be up to date. The standard usage we are urging them to learn for the times they'll need it is *modern* usage. People used to say "deef" for *deaf,* but standard usage today prefers "def." People used to say "the news are bad," but today *news* is treated as a singular. People (including George Washington and John Adams) used to say "you was," and some people still do, but the majority have shifted over to "you were." Uncle Jake may say "tooken," as well as "holp," but almost all young people today say "took" or "taken" and "helped." Chaucer used double, triple, or even quadruple negatives, and Shakespeare was using the standard English of his time when he wrote "the most unkindest cut," but today we say things differently if we don't want to be considered old fashioned.

We aren't asking our students to use standard English at times when doing so would put them out of step with others in their surroundings. (A mechanic tells me that his fellows didn't accept him until he started saying "them pliers" instead of "those pliers.") As Tom Burnam wrote a quarter-century ago, ". . . the trouble with Miss Higginbotham [an excessively starched teacher] is that she leaves her students with the impression that full-dress is the proper costume for breakfast, lunch, dinner, the athletic field, the classroom, and the grocery store." [6] We are today recommending the linguistic equivalent of full-dress for those times when anything else would be inappropriate.

References

[1]Bergen Evans and Cornelia Evans. *A Dictionary of Contemporary American Usage.* New York: Random House, 1957.

[2]Margaret Bryant. *Current American Usage: How Americans Say It and Write It.* New York: Funk & Wagnalls, 1962.

[3]Roy H. Copperud. *American Usage: The Consensus.* New York: Van Nostrand Reinhold Company, 1970.

[4]Robert C. Pooley. *The Teaching of English Usage.* Urbana, Illinois: National Council of Teachers of English, 1974, p. 206.

[5]V. Louise Higgins. "Approaching Usage in the Classroom." *English Journal,* 49 (March, 1960), p. 183.

[6]Tom Burnam. "A Note for Miss Higginbotham." *English Journal,* 40 (Oct., 1951), p. 438.

Question VII, 4

How can one best teach standard language usage to a high school student who does not read well and who comes from an area where standard English is not used?

Lucy Ellis Parker, South Granville High School, Creedmoor, North Carolina

Answer by:

VIRGINIA G. McDAVID, Professor of English at Chicago State University, whose specialties are dialectology and usage. Mrs. McDavid is the author of many articles and several books, of which the most recent are *American English* and *Basic Writing.*

Although we do not have any sure method for teaching standard English usage, we do know that many speakers of nonstandard dialects acquire a command of standard written and spoken English, and we know some elements in their success.

First let us break down what is meant by a command of standard English. Involved in it are *comprehension*—understanding the spoken and written forms—and *production*—writing and speaking these forms. We need give little attention to the comprehension of standard spoken English. The vast body of grammatical structures is common to all varieties of English, and unfamiliar vocabulary is a matter of lack of experience rather than of using a nonstandard dialect. Radio and television, urbanization, and education have been responsible for the widespread dissemination of standard forms.

Reading standard English is another matter, and few would argue that the most important language skill that a student can acquire is the ability to read. Reading is central for mastering the content of almost all subjects. And any experience with competent writers almost always reveals them to be competent readers and interested in reading. Mastery of reading is thus important in expanding control of language and standard usage. It should be emphasized that control of the *production* of standard written and spoken forms is not a preliminary to learning to read. Speakers of very divergent English dialects have been learning to read in their own dialects for a long time. Nor should the teaching of reading, at least in the early stages, be made the vehicle for teaching standard pronunciation and grammar.

The production of standard written forms comes next. Just as reading develops with practice, so does writing. Whatever we know about teaching composition, we know it is a skill, and skills are developed by practice. The reason that composition teachers complain that their students cannot write is often the students' almost total lack of experience in writing. (This lack of experience) is sometimes owing to the teacher's never having had a writing course beyond freshman composition or a course in the teaching of writing.) Practice in writing can be of many kinds, developing skills in organization, sentence structure, standard usage, and punctuation, and can take many forms, from drills to the writing of entire compositions.

Writing standard English, like reading, is not necessarily dependent upon speaking standard English, though acquiring writing skills becomes more difficult for those who speak a sharply divergent dialect of English. But given skill in reading, practice in writing, and motivation, many students can develop some competence in writing.

Many authorities believe that teaching standard spoken English is best delayed until after reading has been taught and until the student is motivated. Without motivation, success is unlikely. Again, many authorities agree that it is best to supplement the student's normal spoken usage with standard forms rather than to seek to eliminate it entirely. Even if it were possible to eliminate his habitual usage, which it almost never is, such action would have the undesirable effect of alienating him from his culture.

A teacher who is going to work effectively to teach standard written or spoken usage must have considerable information about language, regional and social dialects, and usage. While all teachers should have such information and increasingly are coming to have it, it is essential for the teacher whose students use nonstandard English.

The teacher should know that the most important usage problems in this country involve grammar rather than pronunciation. He should know whether a usage problem is a systematic one, one that occurs with a large number of words, such as omitting the -s on the third person singular, present tense, on verbs, or whether it is an isolated one, such as substituting *to home* for *at home*. It is more essential to concentrate on the systematic features.

The teacher should also be sure that what he identifies as a usage problem actually is one. Pronouncing *which* and *witch* alike, or *whether* and *weather*, is entirely standard, as is *like* as a conjunction in spoken English.

Considerable information is available for teachers on matters of dialect study. Almost every issue of such NCTE publications as *English Journal, College English,* and the *CCC Journal* contain discussions on these matters. NCTE offers many other relevant publications as well. All teachers should be familiar with Robert C. Pooley's *The Teaching of English Usage* (Urbana, Illinois: NCTE, 1974), which has an extensive bibliography. For teachers whose students use nonstandard forms, William Labov's *The Study of Nonstandard English* (Urbana, Illinois: NCTE, 1970) and Rawlins Burling's *English in Black and White*, New York: Holt, 1973, are indispensable. For the historical background of usage questions—and most usage questions involve language change and hence history—Jack Lambert's *A Short Introduction to English Usage,* New York: McGraw-Hill, 1972, is essential.

Almost all collections of readings about language have sections on dialect study. Four excellent ones are Roger Abrahams and Rudolph Toike, eds., *Language and Cultural Diversity in American Education,* Englewood Cliffs, New Jersey: Prentice Hall, 1972; Harold B. Allen, et al., eds., *Focusing on Language*, New York: Crowell, 1975, John F. Savage, ed., *Language for Teachers,* Chicago, Illinois: SRA, 1973, and David L. Shores, ed., *Contemporary English: Change and Variation,* Philadelphia, Pennsylvania: Lippincott, 1972.

Question VII, 5

Those of us who teach in this small rural community in southwest Virginia wonder which area or areas of concentration should be stressed most strongly—skills in written communication, oral communication, or a greater understanding of literature of all types. We face a difficult situation in trying to remove from the speech patterns of our students those illiterate expressions—*ain't, ain't got no, theirselves, hisself*—that limit one's upward social and economic mobility.

Madeline Hurt, Tazewell Senior High School, Tazewell, Virginia

Answer by:

RAVEN I. McDAVID, JR., Professor of English at the University of Chicago. Mr. McDavid is a noted expert in the field of dialectology. He is co-author of *Structure of American English* (1955), editor of H. L. Mencken's *The American Language* (1963) and senior editor of the *Linguistic Atlas of the United States and Canada.*

First of all, I suspect that skills in written composition are likely to be the most productive area of concentration, especially if the teachers are concerned about the social amenities of language. It *is* possible to teach a kind of written competence even if one does not directly affect the oral performance. Moreover, I suspect that this is a way to sneak in a bit of a message in behalf of the kind of oral performance one would like students to have. Their achievement in understanding literature is something ultimately desirable, and I would be the last to disparage it. But the concentration on literature at the expense of composition seems at best a social palliative,, and at worst a confession of failure for both the teacher and the student—the latter being condemned to perpetuate the situation in which they find themselves. I do not wish English teaching to be mainly utilitarian, but a command of the written idiom of standard English is going to help immensely in getting the students to understand literature; anyhow, it is unlikely that the reverse is going to work.

The second point concerns the eradication of non-standard forms that "limit one's upward social and economic mobility." I think it is a mistake (Jim Sledd would be far more sulphurous in his labeling) to feel that the teachers can—or should—"eradicate" such forms; the eradicationist position puts the teacher in opposition to all the social pressures in which the student is normally immersed—playground and home and community. And there is so little time in the English classroom anyhow: there are several other class periods (do the other teachers reinforce what the English teacher is trying to do?); there are the various extra-curricular activities (do such more prestigious figures as the football coach emulate the kinds of sanitized English the English teachers apparently want?); there are the home and the playground (what kinds of English does the student use in daily communication after leaving the school building?). There is also the great danger of the student's becoming alienated from his natural environment if the teacher is too belligerently insistent on certain shibboleths.

What apparently this situation calls for is a greater understanding of language variety on the part of the teacher, a little bit of which may be absorbed by the student, a little bit of which might be useful in the actual classroom (from what I know of the kinds of language varieties found in southwest Virginia, the teacher could make a part of the course language-centered, with emphasis on what the students bring with them); like the areas of southern West Virginia and southeastern Kentucky it would seem to be a sort of linguistic crossroads where various streams of migration intersected.

The four forms that were cited in abhorrence would themselves make the kernel of a lesson in linguistic variety:

Hisself, theirselves are more systematic than the so-called "standard" forms *himself, themselves:* like *myself, ourselves, yourself, yourselves,* they present the "modern" classification of *-self* as a nominal, requiring the genitive before it, rather than the old classification as an adjective to be postponed after nouns or pronouns: *I self, ye selves, the boy self* (note that *herself, itself* can be interpreted either way, but certainly not *against* the genitive plus nominal analysis). Why *myself* is now accepted and *hisself* not is something one cannot explain on the basis of logical correctness, only because that's the way it happens to be.

Ain't is a historically legitimate contraction of *am not,* and in various dialects and stylistic situations also of *are not, have not;* extension in place of *is not, has not,* is again an analogical matter. It is probably, again, a more efficient negative contraction, since it can be used in all situations with the present tense of *be* or *have.* What is "wrong," if anything, is that it isn't accepted; I suspect that harping on it may make people more likely to use it, rather than observe the situations where it may and those where it may not be used (there are stylistic situations where it is perfectly naturally used in educated speech, though it is almost never written, even by the least educated).

The multiple negative can be cited as a legitimate form in literary English in Chaucer; it is traditional in the language. Somewhere between Chaucer and Dryden it became proscribed in standard written English, but millions of people just go on using it.

I am sure you know all of Jim Sledd's arguments against imposing "standard" forms from the outside; I suspect it would be far more useful for the teacher to present good models, themselves, of naturally used standard English that might be worth emulating. I am certain that in some cases there will be a prejudice against the person who occasionally uses a non-standard form (or a form that some others think is non-standard—though it might be standard for the student), and it may occasionally be the straw that tips the beam. But practically speaking, it is more important for the student to learn to use the language positively, with facility, fluency and versatility, and to become as widely learned as possible, including mathematics and the physical and biological sciences. The paper I gave to the Nebraska Council, I think back in 1968 (later it was published in the *Nebraska English Counsellor*) gives this in far more detail than I can give it here. The audiotapes I prepared last year for the WBZA (the Chicago Board of Education station) and the videotapes on dialect now available from The Windhover, Inc. (Box 43276, Cleveland 44143) provide fruther background information.

Question VII, 6

Should a Black student be penalized for using Black English rather than standard English in his writing in the English class?

Reba Dianne Boiter, Belton-Honea Path Senior High School, Honea Path, South Carolina

Answer by:

DONALD NEMANICH, Chairperson, Division of Humanities, West Virginia Northern Community College, Wheeling, W.V. Dr. Nemanich has written more than thirty articles on grammar, usage, dialects, stylistics, spelling, composition, and children's language.

Until recently nobody would have asked this question. Everyone knew that it was the responsibility of the English teacher to be a teacher and enforcer of standard English. Although it was difficult to define standard English, we knew that we could find it in newspapers, magazines, books, business and institutional documents, broadcasting, and in the speech and writing of most well-educated people.

Recently, however, some people, especially James Sledd, Wayne O'Neil, and Geneva Smitherman, have challenged either the teaching of standard English or the way it is being taught. In addition, the Conference of College Composition and Communication of the National Council of Teachers of English has issued a statement on "Students' Right to Their Own Language" which argues that all dialects are equally effective for communication and, therefore, students should retain their own language patterns rather than being taught a "mythical" standard English.

Nevertheless, even those who have been most critical of teaching standard English to Black children admit the value of knowing standard English. James Sledd, for example, admits that "there is not, moreover, and there never has been, a serious proposal that standard English should not be taught at all, if for no other reason than because its teaching is inevitable."[1] Elsewhere Sledd, the writer most outspoken against present methods of teaching standard English, comments: "there are also plenty of good reasons why many Blacks do value the mastery of an appropriate form of standard English and why the schools should do what they can to cultivate such mastery."[2]

The "Students' Right to Their Own Language" document also admits that some students wishing to prepare for certain kinds of employment should acquire standard English. "Students who want to write EAE (Edited American English) will have to learn the forms identified with that dialect as additional options to the forms they already control."[3] Among all the arguments for competence in standard English, probably the economic ones are most persuasive. Many jobs are not open to people who use nonstandard English, especially in writing.

David Eskey[4] makes a strong case for teaching standard English since it has been the medium of communication for millions of English-speaking people throughout the world because of its uniformity. And J. Mitchell Morse reminds those who argue for Black English that "Black English has seldom been the spoken language and never the written language (except by way of quotation and fictional dialogue) of any Black leader. . . . Can the advocates of Black English name one Black leader or spokesman with more than a neighborhood following who habitually expresses himself in Black English?" [5]

There are more important things in writing than the use of standard English—clarity, organization, logic, ideas, paragraphing, and effective use of details, among others. Nevertheless a writer will be reducing or alienating his audience if he does not use standard English. Students will be handicapped in school or on the job if they cannot write in standard dialect. For some kinds of writing, especially personal, narrative, or descriptive, there is little need for standard English. For more public kinds of writing like the business letter, research paper, or report, however, anything other than standard English is totally inappropriate. Leading sociolinguists[6] agree that as students progress through school they should do increasing amounts of writing in standard English, and there should be greater penalties for the use of Black English or other nonstandard dialects.

References

[1]James Sledd. "Doublespeak: Dialectology in the Service of Big Brother." *College English*, 33 (1972), p. 455

[2]James Sledd. "After Bidialectalism, What?" *English Journal*, 62 (1973) p. 771

[3]"Students' Right to Their Own Language." Special Issue. *College Composition and Communication*, 25 (1974), p. 15.

[4]David E. Eskey. "The Case for the Standard Language." *College English*, 35 (1974), p. 773

[5]J. Mitchell Morse. "The Shuffling Speech of Slavery: Black English." *College English*, 34 (1973), pp. 838-9.

[6]Alfred Aarons, editor. *Linguistic-Cultural Differences and American Education*. Special issue. *Florida Foreign Language Reporter*, 7 (1969); Joan Baratz and Roger Shuy, editors. *Teaching Black Children to Read*. Washington, D.C.: Center for Applied Linguistics, 1969; Robert Bentley and Samuel Crawford, editors. *Black Language Reader*. Glenview, Illinois: Scott-Foresman, 1973. See especially the articles by Kenneth S. Goodman, William Labov, Ralph Fasold, Walter Wolfram, William Stewart.

SECTION VIII

SPEAKING
AND
LISTENING

Question VIII, 1

Is oral communication in the classroom as important as written? Is there any connection between the two?

Bonnie B. Barefoot, Reid Ross High School, Fayetteville, North Carolina

Answer by:

ELMER U. CLAWSON, Assistant Professor of Education and SHIRLEY M. JENNINGS, Associate Professor of Education; both of the University of the Pacific, Stockton, California. Drs. Clawson and Jennings are authors of numerous articles in the fields of curriculum, reading, social science, and educational research.

To answer your first question, as to the relative importance of oral and written communication, it will help to explore your second question which relates to the connection between the two. That there is a sequence of language development skills of first listening with understanding, then speaking, reading, and finally, writing, is given almost universal credence today.[1] Robert B. Ruddell,[2] in summarizing the research evidence concerning the relationship between oral language and writing, concluded that the studies point to similarities in the growth patterns of oral and written language development. He emphasized that the interrelationships among the language arts skills are very much apparent, and that these interrelationships deserve careful consideration by the classroom teacher, particularly if full utilization is to be made of the learning transfer potential in the language skills.[3]

The theory of the sequential development of language arts skills implies that without the successful development of the basic skills of oracy—listening and speaking—efforts to teach the more advanced literacy skills of reading and writing are almost doomed to failure. It seems, therefore, self-evident that to have an idea to write about, one must first have the words to express and communicate that idea. The development of all writing begins in the cultivation and extension of the use of oral language.[4]

The research of Strickland[5] and Loban[6] supports the hypothesis that oral competency is a vital prerequisite to the literacy skills of reading and writing. Since oral language is, in effect, the base on which you build, it must be an important consideration in program planning. The classroom teacher has the double task of assessing the oral language development of students and for providing needed skill development activities. If your students have the prerequisite listening and speaking skills, you can base your language arts curriculum on these skills. On the other hand, if your students do not have this basic background, more emphasis will need to be placed on developing it.

References

[1] Roger L. Cayer, Jerome Greer, Elmer E. Baker Jr., *Listening and Speaking in the English Classroom: A Collection of Readings.* New York: The Macmillan Company, 1971, p. 183.

[2] Robert B. Ruddell, "Oral Language and the Development of Other Skills." in Hal D. Funk and DeWayne Tripplett, *Language*

Arts in the Elementary School: Readings. Philadelphia, Pennsylvania: J. B. Lippincott Co., 1972, pp. 297-298.

[3]*Ibid.*, p. 299.

[4]Oscar T. Jarvis and Marion J. Rice, *An Introduction to Teaching in the Elementary Grades.* Dubuque, Iowa: Wm. C. Brown Co., 1972, p. 218.

[5]Ruth Strickland, *The Language of Elementary School Children: Its Relationship to the Language of Reading Textbooks and the Quality of Reading of Selected Children.* Bloomington, Indiana: School of Education, Indiana University, 1962, p. 5.

[6]Walter Loban, *Language Ability; Grades Seven, Eight, and Nine.* Washington, D.C.: U.S. Department of Health, Education, and Welfare, Office of Education, 1966, pp. 90 and 92.

Question VIII, 2

Is it necessary to give formal instruction in the development of listening skills in the English classroom? If so, what activities work best in helping students to develop skill in listening?

Geraldine Sykes, Princeton High School, Princeton, North Carolina

Answer by:

BETTY CLEAVER, Director of the Instructional Materials Center, School of Education, University of North Carolina at Chapel Hill. Mrs. Cleaver is author of articles dealing with such aspects of the curriculum as population education, reading, and values education.

Educators doing research in the field of listening emphasize that listening is not synonymous with hearing. Listening is not a simple skill but an additive, complex series of skills. Smith and Dechant reported data supporting what experienced teachers already believed—that reading and listening skills involve the same mental processes and that instruction in either skill affects the other favorably.[1] Listening skills can be significantly improved through both direct and indirect (but not incidental) instruction, Canfield reported.[2] Hogan concurred, writing, "Continuous systematic instruction in listening is necessary to achieve maximum returns."[3]

Almost fifty years ago Rankin reported that 70% of the waking day in America is a "verbal communication day." His study suggested that of this day, we devote 45% of the time to listening, 30% to speaking, 16% to reading, and 9% to writing.[4] Although these figures have never been challenged, Burns, in a 1972 study, concluded that "little, if any, emphasis upon the teaching of listening skills is given in most language arts courses in teacher training institutions." [5]

The teacher who wishes to initiate instruction in listening skills may have access to commercially prepared listening kits; he still needs some understanding of both research and methodology. Where will he begin?

Hogan suggested that he begin with his own style of teaching. Listening instruction should be a part of all teaching. To improve this instruction, the teacher should : (1) reduce the amount of talking in the teaching act; (2) serve as the model of a good listener; (3) vary the stimuli in presenting material; (4) use different communication techniques to arouse and maintain interest; and (5) make frequent appraisals of listening growth.[6]

The hierarchy of listening skills has been variously constructed in the listening literature, but most experts agree on the general levels or categories of skills. At the lowest level of skill is auditory discrimination —the simple ability to differentiate between sounds. Next comes listening for directions or information; then listening for pleasure, or appreciation; and finally, listening with a critical or evaluative attitude. All listening activities can be fit into such a framework.

"What activities work best in helping students to develop skill in listening?" For 24 hours have each student keep a "listening log," entering such information as: "7:00 Heard alarm ring; 7:15 a.m. Listened to news on radio: 7:30 a.m. Mom and I argued about why I had to wear a raincoat," etc. Students will probably report listening to teachers, family, television, radio, household noises, music, traffic, conversation, and discussion. When the logs are completed, the class will be divided into groups to analyze them, classifying the kinds of listening reported, e.g., listening for instructions, sounds, enjoyment, or other categories deduced. When this is done, a listening profile of the class can be made. The teacher might then compare it with Rankin's "verbal communication day."[7]

For simple training in attention or sound discrimination, students might be divided into groups and instructed to record on audiotape a meaningful sequence of sounds. This sequence could be a trip to the circus, a birthday party, rush hour traffic, etc. The class would then listen to each audiotape and interpret it. Schwartz suggests to teachers that sections of sound should run no longer than is necessary to convey an idea; that they consider the use of various editing techniques, such as fading sound in and out, overlaying narration on the beginning and end of sounds, and juxtaposition of sounds; that they make sure that any segment of sound they use is complete so that listeners will not feel they have cut off something in the middle of a significant statement or feeling; and, that they ask themselves if this material would be clear to someone listening to it for the first time.[8]

Actors and sensitivity groups are trained to focus attention and develop empathy. Erway suggested adapting these strategies to the teaching of listening.[9] One way to do this would be to set aside a class period for "communication *a la* Carl Rogers." The teacher would group his class in threes. In each group, one student would be the observer, one the man with a problem, and the third would be the listening friend. The troubled man would tell his problem to the friend, who would be charged with listening carefully and then restating the problem to be sure he understands it. Conversation and discussion could go on for five minutes. The observer would then render a verdict on whether the friend had listened and projected himself into the other's problems enough to reach an understanding.

Other listening activities could center around following directions, analyzing television or radio commercials, listening to a story with the intention of retelling it, or entering into creative dramatics. Cayer and Green's *Listening and Speaking in the English Classroom*[10] and Duker's *Teaching Listening in the Elementary School; Readings*[11] offer a variety of activities and lesson plans which can be used verbatim or adapted to specific needs of the class.

Ralph Nichols, one of the pioneers in the teaching of listening skills, defined listening as "what we hear, what we understand, and what we remember."[12] Listening is more than hearing sound—it includes interpretation of sound—it is a vital part of the process of communication. Just as we teach the skills of reading, writing, and speaking, so, too, should we teach the skill of listening. The English classroom is an appropriate place to emphasize this in systematic, formal instruction designed to be an integral part of the English curriculum. Listening skills are needed by every student in every class and in all his experience.

References
[1]H.P. Smith and E.V. Dechant, *Psychology in Teaching Reading.* Englewood Cliffs, New Jersey: Prentice-Hall, 1961, 143-146.

[2]Robert G. Canfield, "How Useful Are Lessons on Listening?" *Elementary School Journal,* 62 (1961), 147-151.

[3]Ursula Hogan, "Listening—Our Ally in Teaching and Learning," *Learning Through Listening: Applying Listening Skills to the Curriculum,* Georgie L. Abel, et al., ERIC Report, ED 083 774, 1973.

[4]Paul T. Rankin, "The Importance of Listening Ability," *English Journal: College Edition,* 17 (1928), 623-630.

[5]Paul Burns et al., *Language Arts Concepts for Elementary School Teachers.* Itasca, Illinois: F.E. Peacock, 1972.

[6]Hogan, *op. cit.*

[7]Rankin, *op. cit.*

[8]Tony Schwartz, notes accompanying the recording "Tony Schwartz Recording the Sound of Children." Folkways Records, FH 5583, 1967.

[9]Ella Anderson Erway, *Listening: The Second Speaker,* ERIC Report, ED 084 574, 1972.

[10]Roger L. Cayer, et al., eds., *Listening and Speaking in the English Classroom.* New York: Macmillan, 1971.

[11]Sam Duker, ed., *Teaching Listening in the Elementary School: Readings.* Metuchen, New Jersey: Scarecrow Press, 1971.

[12]Ralph G. Nichols and Thomas R. Lewis, *Listening and Speaking.* Dubuque, Iowa: Wm. C. Brown, 1954, p. 1.

SECTION IX

SPELLING AND VOCABULARY

Question IX, 1

What is the best approach to teaching spelling to secondary school youngsters?

Vera B. Hoyle, Cherryville Senior High School, Cherryville, North Carolina

Answer by:

BERTRAND F. RICHARDS, Associate Professor of English at Indiana State University where he teaches methods and composition courses; he has written numerous articles on these subjects and on the interpretation of literature.

It has long been a contention of mine that there is really no problem as to how to teach spelling. There are numerous ways, and the teacher need only select the one he/she thinks will work. The real problem lies in getting the students to want to learn to spell. It is as simple as that; unfortunately, it is not as easy as that.

Students can and will learn anything they want to learn. They also will want to learn only that which they perceive as useful—and immediately useful—not in some vague future, not next year or even next summer, but useful now. If you have any doubts about it, consider driver-training for a group of kids approaching sixteen. Is there any lack of motivation? The teenagers will learn the facts they need but they will also learn to spell the words they need if they think they might have to write them.

But how can you achieve this same will to learn in other situations? Teach them only subjects which they recognize and accept as needed and applicable to their daily lives? There is some truth in this ambition, and the best learning will undoubtedly result from such teaching, but is it always, or even often, possible? The best advice I can muster is not to make a big deal of spelling—at least not to start off. And by no means attempt to teach spelling to a group of reluctant learners by using "traditional" spelling lessons.

I firmly believe that the best way to teach spelling is through writing; writing that is free and uninhibited, and in which spelling is venerated only for what it actually is—a standardized mechanical convention applicable only to the written language and intended solely to assure the best possible communication among transmitters and receivers of a code.[1]

Spelling, like any code, whether it be Apache smoke signals or the binary code of a computer, must be learned to be of any benefit to its user. The better a code is learned, the more efficient will be its employment, and in the case of the graphemic code of the English language—spelling—the more nearly perfect will be the communication achieved through it.

If the use of a tool is necessary to the accomplishment of a desired task, the mastery of the tool is achieved, not without effort, but cheerfully rather than begrudgingly. The sculptor eagerly learns the use of his mallets and chisels, the hopeful guitarist willingly masters picks and fingers, scales and chords. So, too, will the amateur writer master not only spelling, but also grammar and punctuation once he comes to want to use them as tools. Therefore, before you can inspire your students to spell, you must get them into writing and into wanting their writing actually to communicate. Every kid has something to say and the ability to say it quite well. Unfortunately, he does not have, or seems not to have, the ability to write it as well.

But by whose standards is this student unable to write? Suppose we forget *our* standards and judge his writing by his. We might be surprised to find that he can write almost as well as he can talk. If you continue to give him constant practice in writing along with the encouragement of knowing that you consider his writing worthwhile, then he may become as "fluent" in writing as he is in speech, only slower.[2]

In teaching language mastery through use—that is through writing—one of the best approaches is to point out to students that they know much more than they do not know and to build on their capabilities rather than accenting their incapabilities.

One device reported by this writer elsewhere[3] is to "grade" an initial set of papers with a score based on the number of words right rather than those spelled wrong. Give kids the confidence of knowing that for the most part they do well; that will give them the courage, and perhaps the will, to conquer the little that they do not do well.

Next, acquaint them with their language. Point out that the vagaries and seemingly illogical nature of English spelling are not so senseless after all. Let them know something of the historical progress of English orthography, and that the same lawlessness which makes English spelling so difficult has also made English the most flexible and efficient language existent today.

One of the first complaints of kids eager to spell correctly is that they should be able to spell words as they sound, but that they can't. Well, no! But point out that if one does not know how to spell a word and does not have a source at hand for finding out, sound is still the best guide. But also point out that they aren't really being honest. For there are thousands of words that they know perfectly well and which they would hardly recognize spelled "as they sound":[4] *brawt, ankshus, muny, onur, hwair, huz, sehvehn, hwail, anser, soard, kawt, kawf.* But if they do not see these spellings and you give them the list orally, they automatically write: *brought, anxious, money, honor, where, whose, seven, whale, answer, sword* (or *soared*), *caught,* and *cough.*

Through familiarity, most students have already mastered the most erratic word group in English—the *-ough* syndrome. Still, one of the commonest confusions is among *thorough, through,* and *though.* Note, however, that it is not the *ough* that causes these alternate choices so much as not reproducing the sounds that are heard.

Above all, don't let the students get the notion that you sprung fully spelled from the forehead of Zeus. Too often, teachers are unwilling to admit their own imperfections to students. Let them know that spelling was/is no easier for you than for them. Let them know that you quite frequently have to look up a word, and let them know some of the steps you took to become the adequate speller you are. If you have any "crutches" that you use to help you spell, reveal them to your students—perhaps they have, or can develop, some of their own. For instance, there is "a rat" in *separate*. Remember that and you cannot spell it *sep-e-rate*. *Science* occurs in *conscience* but not in *conscious*. *Definite* is a "finite" word and cannot be *definate*. The three l's in *parallel* will not be confused if you think of them as a railroad bordered by a telegraph line. The list of such helps is almost endless and quite individual. Get students to work on foolproof aids to spelling.

Along the same line but a little different is settling the question of spelling by thinking of other words in the same family where pronunciation shifts make spelling clear. Suppose you weren't sure whether it was *humen, humin,* or *human;* thinking of *humanity* would make it clear the *a* is the only possibility. And the silent *b* of *bomb* is certainly heard in both *bombard* and *bombardier*.

My final answer to your question is not very satisfactory consisting as it does of oft-repeated advice: be aware of your problem, keep your teaching student-centered, and employ any means your intuition tells you might work.

References
[1]Stephen Judy. *Explorations in the Teaching of Secondary English.* New York: Dodd, Mead and Company, 1974, p. 37.
[2]Jayne Karsten. "Technique and Tactics." in Patricia A. Geuder et al, eds. *They Really Taught Us How to Write.* Urbana, Illinois: National Council of Teachers of English, 1974, pp. 68-71.
[3]"Spelling, Punctuation, and Vocabulary." in R. Baird Shuman, ed. *Creative Approaches to the Teaching of English: Secondary.* Itasca, Illinois: F. E. Peacock Publishers, Inc., 1974, p. 188.
[4]John Kenyon. "Spelling Pronunciation." in Wallace Anderson and Norman Stageberg, eds. *Introductory Readings on Language.* New York: Holt, Rinehart and Winston, 1966, pp. 319-20.

Question IX, 2

What can I do to make spelling come alive for ninth graders who are poor spellers and resent doing any further work in spelling?
Ruth Stroup, Cherryville Junior High School, Cherryville, North Carolina

Answer by:
ANTHONY ROY MANGIONE, Associate Professor at the School of Education, Brooklyn College, CUNY, New York City, N.Y., whose specialty is English Education. Mr. Mangione is author of nearly thirty articles and co-author of one book, an annotated bibliography: *The Image of pluralism in American Literature. An Annotated Bibliography on European Ethnic Group Life.* National Project on Ethnic America. A Depolarization Program of the American Jewish Committee, New York City, New York. Emphasis: Secondary and College.

Spelling must be motivated. Bernstein [1] suggests that teachers first "motivate the willingness [of the students] to be observant," testing, for example, whether they remember the color of the teacher's tie or the number of steps on the stairway leading from the school's main entrance to the street. Loban [2] re-enforces the importance of motivation, recommending that "those who spell competently should be released from spelling lessons to do other things." Hillocks [3] stresses the need for spelling instruction on an individual basis, focusing on specific spelling problems, one at a time. To undertake individualized pre-tests, drills, and conferences motivates the teaching of spelling. Since students vary so much in spelling difficulties, provisions for individualization become imperative by junior high school.

Beyond motivation and individualization, Hillocks recommends the teaching of a "limited number of orthographic rules that have broad applicability"; [4] for example, the conventions of forming the plural, uses of the apostrophe, and conventions associated with adding various kinds of suffixes. The Commission on the English Curriculum of the National Council of Teachers of English [5] concurs with this recommendation, adding that students be shown how words are formed: *cordially,* for example, formed from *cordial* and *ly,* is one of many words ending in *ly* that follows a definite orthographic rule. Regardless of the rules taught, authorities advocate different lists of spelling words for each student by the junior high school grades.

The Commission recommends, among other teaching techniques, that students be alerted to the various steps necessary for learning new spelling words: seeing the word, hearing the word, comparing what one sees with what one hears, recalling the word, writing the word, and knowing the meaning of it in the context of one's own written expression. [6]

Most authorities affirm that spelling should be taught, not taken for granted or shrugged off as hopeless. More importantly, they urge that more time be spent teaching alternative methods of learning how to spell correctly than drilling students in correct spelling. More time should be spent having students study words and identify effective ways of attacking them than in being tested on spelling words. As Loban points out, good spellers do not use the same method of achieving success, but all good spellers use *some* method. [7] Few good spellers spell well instinctively.

The answer to the question as to how to make spelling come alive for ninth graders who are poor spellers is not simple or one-dimensional. Teachers should motivate, individualize, entertain (e.g., by using the traditional spelling bee, Scrabble, crossword puzzles, and such games as Ghost and Hangman, described at length by Hillocks [8]), and teach—above all, teach. If you prefer, have your students use Harry Shefter's *Six Minutes a Day to Perfect Spelling* and teach themselves.

References

[1]Abraham Bernstein. *Teaching English in High School.* New York: Random House, 1961, p. 78.

[2]Walter Loban, *et. al.* *Teaching Language and Literature* (Grades 7-12). Second Edition. New York: Harcourt, Brace and World, Inc., (1969) p. 725.

[3, 4]George Hillocks. *The Dynamics of English Instruction* (Grades 7-12). New York: Random House, 1971, pp. 481–482.

[5, 6]Commission on the English Curriculum. *The English Language Arts.* New York: Appleton-Century-Crofts, Inc., 1956, pp. 392-393.

[7]*Loban*, p. 727.

[8]Hillocks, pp. 618-619.

Question IX, 3

Do vocabulary words lists, studied out of context, have much lasting benefit for high school students?

Margaret Dixon, Bessemer City Senior High School, Bessemer City, North Carolina

Answer by:

ROBERT E. THORNE, Associate Professor of English at the College of The Albemarle, Elizabeth City, North Carolina.

Many English teachers will generally agree that wide reading accompanied by adequate dictionary skills and competence in the interpretation of context clues—that is, incidental instruction—will enable our long-range-goal-oriented, intrinsically motivated, highly intelligent students to build an extensive vocabulary. How many of these teachers, however, are fortunate enough to have such students filling the majority of the seats in their classrooms?

Ay, there's the rub! What we have is a problem in need of a practical solution. Wide reading, in and of itself, does not seem to provide that solution. In concluding their separately conducted research on vocabulary building through wide reading at the high school and freshmen college levels respectively, Traxler[1] and Sachs[2] painted a rather discouraging picture of the value inherent in reading as a means of increasing vocabulary.

What method then? Although publishers have flooded the market place with self-justifying how-to books on vocabulary building, little in the way of scientifically proved research exists in conclusive support of any one particular method of vocabulary instruction. However, direct instruction, defined by McCullough as "lists of words or sentences containing words [which] are studied deliberately for the development of word power,"[3] seems at present to be more highly regarded and effective for the average high school student than either wide reading or incidental instruction.

Taught properly, master word lists can have lasting benefit for students. In an investigation designed to measure the residual benefits of one semester of vocabulary study, I. W. Miles[4] discovered that the devotion of ten minutes a day to the discussion of meaning, use, and grammatical classification of words produced significant gains in oral vocabulary when students were retested two and one-half years later. From this study, and other similar ones, Miles estimated that direct word study is approximately three times as effective in terms of retention as incidental word study.

The selection and ordering of words used in the direct study method is extremely important. DeCecco found that the higher the meaningfulness, that is, word frequency or familiarity, "the more rapid the learning and the longer the materials are retained." [5] Numerous word lists based on the most frequently used words have been compiled and should be consulted before the teacher initiates vocabulary study. One should find the Thorndike-Lorge *Teacher's Work Book of 30,000 Words* [6] useful. Ordering of words can also be based on frequency count and can be easily geared to match the interest of individuals or groups.

The teacher must be aware of the learn-quickly, forget-quickly technique of word acquisition employed by students oriented to short-term test results. If vocabulary study is to have any lasting benefit, then it must lead the student to retain the newly acquired words in such a way that they become a part of his "living" language, applicable to increasingly more difficult matters and materials.

Retention cannot be left to chance. Students should be informed at the onset of vocabulary study that reviews and periodical follows-ups will ensue. Numerous studies have proved that intentional learning of meaningful material is more effective than incidental learning in terms of initial mastery and long-range retention.

A randomly selected word list, void of any implied or at least inferrable context, seems destined to perpetuate inefficient learning. Without a variety of contexts for each word on the list, there exists the danger of what Hayakawa calls the "one word, one meaning fallacy." [7]

In conclusion, the answer to the question seems not to be an answer at all, merely a suggestion. Vocabulary word lists can be beneficial for long-range retention, if they are taught intentionally, meaningfully, and through a variety of contexts.

References

[1] A. E. Traxler. "Improvement of Vocabulary Through Drill." *English Journal,* 27 (1938), pp. 491–94.

[2] H. J. Sachs. "The Reading Method of Acquiring Vocabulary." *Journal of Educational Research,* 36 (1943), pp. 457–64.

[3] Constance M. McCullough. "What Does Research Reveal About Practices in Teaching Reading?" *English Journal,* 46 (1957), p. 477.

[4] I. W. Miles. "An Experiment in Vocabulary Building in a High School." *School & Society,* 61 (1945), pp. 285–86.

[5] John P. DeCecco. *The Psychology of Learning and Instruction: Educational Psychology.* Englewood Cliffs, New Jersey: Prentice-Hall, Inc., 1968, p. 339.

[6]Edward L. Thorndike and Irving Lorge. *The Teacher's Work Book of 30,000 Words.* New York: Teachers College Press, Columbia University, 1944.

[7]S. I. Hayakawa. *Language in Thought and Action.* New York: Harcourt Brace Jovanovich, Inc., 1972, pp. 54–58.

Question IX, 4

I am teaching a nine-week mini-course in the development of vocabulary skills, and I am finding it difficult to know how to proceed effectively and to know what words should be stressed in vocabulary building. My students are in grades 10, 11, and 12. What do you suggest?

Sandra M. Perkinson, Smithfield-Selma Senior High School, Smithfield, North Carolina

Answer by:

GENE STANFORD, Assistant Professor of Education at Utica College of Syracuse University, Utica, New York. Dr. Stanford is author of numerous books and articles in the field of education, the best known of which are *Human Interaction in Education, Steps to Better Writing, Learning Discussion Skill Through Games,* and the *Stanford/McGraw-Hill Vocabulary Series.*

The first step in designing a vocabulary building program is to determine exactly what your purpose is. For some teachers the goal is to enable students to recognize previously unfamiliar words when reading and listening. For others, the goal is to enable students to use new words in their writing and speaking. Both goals are legitimate, and both should probably be a part of your course; but they require very different approaches.

When your goal is to improve the students' recognition of unfamiliar words, teaching word attack skills has far more payoff than teaching any list of particular words. It's impossible to predict what unfamiliar words a student will encounter, but you can equip him/her with a simple set of tools to unlock the meanings of many of them. I would suggest giving a great amount of emphasis to the use of context clues, starting with exercises that teach students the various types of context clues (definition, contrast, example, modifiers, restatement, inference, etc.). Lee C. Deighton's book *Vocabulary Development in the Classroom* [1] is an excellent teacher resource for understanding context clues. After teaching students the different kinds of clues, let them read freely in any books or magazines that interest them, utilizing context clues to guess the meanings of unfamiliar words they encounter.

Word analysis—guessing meaning from Greek and Latin prefixes, suffixes, and roots—is of some value as a word attack skill; but as Deighton points out in his book mentioned above and as I have described elsewhere,[2] this method has been highly overrated. For example, prefixes such as *trans-* and *de-* have as many as four or five different meanings, and there is no way for the reader to know which meaning applies to the unfamiliar word he has encountered. Furthermore, the literal meaning of the prefix or root may have undergone considerable change through the years, so that the current meaning of a word is completely different from what one guesses by looking at the prefix and root. My experience has been that one should concentrate on the 11 prefixes (such as *non-*) that have single meanings and forget the others. Coupled with an ability to find the English base word in an unfamiliar word, knowledge of these invariant prefixes can be useful in guessing the meaning of words encountered in reading.

Although word attack skills may help a student cope with unfamiliar words he or she encounters, that approach does little to increase the student's active use vocabulary. If your goal is for students to become more articulate, to use words that are more precise and more colorful, and to sound more erudite, then you must teach certain words in depth and give the students considerable practice in using them appropriately.

Determining which words to teach is the first step. In my opinion, it is foolish to force students to learn "fancy" words that few educated persons regularly use or even understand. They should learn, as one of my students put it, "real words that are used in the real world." Therefore, your first rule of thumb should be: Teach no word that is not a part of *your* active use vocabulary. For example, the word *jocund* appears on a list of vocabulary words that a well known expert considers essential for high school students to know; yet, neither I nor most of my most literate colleagues regularly use that word. Hence, I would seriously question teaching it to high school students when there are countless other, more widely used words that could be substituted. A second rule of thumb is to try to choose words that are already in the "twilight zone" of the student's awareness. That is, choose words that students may recognize, but which they don't know how to use with precision and therefore don't use regularly. Most of the students in my tenth grade honors class, for example, could pick out the best definition for *impeccable* on a multiple choice test, but none of them was comfortable using it in their speaking and writing. Therefore, it was one of the first words I chose to add to their active use vocabularies.

Of course, in any given class students' verbal ability varies widely, especially if grades ten through twelve are mixed in a mini-course. A word that a bright twelfth grader uses readily may be only in the "twilight zone" for an average tenth grader. It is almost imperative, then, that you provide for several levels of ability within the class—perhaps by giving a pre-test at the beginning of the course to diagnose each student's vocabulary level and providing materials of various degrees of difficulty. Multi-level self-instructional materials make it possible to individualize the course to a great extent, but I would caution you against limiting the course to students working alone in their workbooks day after day.

As important as choosing which words to teach is deciding how to teach them. Handing out a long list of words (and by long I mean twenty-five per week) for students to look up in the dictionary is *not* an effective way to build vocabulary. I have found that teaching two new words each day gets results; any more than that overwhelms most students.[3] The two words should be introduced in detail—with a definition in words the student can understand, with sample sentences, with synonyms, antonyms, related forms, and perhaps with a bit of information about the origin of the word. This complete explanation is far more helpful than the kind of misinformation that most students get from a dictionary definition.

After students understand the meaning of the two new words, they should work various kinds of exercises with those words including writing original sentences with them. Words from previous days should be included in the exercises to help students continually review them.

A nine-week course would be deadly if you have students do nothing but work pencil and paper exercises. A great variety of classroom activities is imperative. If I were teaching such a course, I would probably have all students spend approximately fifteen minutes each day learning their two new words, then each day I would vary what I planned for the remainder of the period. On some days, I might use workbook exercises on context clues or word analysis. On others I'd have students read for pleasure, practicing their word attack skills whenever they ran across an unfamiliar word. On still other days students could play some of the many commercially produced word games or some that I devised myself. And I'd not overlook oral communication activities—structured opportunities for students to practice the new words they've learned.

References

[1]Lee C. Deighton. *Vocabulary Development in the Classroom.* New York: Teachers College Press, 1959.

[2]Gene Stanford. "Word Study That Works." *English Journal,* January, 1971.

[3]Gene Stanford. "The Effectiveness of Vocabulary Improvement Workbooks Compared to Dictionary Study of the Same Words." *English in Texas,* Winter, 1972.

SECTION X

ARTICULATION WITH HIGHER INSTITUTIONS

Question X, 1

As a teacher of high school juniors and seniors I wonder what I should be stressing with my college-bound students. What do colleges presume their entering students will be able to do in such areas as composition and critical reading?

Thomas R. Cox, North Central High School, Indianapolis, Indiana

Answer I by:

JOHN K. PRATT, Assistant Professor of English at Tarleton State University, Stephenville, Texas. Mr. Pratt teaches an English methods course.

There is no single answer to the question: "What do colleges presume their entering students will be able to do in such areas as composition and critical reading?" Teachers of freshman English are as varied and more various than animals in a zoo. Whatever the syllabus indicates, they range from grammarians (or worse, *moral* grammarians) to amateur psychologists whose class sessions consists of orgies of ego stroking. However, assuming that your students will draw an instructor within the sane middle range, I risk a few suggestions.

First, do not labor over distinctions in usage which may no longer be valid in the real world. Who will accomplish what with whom? You may do more harm than good. Who can tell? Try to eradicate such illiteracies as "I seen" and "I set," but be aware that "Loan me a dollar" may raise no money but will seldom raise an eyebrow.

Also, certain niceties of punctuation can safely be ignored or at least be placed so far down on the priority list that you will never reach them unless your students are gifted indeed. For example, your rhetoric text may still command that a semicolon be used before every conjunctive adverb, yet you will find the comma substituted frequently by accomplished writers.

Help your students to learn to spell the commonly-used words— the ones each individual tends to misspell. Encourage them to compile individual lists which might include "separate," "usually," and "writer" but not "sieve" or "fossiliferous." In matters of usage, punctuation, and spelling, work on "everthing" but not everything.

So much for the relatively superficial aspects of composition. When I was teaching high school English, one of my graduate school English professors remarked, "*Just* teach them to write a good paragraph. That's *all* we ask." I resented his implication that teaching students to write good paragraphs is a simple matter. I knew then and I know now how difficult it is, but I also believe that, after the principles of paragraph composition are learned, the rest is easy. My advice is that you take your students as far as you can in learning to write effective paragraphs, a somewhat more modest proposal than that of the university professor.

In my experience, the most serious defect in paragraphs written by beginning college students is that they lack what I call guts. In expository and persuasive writing, a paragraph topic statement is an assertion which requires additional information of illustrative and/or evidential nature. If a student writer, after having read James Thurber's "The Secret Life of Walter Mitty," commits himself to the assertion that Walter Mitty is henpecked by his wife, he needs to know that he must follow that assertion with specific examples of Mrs. Mitty's behavior. And he needs to know why. These examples will clarify the meaning of "henpecked" and will prove that the assertion is true. If his assertion is that most of the students in his English class oppose further U.S. involvement in Southeast Asia, he needs to understand that he must gather statistical information and accurate, typical quotations to supply the necessary guts. In short, the student writer must understand that the guts of the paragraph are the means by which the writer shows the reader that his assertions are valid.

A short word about free writing or personal writing, journals, creative writing, etc. Although not every student (or adult either) wants to leave his soul to the teacher, students who are interested may benefit considerably from these kinds of writing as long as they do not neglect the skills involved in more practical exposition and persuasion.

As for reading, any college instructor I know would be delighted with students who could read, to a reasonable degree, closely and accurately, which is another large order. If you have not already discarded chronologically-organized American and British literature textbooks, I suggest that you do so as soon as possible. The important thing is reading skill, not knowledge of the classics. Most students will be better motivated to read with Karl Shapiro's "Auto Wreck" than Bryant's "To a Waterfowl." Make use of films and TV drama to help your students make the shift from dependence on multi-media to the printed page. Discard all of the memorizing, such as author-title matching and definitions of literary terms. Study advertising copy for examples of Doublespeak. Urge your students to talk about literature in open class discussion and in small groups. Encourage debate: "Mrs. Mitty is justified in dominating her husband"; "Mrs. Mitty is not justified in dominating her husband." These are, of course, matters of opinion, but students will need to go back to the details of the story to support whichever opinion they choose.

In order to evaluate a literary selection, any reader must establish standards by which he makes judgments. Encourage your students to establish their own individual standards; do not dictate them yourself. Encourage discussion. What are the essential qualities of a good short story or poem? How does this particular poem or that story measure up? What is the specific evidence which reveals a quality or a defect? The individually established standards will vary. Good. Individual students will alter their standards. Better. And there will be little if any literary jargon involved. Excellent.

You have asked me to "presume," and I have no doubt been presumptuous. Don't let me or anyone else set your standards. What if you never see your students again after next Friday?

***Answer II by*:**
HENRY VAN SLOOTEN, Professor of English, California State University, Northridge, California. Mr. Van Slooten has taught college composition for almost thirty years, is co-editor of a reader published by Harper & Row, has been reader and table leader of composition exams administered by the College Board, and is, this year, one of two question leaders on the English Equivalency Examination for the California State Universities and Colleges.

It seems to me that a college-bound student needs, above all, to be able to use detail in support of an idea. Common to placement examinations I have read is the instruction to the student to develop his essay by using illustrations from his reading or from his own experience. College teachers hope that their composition students not only will have done some reading in which they have learned to value the positive effect of well-organized detail but also will have learned to detail their life experience in meaningful ways.

As an aid to getting students to value their own experience, I have recently begun my classes in advanced exposition by reading a brief, recently published essay that I tell them frankly has special meaning for me. One I have used effectively for this purpose during the past year is a concise essay by L. E. Sissman, entitled "The Crystal Year." It appeared in *The Atlantic* in November, 1973. During the first class meeting of each of the last two semesters, I have read this essay to students as an example of meaningfully stated experience that has spoken directly to me. Without talking it into extinction I have tried to show, in general, how it has been effective. I have then asked each member of the class to bring me a short essay of similar length which he believes has spoken directly to him. From the essays I have received, I have been able to get some idea of what each student values as experience and what each student believes to be an effective presentation of it in words. Although I have not yet done so, I plan in future semesters to use some of the best of these essays to invite class discussion of what words can do to convey the meaning of experience. This is one way, I believe, to move toward what is fundamental to teaching essay writing based (as it very vitally can be) on experience—the development in students of a sense of the special value of a teacher's experience and the creation reciprocally in a teacher of a sense of the special value of each student's experience.

Discussion of essays selected in this manner or of essays, stories, or poems to be found in readers must further lead to the important idea that for details to function effectively, they must be well-selected, well-arranged, and sufficient in number to flesh out the idea they are intended to support. Thus, the young writer learns, if teaching is successful, the essential logic of writing—that belief is instilled in a reader only by substantial and well-planned detailing. But one more concern is left, more a matter of the aesthetics of writing—that to keep a reader from nodding over his essay the writer must use details that are interesting and fresh.

Question X, 2

Is there any correlation between success in writing term papers or research papers in college and having had practice in writing them in high school? If research papers are written in high school, how many should a college-bound student write, how long should they be, and what should the teacher stress?

Mary H. Deason, Wilkes Central High School, Wilkesboro, North Carolina

Answer by:
ROBERT E. PROBST, Associate Professor of English Education at Georgia State University. Dr. Probst is especially interested in the teaching of literature, and has recently published a chapter on that subject in Shuman's *Creative Approaches to the Teaching of English: Secondary.* He is one of the editors of the revision of Ginn's *Voices Series.*

Opinions on teaching the research paper in high school are sharply divided. Neman, a high school English teacher, says, without reservation, that "Every college-bound student should have the opportunity during his last year in high school to learn the skills necessary for the construction of a scholarly research paper." [1] Stevenson, a college teacher of English, says, without reservation, "I am opposed to the 'research' paper because it is pretentious; it serves no real value as an 'English' assignment; and it promotes dishonest writing." [2] The strong, unqualified language reveals more about the strength of the writers' convictions than about the validity of their positions.

There is little evidence in the literature to indicate that high school training in the research paper significantly influences a student's performance on research papers in college. Nonetheless, the most frequently offered reason for its inclusion in the high school curriculum is that it helps to prepare the students for college work, and it does seem reasonable to assume that good training and adequate practice at one level should yield benefits at the next. There are other considerations besides the demands of college courses, however, that may influence the English teacher's decision about whether or not to teach the research paper.

There is increasing evidence, for instance, that encouraging the more personal, informal modes, drawing heavily upon the students' own experiences and perceptions, is resulting in improved writing. The recommendations of Ken Macrorie[3], whose composition program begins with free writing and remains personal throughout, have been enthusiastically received by many teachers. Slotnick, discussing the vast National Assessment of Educational Progress, observes "that students will no longer write simply because they are asked (or told) to, and that if they do, they will write less well, less readily about things that do not interest them." [4] The most important implication of the study, he says, is "that the best writing is produced when students are asked to write about subjects they find interesting or important." [5]

One of the objections expressed by Stevenson and other critics of the high school research paper is that the paper usually is not on an issue that draws upon the student's experience or that deeply interests him, and so he finds himself borrowing and paraphrasing rather than seriously thinking about his research problems, processing the thoughts of others rather than trying to find and clarify his own. Rosenblatt warns about encouraging students to ignore their own perceptions in favor of those of experts. Those students may become "anxious to have the correct labels—the right period, the biographical data, the correct evaluation. They read literary histories and biographies, critical essays, and then, if they have time, they read the works." [6] The research paper may encourage students to adopt this approach.

The critics argue, further, that the term paper occupies a disproportionate amount of time in the high school curriculum. Frazier remarks, "In high school the skills needed for the construction of a longer paper can be learned and more readily checked in the short paper." [7] If that is correct, then it is unwise to devote four to ten weeks to intensive work on the term paper.

Training the students to prepare research reports is a less important responsibility than helping the students to realize the potential in the act of writing for pleasure and for discovery. Guth argues that "The most basic task in teaching composition is to convince the student of its *rewards*," [8] and that may be more easily accomplished through other modes than the research paper.

Although the research paper, in its time-consuming, ten to twenty page form, might well be abandoned by high school English teachers, some modification of it might profitably be taught. It is important for students to learn to use the library and to write objective, reasoned prose. Hipple recommends "short papers, ideally, of three or four pages that utilize a very limited number of sources, perhaps three." [9] In such short papers the students can be expected to deal with several points of view on a question, and attempt to come to some resolution. The short papers on very limited topics might be more honest research than students would be likely to produce in longer, more complicated undertakings, since the questions would be easier to handle and less likely to tempt the students to plagiarism. The students could as well learn the techniques of library research and objective writing in the short papers as in the full-term project.

Jordan reports a slightly different effort to reform the research paper. He explains that he and his staff "wished to retain the basic skills and study habits designed and developed to accompany the preparation of the research paper, but we wanted to take into consideration topics which had the potential for more student interest and more firsthand student involvement in the development of research and ideas." [10] To achieve this, Jordan urged his students to prepare "documentaries" rather than papers. The documentary was to include research into matters of local interest, so that students would be dealing with primary as well as secondary sources. The students undertook such projects as an analysis of the mayor's fulfillment of certain campaign promises, and a study of the future transit needs of the area.

The research paper, as it has been traditionally taught, probably does not do enough good to justify the time and energy it demands. Its goals—objective, informed, logical thought and writing—remain, however, valid goals for the English classroom, and so teachers might well be encouraged to devise alternatives to, or modifications of, the traditional term paper.

References
[1]Beth S. Neman. "A Handbook for the Teaching of the Research Paper." *English Journal*, 56 (1967), p. 263.

[2]John W. Stevenson. "The Illusion of Research." *English Journal*, 61 (1972), p. 1030.

[3]Ken Macrorie. *Uptaught*. Rochelle Park, New Jersey, Hayden Book Company, 1970.

[4]Henry B. Slotnick. "On the Teaching of Writing: Some Implications from National Assessment." *English Journal*. 62 (1973), p. 1252.

[5]*Ibid.*, p. 1253.

[6]Louise M. Rosenblatt. "The Acid Test for Literature Teaching." *English Journal*, 45 (1956), p. 71.

[7]Alexander Frazier, ed. *Ends and Issues: 1965-1966*. Champaign, Illinois: National Council of Teachers of English, 1966, p. 16.

[8]Hans P. Guth. *English for a New Generation*. New York: McGraw-Hill Book Company, 1973, pp. 135-6.

[9]Theodore W. Hipple. *Teaching English in Secondary Schools*. New York: Macmillan, 1973, p. 175.

[10]Kurt M. Jordan. "The Community Documentary: An Alternative to the Library Research Paper," in *They Really Taught Us to Write*. Ed. by Patricia A. Geuder, et. al. Urbana, Illinois: National Council of Teachers of English, 1974, p. 77.

Question X, 3

How may high school English departments and colleges achieve greater articulation in the planning of curriculum?

Angela Raffel, Greenwich Senior High School, Greenwich, Connecticut

Answer by:

FREDERICK B. TUTTLE, Jr., Associate Professor of Education at the State University College of New York at Brockport. Mr. Tuttle is the author of over 30 articles and speeches and two books. His specialties are teacher education and using visuals in teaching language arts.

Many assume curriculum planning is an esoteric task dependent on secrets possessed by those few who have devoted their lives to examining the inner mysteries of course structure and content. Some believe the best way to revise curricula is to search out these authorities, take their suggestions, and impose them directly on their school system. Others merely adopt curricula developed by "model schools" or curriculum planning centers. Each of these approaches assumes the only value of curriculum planning lies in the derived system of delivering concepts to students. This, however, is only one goal of curriculum planning. Perhaps an even more important goal is the process which teachers go through while developing their own curricula.

Throughout their struggle to develop a curriculum valid for their school, teachers should have to state their philosophies, form arguments, and make compromises, adjusting to realities of their particular physical and intellectual environments. By this process teachers not only derive a curriculum that is most appropriate for their situation, but, more importantly, they share in forming the philosophical basis for that curriculum. Without this basis, the curriculum is hollow, since it is the attitude and the approach of the individual teacher that ultimately determines what concepts and attitudes the students will really learn, not the overall structure under which teachers operate. Consequently, the process itself should receive at least as much attention as the end product.

The procedure for developing a curriculum will certainly vary from one school to another since each situation has its own power structure, personalities, modes of communication, and assumptions. Teachers have to take these into account when deciding how best to approach the process. The procedure for curricular revision described below worked well for an English department in which most curricular decisions are determined through departmental discussions.

Prior to adopting the procedure, several factors were considered. First, the primary task was to discuss the department's goals for teaching English and to examine the current curriculum in light of these goals. Second, to initiate this articulation and examination, discussions had to occur in an open atmosphere where each teacher felt free to express his opinions yet where he also felt a sense of direction and progress. Third, to encourage different individuals to participate, discussion formats had to vary. While some teachers are confident in large group discussions, others participate more freely in small group or individual sessions. Fourth, the procedure had to allow for new ideas and directions, but this flexibility could come only from having an initial structure from which they could deviate. Otherwise, discussions ran the risk of degenerating into "bull sessions," which, although exciting, too often dissipate energies and, through lack of direction, alienate many.

Because the entire department was invited to participate in all discussions, a few members had major responsibility for coordinating ideas and leading small group discussions. While this relieved some of unwanted work and responsibilities, it limited the major burden to productive volunteers. In addition, a discussion leader from outside the school coordinated all the work and led the large group discussions, providing additional information and ideas when appropriate. He also had the necessary distance from the internal power structure and concerns of the school and department to lead the discussions objectively. The discussion leader and department chairman devised the following three-stage procedure for examining and revising the curriculum.

The first stage of the procedure was a series of large group discussions in which the limitations of revision and the departmental objectives were discussed. Since this department had recently converted from a traditional four-year program to one of electives, neither the administration nor the teachers would consider returning to the former system. It was necessary for teachers to realize the restrictions early in the discussions in order to avoid later frustration and resentment. During the initial meetings the group also discussed the factors stated above and the general approach they would use to examine their curriculum.

With these understandings, the department considered what they wanted their students to be able to do as a result of studying under their curriculum. By stating their departmental objectives in terms of student behavior, they formed clear pictures of what they were really teaching. "Appreciation of literature" sounds ideal, but if all one requires is "identification of famous authors," the result will be unsatisfactory. The ideas presented during this stage were not binding, but rather were taken as tentative thoughts which would continually be re-examined and revised. This attitude toward the ideas was important, since it motivated teachers to state their opinions freely even if they were not yet fully committed to them. On the other hand, the constant re-examination was essential, for too often tentative ideas accepted during initial meetings solidify because of neglect rather than through critical evaluation and conscious agreement. Once these departmental objectives were aired, initially examined, and categorized, the group moved to the second stage.

During the second stage, the teachers worked in small groups to examine the current curriculum in view of the departmental objectives. Each small group listed specific courses and objectives under appropriate departmental objectives, changing wording where necessary. This comparison of course and departmental objectives gave the teachers several insights into their current structure. First, they found that several departmental objectives were just taken for granted and were not dealt with specifically in any courses. Second, they located many course objectives which they had failed to account for in the departmental list. Finally, teachers found that they had to re-write many of the course objectives which were too nebulous for comparison with the departmental objectives. These discoveries and the realization of the need for revision resulted from the comparison of what was with what should be.

Although much of the comparison and articulation was conducted in small groups, the entire department met periodically to discuss results and questions. These large group meetings were necessary both to share information and to provide opportunity for input from all members of the department. This sharing and coordination of effort was supplemented by the discussion leader's meeting with individuals and small groups, providing directions and information where necessary.

After the teachers articulated and compared their current curriculum with departmental objectives, they moved to the third stage: examination of alternative methods of achieving their objectives. With this department, the major changes were made within the existing structure, so an extensive search was not necessary. Where a greater discrepancy between departmental goals and current structure occurs, however, teachers would have to conduct a more thorough examination of alternatives. As they consider curricula developed by others, they should not lose sight of those objectives and experiences they believe are important for their students. The management system for delivering concepts should adapt to the philosophy behind the instruction, not vice-versa. Consequently, teachers should not conduct the examination of other curricula until they have completed the first two stages and know what they want as well as what they already have. Otherwise, the department might simply impose a new shell over the old core without considering the essential elements of the curriculum, the teachers' own views and objectives.

How can the curriculum be articulated? By involving the teachers in a sharing of their philosophies, in a close examination of their current structure and objectives, and in an exploration of different ways to meet their goals. Although an "expert" in the field can provide valuable assistance as a discussion leader and source of information, the articulation, examination, and final decision have to come from within the department. Regardless of what a curriculum looks like on paper, it can only reflect what the teachers do with it in their own classrooms.

SECTION XI

A
BIBLIOGRAPHICAL
AFTERWORD

A Bibliographical Afterword

The individual contributions to *Questions English Teachers Ask* contain substantial bibliography; therefore it would be superfluous to present any extensive bibliography here. It is presumed that most English teachers are familiar with the publications of the National Council of Teachers of English and of the International Reading Association, whose journals, monographs and other studies are of continuing use to teachers in the field. The publications of these two organizations will not be included in the following bibliography, which will be brief and highly selective. Essentially it consists of titles which the editor and the teachers with whom he works most closely have found of particular use to them.

Barber, Charles. *Linguistic Change in Present-Day English.* University, Alabama: University of Alabama Press, 1964. Barber emphasizes the importance of spoken language as a means of studying linguistic change and chronicles recent changes in English usage.

Britton, James. *Language and Learning.* London: Penguin Press, 1970. Presents language as central to all learning processes.

Burton, Dwight. *Literature Study in the High Schools.* 3rd ed. New York: Holt, Rinehart and Winston, 1970. Especially valuable for its extensive bibliographies of books to use with secondary school students.

Cassirer, Ernst. *Language and Myth.* New York: Dover Publications, 1946. A brilliant consideration of the symbolic functions of language.

Ciardi, John. *How Does a Poem Mean?* Boston: Houghton Mifflin, 1958. A careful and engaging consideration of how poetry achieves its effect.

Commission on English. *Freedom and Discipline in English.* New York: College Entrance Examination Board, 1965. A balanced consideration of the English curriculum and of the responsibilities of English teachers.

Dixon, John. *Growth Through English.* Oxford: Oxford University Press, 1969. A report of the Anglo-American Conference on the Teaching of English held at Dartmouth College in 1966. See also Herbert Muller.

Eliade, Mircea. *Rites and Symbols of Initiation.* New York: Harper and Row, 1965. Contains a valuable chapter on the initiation theme in literature. Particularly useful to high school English teachers seeking new approaches to dealing with adolescent literature.

Fast, Julius. *Body Language.* New York: Pocket Books, 1974. Considers the role of gesture as a part of language, an indispensable adjunct to verbal expression.

Francis, W. Nelson. *The Structure of American English.* New York: Ronald Press, 1958. See particularly Raven McDavid, Jr.'s chapter on regional dialects.

Gordon, Edward J. *Writing and Literature in the Secondary School.* New York: Holt, Rinehart and Winston, 1965. Stresses the interrelationships among reading, writing, and thinking.

Guth, Hans P. *English for a New Generation.* New York: McGraw-Hill, 1973. A good overview of English teaching in today's schools.

Hall, Edward T. *The Silent Language.* Greenwich, Conn.: Fawcett, 1968. Silent language, based on traditions, taboos, and cultural milieu, is presented as a communication mode as effective as verbal communication.

Hook, J. N. *The Teaching of High School English.* New York: Ronald Press, 1965. A comprehensive overview of English instruction, particularly useful for its practical teaching suggestions in the "idea boxes" which are a part of each chapter.

Jenkinson, Edward B. *What Is Language?* Bloomington, Indiana: Indiana University Press, 1967. A strong overall approach which considers American dialects, language change, use of the dictionary, and semantics. Provides useful teaching units for grades 7 through 12.

Joos, Martin. *The Five Clocks.* New York: Harcourt, Brace and World, 1967. A carefully prepared and infinitely readable presentation of the types of English usage practiced in various language situations.

Katz, John. *Perspectives on the Study of Film.* Boston: Little, Brown, 1971. One of the more comprehensive studies of the use of film as a teaching device.

Macrorie, Ken. *Uptaught.* Rochelle Park, New Jersey: Hayden Book Co., 1970. A readable and witty collection of vignettes related to English teaching and to writing.

———. *Writing to Be Read,* rev. 2nd edition. Rochelle Park, New Jersey: Hayden Book Co., 1976. Gives special emphasis to considering the audience for whom students are writing. Suggests ways of getting students' work into a form in which it can be shared by other people.

Marckwardt, Albert H. *Linguistics and the Teaching of English.* Bloomington, Indiana: Indiana University Press, 1966. A clear and relevant presentation of linguistic science and how it relates to English teaching.

Muller, Herbert J. *The Uses of English.* New York: Holt, Rinehart and Winston, 1967. A report on the Anglo-American Conference on the Teaching of English held at Dartmouth College in 1966. See also John Dixon.

Postman, Neil and Charles Weingartner. *Linguistics: A Revolution in Teaching.* New York: Delacorte Press, 1966. Part I provides a rationale for the linguistic approach to teaching language and Part II discusses grammar, usage, semantics, lexicography, and dialectology. A practical approach.

Richards, I. A. *Practical Criticism.* New York: Harcourt, Brace and World, 1939. A central work of modern criticism which identifies difficulties university students experienced in approaching a broad range of poetry. Has good carry-over value for English teachers at all levels.

Rosenblatt, Louise. *Literature as Exploration.* New York: Noble and Noble, 1969. Perhaps the most convincing rationale extant for the teaching of literature, giving special attention to reader response.

Skinner, B. F. *Verbal Behavior.* New York: Appleton-Century-Crofts, 1957. A behaviorist's approach to language.

Sohn, David. *Film: The Creative Eye.* Dayton: George A. Pflaum, 1971. An imaginative approach to using film and film-making in English classrooms.

Squire, James R. and Roger K. Applebee. *High School English Instruction Today.* New York: Appleton-Century-Crofts, 1968. Analyzes English programs in 158 high schools in 45 states. A perceptive presentation of the data.

Stewart, William A. *Non-Standard Speech and the Teaching of English.* Washington, D. C.: Center for Applied Linguistics, 1954. A useful book for teachers whose students normally speak non-standard dialects.

Strunk, William, Jr. and E. B. White. *Elements of Style.* New York: Macmillan, 1972. Of particular interest and value is White's chapter on writing.

Vygotsky, Lev. *Thought and Language.* Cambridge, Mass.: M. I. T. Press, 1969. A sound scholarly consideration of the relationship between thought and language.

Whorf, Benjamin Lee. *Language, Thought, and Reality.* John B. Carroll, ed. New York: Technology Press of M. I. T. and John Wiley, 1956. A provocative presentation of language as a means of understanding people from other cultures and their value systems.